Ensuring that children and young people with complex needs are enabled by professionals to make their own decisions and lead independent lives is crucial and at the centre of the SEND reforms and good practice. This guide is indispensable for any professionals working with children, young people and families in navigating policy and practice in this complex area. It also supports developing practice around ensuring that parents are kept fully involved and support the process. There are few more knowledgeable experts on both the law and the practice in this area and this should be required reading for professional development for anyone working in this field.

Brian Lamb, Visiting Professor of SEND, Derby University,
Chair of Achievement for All

With the rise in mental health issues and subsequent awareness in children and young people – particularly those with special educational needs, this book couldn't have come soon enough! As health and education professionals we must be made more aware of the impact a lack of independent and well supported decision making can have on a child and young person's feeling of mental well-being and belonging. As an SLT promoting joint decision making with parents and children and young people through a health coaching approach, this book will be invaluable in complementing your rationale, planning and execution of child centred intervention and get you thinking about the ways you can support the children and families you work with in a more holistic approach to gain the results that are collectively strived for.

Hana L Haziem (BA/PGCert), Service Manager, Children's Speech and Language
Therapy, Leeds Community Healthcare NHS Trust

As a QTVI, and Sensory Service Manager, I found this book extremely useful and thought provoking, and recommend it to all specialist professionals working with CYP with SEND, and their families. It provides a direct link between the legislative framework of the SEND CoP and EHCPs, and the importance of empowering CYP to make their own decisions, whilst supporting parents to encourage and allow them to become independent in their decision making, as far as possible. The book has a useful framework for how to teach decision making skills from the earliest years, and the approach will be easily embedded into a professional's armoury.

Anne Lomas, Head of Sensory and PD Services (retired)

This book shines a light on an overlooked area and appeals to a wide range of professionals working within the education sector. The book explores how to support children and young people to develop their decision-making skills, providing the reader with examples of practical applications along the way.

Dr Suzanne Devereux, Nicola Blackwell and Katherine Lucor,
West Sussex Educational Psychology service

Increasingly occupational therapists are contributing to Education Health Care Plans to support children and young adults maximise their learning and development. Therapists must juggle busy case work and their continuous professional development requirements related to keeping up to date with clinical evidence. This can result in limited capacity to research legislation and government guidance related to EHCPs.

This book brings together the key relevant legislation in an accessible format for health professionals working in education and provides the reader with essential information around the legal framework. The author discusses in detail the challenges of enabling children and young people develop decision making skills. The topic will stimulate occupational therapists to consider how they can enable this skill development when working with children and setting treatment goals and planning programmes. The book contains varied and interesting case studies which give practical examples on how to support choice and provide opportunities to develop essential decision-making skills. The book will be a valuable resource for therapists.

Jane Oxnard Jay, Occupational Therapist

DEVELOPING DECISION-MAKING WITH CHILDREN AND YOUNG PEOPLE WITH SEN

We all make decisions every day, but are you aware of the process you use to make a decision? This essential practical guide for education and associated professionals, using education-focused case studies throughout to illustrate key points, explains the mechanics of decision-making, introducing the associated language and concepts. It presents both a practical decision-making framework based in the Mental Capacity Act decision-making process, and a decision-making syllabus, from which education professionals can create their own curriculum.

Being able to make decisions is an important life skill, which can have a positive impact on well-being. However, many children and young people with SEN will need direct teaching and guidance to develop this ability, from the earliest age. The book explores the types of important decisions children and young people may need to make in relation to their education, with particular focus on choosing a new educational placement, providing practical guidance about how education professionals can support young people to make this decision. There is reference throughout the book as to the ways in which practitioners can work in partnership with parents to support and develop children and young people's decision-making ability. Appendices provide completed decision-making frameworks and associated guidance.

Jane L. Sinson is an HCPC registered educational psychologist (EP) and Chartered Educational Psychologist. Having attained a degree in Psychology, she taught pupils with special needs in a range of mainstream, resourced and special schools before training as an educational psychologist. She worked as a local authority (LA) educational psychologist for over twenty years, supporting pupils and staff in a range of mainstream, resourced and special schools as well as delivering training to school staff and parent workshops. Additionally, Jane was the EP representative on the CAMHS school-aged autism protocol panel, and course tutor for the LA teaching assistant accredited training. Whilst an LA EP she lectured in the UK to psychology undergraduates and education undergraduates in Hong Kong. After leaving the local authority, initially Jane worked for an independent psychological service undertaking dyslexia assessments in further and higher education institutions as well as expert witness work, before becoming self-employed. She has been part of The Ear Foundation multidisciplinary assessment team undertaking assessments of deaf children and young people. Currently, she is mainly commissioned to deliver training to education professionals and parents related to the Mental Capacity Act 2005 and developing children and young people's decision-making ability, as well as writing on the subject. Jane also undertakes voluntary work as an EP in a school for children with severe learning difficulties in St Lucia, Caribbean.

DEVELOPING DECISION-MAKING WITH CHILDREN AND YOUNG PEOPLE WITH SEN

A PRACTICAL GUIDE FOR EDUCATION AND ASSOCIATED PROFESSIONALS

Jane L. Sinson

Routledge
Taylor & Francis Group
LONDON AND NEW YORK

First published 2020
by Routledge
2 Park Square, Milton Park, Abingdon, Oxon OX14 4RN

and by Routledge
52 Vanderbilt Avenue, New York, NY 10017

Routledge is an imprint of the Taylor & Francis Group, an informa business

© 2020 Jane L. Sinson

The right of Jane L. Sinson to be identified as author of this work has been asserted by her in accordance with sections 77 and 78 of the Copyright, Designs and Patents Act 1988.

All rights reserved. The purchase of this copyright material confers the right on the purchasing institution to photocopy pages which bear the eResources icon and copyright line at the bottom of the page. No other part of this publication may be reproduced, stored in a retrieval system, or transmitted in any form or by any means, electronic, mechanical, photocopying, recording or otherwise, without prior permission in writing from the publisher.

Trademark notice: Product or corporate names may be trademarks or registered trademarks, and are used only for identification and explanation without intent to infringe.

British Library Cataloguing-in-Publication Data
A catalogue record for this book is available from the British Library

Library of Congress Cataloging-in-Publication Data
Names: Sinson, Jane L., author.
Title: Developing decision-making with children and young people with SEN :
  a practical guide for education and associated professionals / Jane L. Sinson.
Description: Abingdon, Oxon ; New York, NY : Routledge, 2020. | Includes bibliographical
  references and index.
Identifiers: LCCN 2019048443 (print) | LCCN 2019048444 (ebook) |
  ISBN 9780367420987 (paperback) | ISBN 9780367821784 (ebook)
Subjects: LCSH: Decision making—Study and teaching (Elementary) |
  Children with mental disabilities—Education. | Learning disabled children—Education.
Classification: LCC LB1062.5 .S56 2020 (print) | LCC LB1062.5 (ebook) | DDC 371.92/6—dc23
LC record available at https://lccn.loc.gov/2019048443
LC ebook record available at https://lccn.loc.gov/2019048444

ISBN: 978-0-367-42098-7 (pbk)
ISBN: 978-0-367-82178-4 (ebk)

Typeset in DIN Pro
by Apex CoVantage, LLC

Visit the eResources: www.routledge.co.uk/9780367420987
Printed and bound by CPI Group (UK) Ltd, Croydon, CR0 4YY

In memory of my sister, who sometimes presented me with the challenge of accepting what, in my view, were her unwise choices, but they were her decisions.

CONTENTS

Acknowledgements		xi
Prolegomenon: setting the scene		1
Part 1	**Decision-making**	**13**
One	Making decisions	15
Two	Mental health perspective	33
Three	Legislative context	44
Four	Making decisions about educational matters	57
Part 2	**Decision-making syllabus**	**79**
Five	Decision-making syllabus	81
Six	The art of writing SMART outcomes	121
Part 3	**The role of education and associated professionals**	**141**
Seven	Educational psychologists (EPs) and associated professionals	143
Eight	Supporting and involving parents	159
Epilogue: reflections and steps forward		171
Appendix 1: Completed decision-making framework for 'important' decisions for education and associated professionals or parents		181

Contents

Appendix 2: Child or young person completed
decision-making form   200

Appendix 3: Statutory 'best interests' checklist
and completed 'best interests' balance sheet   204

Appendix 4: SEND Code of Practice preparation
for adulthood outcomes   209

Appendix 5: Guidelines for undertaking
observations   211

Appendix 6: Sample 'My Activity Passport'   217

Appendix 7: Mechanics of the Talking Mats
style approach   219

Glossary   222

References   225

Resources   229

Index   233

ACKNOWLEDGEMENTS

Grateful thanks are due to:

The participants at the NatSIP parents' workshop 'Young people and decision making' in London (March 2019) and Devon (June 2019) whose thoughts helped shape Chapter eight.

The participants attending the British Psychological Society workshop in November 2018, 'An introduction to applying the Mental Capacity Act (MCA) 2005 in education and developing young people's decision-making ability: exploring issues for educational psychologists', for their encouragement to write this book.

Lindsey Rousseau MBE, NatSIP Facilitator, for her never-ending support and encouragement.

The Hotel Manager and staff aboard the SPV *Royal Clipper* November 2018 Barbados to Panama cruise, who, on days at sea, allowed me to occupy a table in the Tropical Bar overlooking the sea to write undisturbed.

My family, friends and colleagues, for their support and understanding.

PROLEGOMENON: SETTING THE SCENE

Are you an education or associated professional such as speech and language therapist (SLT), occupational therapist (OT), physiotherapist, school counsellor, mental health practitioner, Portage worker or social care employee, working with children and/or young people with SEN aged 0–25 years? If you answered 'Yes', this book is essential reading. Like most education or associated professionals, you will have read the *Special educational needs and disability code of practice: 0–25 years* (SEND COP) sections applying to your role. Undoubtedly, you will welcome the emphasis on children and young people participating in decision-making about their education and being prepared for adulthood from the earliest age, but you may be perplexed by the lack of information, support or guidance as to how to effect this. From your experience you are aware that children and young people with special educational needs (SEN) find incidental learning more difficult, frequently needing direct teaching, overlearning and practise, to develop skills that those without SEN seem to acquire by osmosis. Searching for resources reveals there are few focused on teaching children and young people the decision-making process, even fewer for those with SEN, but lots to practise decision-making.

Since 1 September 2014, the English special educational needs legislation has formally introduced young people's right, from the age of 16, to make their own decisions about their education. However, if the young person has had very limited guidance or opportunities to make decisions prior to this, they are likely to have difficulties exercising this right and achieving the autonomy this gives them. The author's experience, as a panel member for the First-tier Tribunal Special Educational Needs and Disability (SEND Tribunal), is that some young people's parents assume that their young person with SEN is unable to make decisions, suggesting they may have been afforded limited opportunities to make their own choices.

The author has been involved with the notion of children and young people with SEN making their own decisions since September 2014 when she began preparing and delivering Mental Capacity Act 2005 training to education professionals. Yet, when, how and where do we learn to make decisions? The author has no recollection of how she learned to make decisions – do you? It is reflecting on these issues that has prompted the writing of this book to support education and associated professionals to enable children and young people with SEN to make as many decisions for themselves as they are able.

Prolegomenon

Effectively, this book is the precursor to, and preparation for, the provisions of the Mental Capacity Act 2005, Mental Capacity (Amendment) Act 2019, and their accompanying Codes of Practice, which apply from a young person's 16th birthday. However, the impetus came not just from the legal requirements, but also from the research which demonstrates the positive effects on mental well-being for people with learning difficulties when they are enabled to have some autonomy (see Chapters one and two). Children and young people's mental health is a current focus of government research and policy development (see Chapter two), with all education institutions considered to have an important part to play in preventing mental health problems as well as promoting and supporting well-being (DfE 2017a, 2017b; Knightsmith 2019); by implication this means all education professionals. The Mencap website[1] cites statistics showing that 40% of adults with learning disabilities experience mental health problems; this is considered to be about double the estimated prevalence for mental health problems in the general population. Therefore, developing and enabling children's and young people's with SEN decision-making ability is not just cultivating a life skill, but helping to promote and support their mental well-being.

This chapter provides the backcloth for the book, introducing key pieces of English legislation, discussed in more detail in Chapter three, that enshrine the rights of children and young people with SEN to make their own decisions as far as possible, as well as explaining the concepts used throughout and briefly exploring some of the ideas that are discussed in more depth later in the book. Hopefully, this chapter will prompt the reader to reflect on the development of their own decision-making skills and where they feel they are now. It is important that education and associated professionals have some awareness of their own abilities in this area to enable them to support the development of children and young people's decision-making skills.

Although this book focuses on the English legislation, education and associated professionals in Wales may find it helpful as the SEN legislation is changing from September 2020 to extend participation in education to the age of 25 for young people with SEN. Education professionals in Northern Ireland may also find the book useful as from October 2018 the Mental Capacity Act (Northern Ireland) 2016 came into force and 2020 brings the new special needs legislation which emphasises children participating in decision-making.

What makes being able to make decisions an important life skill?

Being able to make a decision enables a person to have control over what happens in their life. Kostikj-Ivanovikj and Chichevska-Jovanova's (2016) research with adults with learning disabilities found a positive relationship between quality of life and opportunities for making everyday choices and advocated the need to design programmes that will develop the ability to make personal choices. The effect of not having this control is illustrated by the concept of 'learned helplessness', coined by the American psychologist Martin Seligman in the early 1970s. 'Learned helplessness' is a state a person reaches when they believe that their actions have no effect on their environment (Kurtycz 2015). The effect of this has been shown to adversely impact on motivation, affect (mental health) and cognition (Abramson, Seligman and Teasedale 1978, cited in Marks 1998). People experiencing learned helplessness cease to make choices, even in circumstances when making a choice would give some control over what happens. Therefore, learning to make choices can be considered a very valuable life skill in preparation for adulthood, which is likely to have a positive impact on well-being and enable children and young people to have some control over what happens in their life.

This book presents a decision-making framework and guidance to support education and associated professionals to develop and enable children and young people's decision-making ability (Chapter one). Additionally, the book sets out a decision-making 'syllabus' to provoke discussion and debate about how to ensure that education professionals embed developing, supporting and promoting children and young people's decision-making into everyday practice, and how this can be supported by associated professionals (Chapter five). Furthermore, both the decision-making framework and 'syllabus' will assist education professionals to support parents to empower their son or daughter to make their own choices.

Children and Families Act 2014

The Children and Families Act 2014 is the special educational needs legislation in England applying to children and young people aged 0–25. More precisely, it is Part 3, of this ten-part Act, 'Children and Young People in England with special educational needs or disabilities', which not only sets out how to meet children's and young people's special educational needs, but also ensures close cooperation between education, health and social care (SEND COP Introduction vi). It is accompanied by the *Special educational needs and disability code of practice: 0 to 25 years* (SEND COP), the statutory guidance that explains in more detail what the relevant part of the Children and Families Act 2014 means, how it should work on a day-to-day basis, and gives practical steps, as well as setting out which roles or jobs must follow the SEND Code of Practice (Introduction iv).

The Children and Families Act 2014 introduced Education, Health and Care Plans (EHC Plan or EHCP) and places an emphasis on preparation for adulthood from the earliest age, including children and young people participating in decision-making about their education. The law and the SEND COP apply to children and young people living in England attending any type of publicly (state) funded education. That is, a mainstream or special school or pre-school, regardless of whether the educational establishment is maintained by the local authority or it is an academy, free school, university technical school, studio school, or non-maintained special school. It also applies to sixth form colleges, general further education (FE) colleges, non-maintained specialist colleges, as well as independent special educational establishments, independent specialist colleges, and post 16 training providers, approved by the Department for Education (DfE) under section 41 of the Children and Families Act 2014. Additionally, the law makes provision for young people aged 16–25 years with special educational needs to retain their EHC Plan if they gain an apprenticeship or traineeship.

In formal recognition of young people's rights to make their own decisions about their education, the Children and Families Act 2014 has incorporated the Mental Capacity Act 2005 (MCA), now including the Mental Capacity (Amendment) Act 2019, legislation wholly concerned with people's right, from the age of 16, to make their own decisions, providing protection for people who are unable to make a particular decision for themselves. The Mental Capacity Act 2005 also has a Code of Practice. See below for more information about the MCA.

SEND Code of Practice (SEND COP)

All education and associated professionals working with children and young people with SEN aged 0–25 years must have regard to the SEND COP. As this is the guidance to be followed there will be references to the relevant sections throughout this chapter and the rest of the book; paragraph and page numbers cited are from the SEND COP published in January 2015. The SEND COP is only available online, and it is free to download.[2] It is essential that all education and associated professionals familiarise themselves with the information, in particular reading the Introduction, Chapters 1, 4 and 8, then, depending on the phase of education you work within, the following chapter(s) – early years practitioners, Chapter 5; education and associated professionals working in schools, Chapter 6; those working in the post 16 sector, Chapter 7 and Annex 1. Chapter 9 provides specific information about EHC Plans, including some guidance about outcomes; the most relevant sections are 9.2, 9.5, 9.21–9.26, 9.61, 9.69 Section E (outcomes), 9.150, and 9.184–9.185. Additionally, health and social care professionals may find it informative to read Chapters 3 and 10.

In relation to this book's subject matter – decision-making – the SEND COP (1.40) states that '**All professionals** working with families should look to enable children and young people to make choices for themselves from an early age . . .' (p28). This is supported in various ways in different chapters in the SEND COP but lacking any specific guidance and, at times, subsumed within the general phrase 'prepare for independent living'. To make decisions, children and young people need access to information; the SEND COP sets out children's and young people's right to receive and give information, to express an opinion and to have their viewpoint considered in any matters affecting them from the early years. However, the latter is qualified with the caveat, 'their views should be given due weight according to their age, maturity and capability' (SEND COP 1.6 p20), but no guidance about how to determine this. This issue is explored in more depth in Chapter four.

Interestingly, despite the emphasis on children and young people participating in decision-making, there is no requirement to include a decision-making outcome in person-centred planning or an EHC Plan. In the author's opinion, this is a significant omission; she believes that education and associated professionals should routinely consider encouraging parents, children and young people to include an age or developmentally appropriate decision-making outcome as part of person-centred planning or in an EHC Plan. Equally important is education and associated professionals including a decision-making outcome in their consultation records, reports, advice for an EHC needs assessment or annual review report. Writing an effective SMART decision-making outcome may be best achieved through collaboration between the education professional and, for example, the SLT or OT. The legislative provisions supporting education and associated professionals developing and enabling children and young people's decision-making are discussed in depth in Chapter three in this book.

Additional Learning Needs and Education Tribunal (Wales) Act 2018

This legislation will be phased in over three years beginning in September 2020. Like the Children and Families Act 2014 it extends the age up to 25 years for additional learning needs support to be provided to young people in an educational setting, as well as ensuring collaboration between education, health and social care to meet children and young people's additional learning needs. It also enshrines the rights of children and young people to participate as fully as possible in decision-making and being given access to information and support. It is proposed there will be a Code of Practice similar to the English SEND COP.

It differs from the Children and Families Act 2014 in the terminology used: special educational need is termed 'additional learning need (ALN)', and an EHC Plan will be known as an Individual Development Plan (IDP).

Special Educational Needs and Disability Act (Northern Ireland) 2016

This legislation comes into force in Northern Ireland during 2020. Like the Children and Families Act 2014 it encourages collaboration between education, health and social care to provide services which will be of benefit to address children's special educational needs. It places a duty on education authorities to have regard to the views of the child when making decisions on special education provision, as well as emphasising the importance of the child participating in making decisions and being provided with information and support to make these decisions. It is proposed there will be a Code of Practice similar to the English SEND COP.

It differs from the Children and Families Act 2014 in some terminology used, an EHC Plan will be known as a statement of special educational needs.

Mental Capacity Act 2005

The Mental Capacity Act 2005 (known as the MCA) is a law applying in England and Wales that gives everyone the right from the age of 16 to make their own decisions. Mental capacity means the ability to make a decision – any decision. Most importantly, the MCA provides a statutory framework to support and protect young people if they are unable to make a particular decision for themselves.

The MCA has five principles; the first three relate to young people making their own decisions, the fourth and fifth give guidance to those deciding on behalf of a young person who is unable to make a particular decision. The first principle is the presumption of capacity; it should be assumed a young person can make their own decision unless it is proved they cannot do so. It sets out the attributes of decision-making and a process to be used to assess a person's ability to make a particular decision, and, like the SEND COP, encourages participation in decision-making.

Like the Children and Families Act 2014, the MCA is accompanied by a Code of Practice. When the young person is aged 16 years and over, all education, health and social care professionals and parents must have regard to the Mental Capacity Act 2005 Code of Practice (MCA COP).[3] Therefore, education, health and social care professionals working with young people with SEN aged 16–25 years, in an education institution or training placement, must have regard to two Codes of Practice – SEND COP and MCA COP.

The SEND COP Annex 1 is the only guidance given by the Department for Education (DfE) regarding education professionals' responsibilities in relation to the Mental Capacity Act 2005. It is brief, incomplete, lacking in definitions and has significant omissions (Sinson 2016).

The Mental Capacity Act 2005 Code of Practice (MCA COP)

The Mental Capacity Act 2005 Code of Practice is a simpler document than the SEND COP, although it may present challenges to education professionals as it was written with health and social care professionals in mind. This is reflected both in the language used to describe a person's functioning, very different terminology from that used in education, and the scenarios presented to illustrate points – adult health and social care issues. All education professionals working with young people are advised to read MCA COP chapters 1–6, 12, 15 and 16.

Sinson (2016) provides detailed guidance specifically for education professionals regarding the legal requirement to follow the MCA COP and SEND COP when formally considering a young person's capacity to make decisions about their education.

Mental Capacity (Amendment) Act 2019

This Act amends the MCA 2005 in relation to the Deprivation of Liberty Safeguards, which has always been a supplement to the MCA. The new scheme, entitled Liberty Protection Safeguards, will apply from the age of 16 years in England and Wales. At the time of writing, in June 2019, this new Act had only just received Royal Assent, the government had yet to announce the date it will come into force, but there is speculation this will be 1 October 2020. The accompanying regulations and Code of Practice need to be written. Since the March 2014 Supreme Court case, known as Cheshire West, the definition of Deprivation of Liberty has been: the young person is under continuous supervision and control and is not free to leave and lacks capacity to consent to this arrangement (see Sinson 2016 for further information). It applies to all publicly funded residential settings, including the residential part of residential schools and specialist colleges, as well as foster placements and supported living.

The relevance of this new law to the subject matter of this book is that it has become mandatory to ascertain the young person's views and feelings in relation to the proposed arrangements, which, under the new Act, may now include placement in a day centre and travel arrangements. The new law sets out those people who **must** be consulted, which include the young person, anyone the young person names, and anyone caring for the young person. Having the experience of making choices enables the development of views and feelings, such as preferences, likes and dislikes. This new law serves to emphasise the importance of young people, particularly those who will always require a high level of supervision from education institution staff, parents, or carers, being able to make everyday and other decisions, and to demonstrate their preferences, as well as those supporting them to know these.

As this new law is part of the Mental Capacity Act 2005 and will have its own Code of Practice, all education and associated professionals working with young people aged 16–25 years will also have to have regard to this additional Code of Practice.

Mental Capacity Act (Northern Ireland) 2016

Like the Mental Capacity Act 2005, this legislation applies from a young person's 16th birthday. It also shares the same principles, definitions of capacity and lack of capacity including how to assess capacity; likewise there will be a Code of Practice. This legislation came into force in late 2018, with full implementation in 2020.

Children and young people

Throughout, this book adopts the terminology used in the Children and Families Act 2014, and the accompanying *Special educational needs and disability code of practice* (SEND COP). 'Child' refers to someone aged 0–16 years who has not completed compulsory education. The end of compulsory education in England and Wales is defined as the last Friday in June in the school year (generally Year 11) in which the young person becomes 16. The term 'young person' means someone aged between 16 and 25 years old who has reached the end of Year 11 (after the last Friday in June). Compulsory education in Northern Ireland is somewhat different (see Glossary – compulsory school age).

Confusingly, the Mental Capacity Act 2005 uses the term 'young person' for someone who has had their 16th birthday but is not yet 18 years old. This is because someone who has had their 18th birthday is legally an adult.

Whilst it may seem odd to use the term 'young person' for someone who is legally an adult, it aligns with the United Nations[4] (UN) definition of a young person as being aged between 15 and 24, although the UN acknowledges that member states may vary this. The disadvantage of using the term 'young person' is that it can be overlooked that a young person who has turned 18 is an adult and all adult provisions apply, especially the Mental Capacity Act 2005. For example, once the young person has attained adulthood, their permission is needed to discuss any matters with their parents. This is often not considered by education professionals who continue to follow the protocols used for those under 18 years even though the student is an adult. Additionally, education and associated professionals frequently make reference to 'adult support' when documenting provision for the 18–25 years age group, forgetting the young people are themselves adults. Once young people are adults, education and associated professionals should be using terms such as 'education institution staff support', 'keyworker support' or 'learning support assistant support', or other appropriate term that defines the person's role in relation to the young person, but not 'adult'.

Education professionals

This book uses the term 'education professional' to mean the same people as set out in SEND COP Introduction iv. That is, all teachers and support staff working in early years settings – maintained, private, voluntary and independent sector – that receive local authority funding; school staff (teachers and support staff), including the governing body, of maintained, academies, free schools, non-maintained special schools and independent schools and independent specialist providers approved under section 41 of the Children and Families Act 2014; education staff (tutors and support staff) in further education colleges and sixth form colleges, state-funded and independent, and local authority officers, e.g. SEN officers, specialist teachers, educational psychologists.

Associated professionals

This term will be used throughout the book to mean a range of health (e.g. SLT, OT, physiotherapist), social care and other professionals (such as education institution counsellors, mental health practitioners, Portage Home Visitors, ABA tutors, Habilitation/Mobility Officers (see glossary)) who are involved with providing special educational provision to children and young people, attending educational or training settings. It is essential that associated professionals understand the importance of developing, supporting and facilitating children and young people's decision-making and consider how they can contribute to this. As noted above, in the spirit of the Children and Families Act 2014, collaboration with education professionals may be the most effective way.

Some children and young people receive support from social care, which may be from a social worker, or from others employed to provide support to the child or young person, such as respite care staff, or short break providers. Depending on the child or young person's social care needs, it may be appropriate for those supporting them to work in collaboration with the education or training setting to develop and empower children's and young people's decision-making.

Parents

This book refers to 'parent' as any person who is the child or young person's parent or who has parental responsibility or who cares for the child or young person.

Education institution

The term education institution is used to denote any educational establishment, be it special or mainstream, such as nursery, school, further education college (general or specialist), whether they are maintained, academies, free schools, non-maintained or independent.

Case studies

The case studies used throughout the book have mostly been made up to illustrate points, and the children, young people, education and associated professionals, parents and education institutions are all fictitious. Where examples or scenarios are based on actual cases, this is indicated, and all the names of people, including children and young people, education institutions and other placements, have been changed.

Digital technology

Throughout the book there is reference to using digital technology to support and enable the development of children's and young people's with SEN decision-making ability as well as being an aid to communication with children, young people and their parents. Education and associated professionals are encouraged to maximise the potential of personal digital technology, as well as education institution-based ICT, to support their endeavours. The use of emojis is mooted, as these now seem to have gone beyond being solely a digital technology communication and are now seen in the wider environment. They appear to have become a universally understood language, suggesting children and young people with SEN should be introduced to emojis and taught to use them to facilitate communication. This raises the question of whether emojis should be used in place of Boardmaker or similar symbol systems. This is something for education and associated professionals to ponder as they read the book.

Talking Mats style approach

Throughout the book, a Talking Mats (www.talkingmats.com) style approach is recommended to assist children and young people with communication difficulties express their views and feelings about the options for important decisions. Talking Mats is an interactive visual communication tool, developed by speech and language therapists in Scotland, and has its own symbols. Talking Mats is run as a social enterprise whose aim is to enable people with communication difficulties to communicate about matters that affect them. The idea of using visual symbols and a mat is not trademarked and it is therefore open to education and associated professionals to use a mat with their own visual materials. Therefore, when the term 'Talking Mats style approach' is used in this book it refers to the use of a mat or digital space and visual materials, such as photographs, to enable a child or young person to express their views and feelings about options related to an important decision (Appendix 7 explains the mechanics of the approach). As noted above, the author is questioning the use of symbols exclusive to a particular provider which are not generalised to the wider world and advocates adopting the now universally recognised emoji symbols from digital technology. Additionally, throughout the book, the author advises taking photographs of the actual items/activities, in particular the child or young person taking their own photographs using digital technology.

No decision about a child or young person's education without a contribution from them

The reader will become aware that this aspiration/mantra/slogan appears throughout the book, alongside its variant, 'no decision about my education without a contribution from me', inspired by an NHS slogan (Department of Health 2012)[5] that the author has taken the liberty of adapting. The author gives her permission for education and associated professionals to use or adapt this aspiration/slogan. Ideally, the author would like to see it incorporated into the vision or mission statement for all education institutions catering for the needs of children and young people with SEN.

Is this book essential reading?

This practical book aims to provide information and guidance, supported by education-focused case studies, to facilitate education and associated professionals to realise the SEND COP aspiration that children and young people with SEN will participate in making decisions about their education. Hopefully, it will help embed opportunities, activities, experiences and support for decision-making into day-to-day practice, including always considering having an age-related or developmentally appropriate decision-making outcome in person-centred planning and EHC Plans. It will assist education and associated professionals' understanding of the SEND COP requirements, and, for those working with the post 16 age group, the MCA COP. It:

- examines in detail the decision-making process, including factors which affect it, as well as providing a decision-making framework aligned to the MCA COP (Chapter 1)
- introduces the language of decision-making (Chapter 1)
- gives an overview of the developmental process in relation to children and young people acquiring the ability to make decisions (Chapter 1)
- explores the benefits to children's and young people's mental well-being to be able to make their own decisions against the backcloth of the education institution's role in supporting and promoting well-being (Chapter 2 and throughout the book)
- explores the legislative background that supports the reasons it is important to develop children and young people's decision-making ability (Chapter 3)
- explores the education professional's role in supporting and enabling children and young people to develop and use their decision-making ability (Chapter 4)
- considers the types of decisions children and young people usually make in relation to their education (Chapter 4)

- discusses in depth how to support and facilitate children's and young people's decision-making ability and proposes a decision-making syllabus (Chapters 4, 5, 6, 7 & 8)
- explores the educational psychologist's and other associated professionals' role in supporting and enabling children and young people to develop and use their decision-making ability (Chapters 6, 7 & 8)
- gives suggestions for ways in which education and associated professionals can work in partnership to support parents to enable their child to make their own decisions (Chapters 4, 5, 7, 8 & Epilogue)

Notes

1 www.mencap.org.uk/learning-disability-explained/research-and-statistics/health-research-and-statistics/mental-health, accessed 15 April 2018.
2 Available from: www.gov.uk/government/uploads/system/uploads/attachment_data/file/398815/SEND_Code_of_Practice_January_2015.pdf, accessed 31 July 2019.
3 The MCA COP can be downloaded free from www.gov.uk/government/publications/mental-capacity-act-code-of-practice, or purchased from some high street or online booksellers or from The Stationery Office at www.tsoshop.co.uk.
4 United Nations (undated) *Definition of Youth.* Available at: www.un.org/esa/socdev/documents/youth/fact-sheets/youth-definition.pdf, accessed 10 March 2018.
5 Department of Health (2012) 'Liberating the NHS: No decision about me, without me.' London: DOH. Retrieved from: https://assets.publishing.service.gov.uk/government/uploads/system/uploads/attachment_data/file/216980/Liberating-the-NHS-No-decision-about-me-without-me-Government-response.pdf, accessed 24 June 2018.

PART 1

DECISION-MAKING

Chapter one
MAKING DECISIONS

We all make decisions every day of our lives; many of those are what could be termed small decisions – everyday decisions – what to eat, what to wear, etc. Other decisions are bigger and perhaps better made after giving the matter some considerable thought. As you are perusing this, you have decided to acquire the book, and now, to find the time to read it. In the author's opinion, that is a good decision; hopefully, you will agree. But, are you aware of the process that you use to make a decision? Perhaps thinking about a recent decision – choosing a sandwich, booking a holiday, buying new clothes – will assist. Write down the process you went through, which, all being well, closely resembles the procedure described later in the chapter.

What is decision-making?

Decision-making is a cognitive process. Research has shown that people tend to think about making decisions in the same way, suggesting there is a common set of cognitive skills (Hastie and Dawes 2001, cited in Beresford and Sloper 2008). The dictionary defines decision-making as 'the process of making choices, especially important choices'.[1] Analysing this indicates the process can be described as 'a series of actions or steps taken to achieve a particular end'[2] – the 'choice'. The implication being that it is an active procedure, which may involve several different actions to arrive at the outcome, suggesting it may take time to arrive at the choice. The definition suggests that this process is more likely to be applied to choices that are perceived to be important; conceivably, for some decisions, importance is a subjective assessment. Choosing a sandwich could be considered a small decision, perhaps not one needing to be subjected to a lengthy decision-making process. However, for diabetics or those with other special dietary needs, picking a sandwich may need to be given more careful consideration. Probably, most people would agree that making a choice that results in a big change to a person's life or involves a significant financial outlay, or personal risk, is an 'important' decision requiring the careful consideration indicated by the definition.

Essentially, the above has presented a theoretical model of decision-making, which gives little clue as to how to make this into a functional framework to assist education and associated professionals in teaching and supporting children and young people with SEN to make their own decisions. Perhaps the starting point for this process would be to scrutinise the heart of decision-making – the choices on offer. Being given a choice implies there are at least two options to consider. The dictionary defines 'choice' as 'a range of possibilities from which one or more may be chosen'.[3] Beresford and Sloper (2008) highlighted that the options offered needed to have a positive value to the person making the choice. They considered that if a person was being given a choice between something they really liked against something they disliked, this was not a real choice. Whilst an admirable aspiration, in real life there are times when the choices are not all highly desirable, or there may be only one real option. Think of Henry Ford's offer to customers – you can have any colour so long as it is black.[4] This is known as Hobson's choice – a situation where there appears to be a choice between different options, but, in reality, there is only one choice.[5] For some children and young people this may be the case in relation to some decisions about their education.

Pondering the attributes of choices gives food for thought in relation to teaching children and young people with SEN to make their own decisions. Intuitively, in the initial stages of teaching the process, it would seem appropriate that the options are all seen as positive, to show the child or young person how to evaluate the choices. However, if decision-making is a life skill, then there is an argument for introducing choices that are not all desirable, as we do not always have a choice between highly desirable options. This perhaps applies more to 'important' decisions than everyday ones. An 'important' decision children and young people will be involved in making is choosing their next education institution; in this case the options may not all be seen positively, but all must be seriously considered. Consider 11 year old Marvin's dilemma, which is based on a real situation the author encountered, many years ago, when working as a local authority educational psychologist (EP). How would you have helped him make the decision?

Marvin's high school choice (part 1)

Marvin is in Year 6, he is a wheelchair user. He is the subject of an EHC Plan due a life-limiting degenerative physical disability and attends his local mainstream primary school. He, like his classmates, is choosing his high school. Most of his friends will be attending Clipper High School, but this school, having been built in the 1960s, has limited access for wheelchair users and no lift. Marvin is aware the local authority would like him to attend Trillian Academy, the resourced high school for pupils with physical disabilities, which is in another part of the city. Marvin's parents took him to visit the school, during which he made his dislike of the school very clear. He was very reluctant to look at the different areas of the school. Clipper High School are willing to consider Marvin attending part-time for lessons he can access on the ground floor, but he would

> not have access to the first-floor science labs, computer and technology rooms. He would need another educational placement, such as the offsite provision for children and young people with medical needs, or for his paediatrician to state he was not well enough to attend school on a full-time basis. The Children and Families Act 2014 (SEND COP 9.85) has provision for children to have a dual placement, mainstream and a special school.

Marvin was being asked to choose between two options, his choice and the local authority's preferred one. In other situations, there may be more than two choices, which raises the question about how many options should be offered to children and young people with SEN – all the actual choices or a reduced number? Mitchell (2012) found that parents facilitated their child making choices by limiting the options presented to those the parents thought best or most appropriate. In real life the number of options is likely to vary depending on the situation, but how will it be decided if all or only a few are offered? If it is a limited number, who will decide and what criteria will be used to determine which are offered? Is offering a restricted number of choices, thereby enabling some autonomy, better than overwhelming the child or young person with all the possible options so they are unable to choose? A rule of thumb for considering the choices being offered is for the education or associated professional or parent to stand in the child's or young person's shoes, that is to see the situation from their perspective, and consider the options the child or young person would wish to be given. The issues around choices will be revisited later in this chapter and throughout the book, particularly in Chapters two, five and the Epilogue.

In summary, the above suggests the issue of choices and the decision-making process could be considered a complex one, with many possible factors to be explored (Mitchell and Sloper 2011). This may now make you think teaching and supporting children and young people with SEN to make their own decisions is a daunting prospect. Perhaps the twentieth-century American cognitive psychologist Jerome Bruner's well-known hypothesis may help us see this is not necessarily the Herculean task it may seem. Bruner (1962, cited in Elkind 1975) stated: 'We begin with the hypothesis that any subject can be taught effectively in some intellectually honest form to any child at any stage of development' (p245). Hopefully, the straightforward framework, founded in the MCA COP decision-making process, presented below, will assist education professionals, supported by associated professionals, turn theory into practice to achieve this important undertaking and help realise the aspiration that there is no decision about a child or young person's education without their participation in some form.

How do we learn to make decisions?

Looking back to her childhood, the author can recall being given choices, and perhaps the first 'important' decision was selecting a high school, which was not straightforward. The fact the author can recall the process and feelings associated with this choice from all those years ago suggests the position she was placed in at a young age had an impact and, perhaps, helped her to be able to make difficult decisions. Can you recall your first 'important' decision? How did you make your choice?

Child development

From a child development perspective, decision-making is a cognitive process which develops from early childhood to young adulthood. Whilst it is aligned to certain areas of the brain, decision-making is a learned behaviour and is reliant on experience for its development. Imaging techniques have shown that the prefrontal cortex, the part of the brain right at the front of the head, plays an important role in decision-making in relation to making advantageous choices when there is uncertainty. This part of the brain is not fully matured until young adulthood, but the area that processes rewards develops early (Levin et al. 2014). Understanding rewards is an important factor in learning, enabling skills to be taught such as decision-making.

A child's development of their decision-making ability should be viewed against the backcloth of adults' decision-making skills, which are variable. Jacobs and Klaczynski (2002) summarise the research into adult decision-making as showing adults are quite accurate making everyday decisions but they are affected by judgement biases, depend on what seem like inappropriate decision-making shortcuts and make less than good decisions across a variety of situations. Levin (2014) considers decision-making sometimes as being a fine balance between reflectiveness and more impulsive processes. This accords with the author's view of her decision-making skill; she can think of poor decisions arrived at by focusing on unimportant factors or being influenced by the media, family, friends, or perceptions, as well as good decisions she has made.

Generally, in child development there are ages when it is expected a typically developing child will have acquired certain skills or behaviours. For decision-making, Levin et al. (2014) cite research supporting the idea that it is a child or young person's cognitive (reasoning) abilities rather than age that is the more important factor in the development of decision-making ability. Jacobs and Klaczynski (2002) also felt trying to ascertain age differences in decision-making competence had led to studies focusing on what children could do under optimal conditions, rather than realistic conditions when there may be other factors such as personal goals, beliefs and prior experience to add to the consideration of a child's decision-making ability. Jacobs and Klaczynski highlight that children's development of decision-making is not a one-direction model of developing logic and efficiency. They consider there are two developmental changes from childhood to adulthood: the first is improvements in reasoning competencies, the second is the increase in the number of and frequency of use of heuristics (strategies); this includes judgement biases. Most researchers distinguish between what is referred to as 'normative reasoning', based on the rules of logic, and 'heuristics', based on the person's own rules or beliefs.

Reasoning abilities

Whittaker (2014) presents an overview of children's development of reasoning and problem-solving skills, including logical reasoning, which begins in infancy, and continues through the pre-school years; these cognitive skills underpin the development of decision-making. Reasoning begins in the first year of life, object permanence develops around the age of 9 months, which is when a child will begin to look for something they drop on the floor. By about a year old a child will find a hidden toy, such as a toy hidden in a cup (Sheridan 1975). Understanding cause and effect begins to develop between 9 and 12 months old (Whittaker 2014). From nursery age to Y1 (6 years old) a child develops the ability to reason and generalise what they find out from their own behaviour or experiences – inductive reasoning. From the age of 3 to 4 years children develop the ability to understand and make comparisons. During the same period children also develop the ability to use facts or general rules to draw conclusions, such as if X happens then Y will also happen – deductive reasoning. For example, a child can work out it is bedtime because they have been changed into their pyjamas.

Heuristics

The American Psychological Association website[6] defines heuristics as 'rules of thumb that can be applied to guide decision-making based on a more limited subset of the available information'. Gigerenzer and Gaissmaier (2011) explain heuristics as a reasoning process, conscious or unconscious, which ignores part of the information. The Oxford dictionary[7] defines heuristic as 'enabling a person to discover or learn something for themselves'. Unlike the decision-making process, which is considered to have a common set of cognitive skills, heuristics, the strategies used to arrive at a decision, vary between individuals. People will use different strategies for different decisions; there is a need to have a range of strategies to apply to decision-making (Beresford and Sloper 2008). Increases in knowledge of the social world lead to judgement heuristics and other biases as factors affecting decision-making. Overall, as age increases so do the number of heuristics and the situations to which they are applied (Jacobs and Klaczynski 2002).

Overlaying the changes in reasoning and heuristics from childhood to adulthood are other factors affecting an individual, such as social, motivational and emotional influences, which can bias reasoning and judgements. A child or young person's use of a particular decision-making strategy, normative reasoning (logic) or a shortcut heuristic approach, may be influenced by a desire to support favoured beliefs (Jacobs and Klaczynski 2002).

Returning to Marvin choosing his secondary school, he wanted to attend the same school as his friends, despite it being an unsuitable placement as he would be unable to access the full curriculum or all the facilities. His overriding desire was to be with his friends. He was determined not to like the resourced high school, even though it had the key facilities he had put on his checklist – lift, physio room and social room at lunchtime. His analysis showed that both schools had the same number of positives; however it was the value Marvin attributed to these that influenced his decision. His values were not the same as the adults'; access to the curriculum and gaining qualifications were not priorities for him. Marvin's decision-making process used his own rules rather than logic.

Language of decision-making

The discussion above has introduced some of the language related to decision-making. It is essential for children and young people with SEN that there is a consistent use of language by everyone, that is education and associated professionals and parents. Teaching, supporting and enabling decision-making is effected through communication, and a shared language will facilitate this process. As noted in the Prolegomenon, the Mental Capacity Act 2005 (MCA) is all about decision-making; it provides a framework, language and model for the decision-making process. Although the MCA does not apply until a child has reached their 16th birthday, developing their decision-making ability should begin from the earliest age, therefore it would make sense to use this language from the outset, thus familiarising children, young people and their parents with the language and concepts. Parents become acquainted with the language of SEN enshrined in the SEND COP; it is equally important they are conversant with the language of decision-making. The SEND COP places an emphasis on collaborating with parents, which can be facilitated by education and associated professionals' consistent use of terminology.

The author is not alone in considering the MCA framework as a useful way to consider a child's decision-making ability. The Honourable Mr Justice Cobb sitting in the High Court in October 2017 pondered a means of assessing a child's competence to consent to her baby being placed for adoption ([2017]EWHC 2729 (Fam)). The parties agreed that a child's competence to make a decision generally uses the principles of Gillick Competency (see glossary and Chapter three). Mr Justice Cobb highlighted there is a difference between assessing a child's competence to make a decision and the capacity assessment set out in the MCA.

He proposed that 'the following principles relevant to decision-making under the MCA 2005 can usefully be applied to Gillick decisions' (para 17). He added weight to this by stating:

> . . . while it is abundantly clear that the MCA 2005 does not apply to those under 16 years of age, there is an advantage in applying the relevant MCA 2005 concepts and language to the determination of competence to the under-16s . . . (para 19)

Mr Justice Cobb set out five components for his model, which are effectively the same as the four elements set out in the MCA COP and SEND COP Annex 1 ('four key questions'). These are to:

- understand the information
- retain the information
- weigh and use the information
- communicate the choice

Exploring the language of the MCA starts with the title concept 'mental capacity', often referred to as 'capacity' – the terms are used interchangeably. 'Mental capacity' means the ability to make a decision – any decision, big or small. As noted above, a child's ability to make a decision is known in the UK as 'competence', however 'capacity' is the internationally recognised term, and this is used by the UN in the United Nations Convention on the Rights of the Child, known by the acronym UNCRC (UNICEF 1990). As Mr Justice Cobb proposed using the language and concepts of the MCA when referring to a child's decision-making ability, the term 'capacity' will be used in this book.

The MCA COP (4.1) categorises decisions as:

- *everyday*, which so far have been termed 'small decisions', such as what to wear, what to eat, which computer game to play, who to sit next to, who to play with. Developmentally, everyday decisions are the first choices a child is given, milk or water, paint or crayons, red or blue jumper. The importance of giving children and young people these choices is further explored in Chapters 2 and 3.

- *'more serious or significant'*: earlier in the chapter these were referred to as 'important' decisions, characterised as resulting in a big change to a person's life or involving a significant financial outlay or personal risk. Effectively, this type of decision will have a long-term consequence or involve a risk. Additionally, these decisions are more likely to be concerning a future event rather than something that will happen immediately as with everyday decisions. In relation to education these may be decisions about choosing a new education institution or placement, selecting options, how to be supported, whether to go on a residential trip, or the content of the EHC Plan. For many 'more serious or significant' decisions that will be made by children or young people, financial outlay may be less likely to be a consideration, although this may become more of a factor for young people.

This book will use the terms 'everyday' for small decisions and 'important' for the 'more serious or significant' decisions. The MCA COP refers to 'use and weigh the information' as the process by which the decision is reached, and this terminology will be used throughout this book. In day-to-day work, education or associated professionals will probably be teaching and supporting children and young people with SEN to make everyday decisions. Within an educational context the 'important' decisions probably, generally, occur less frequently. There is further discussion about making educational decisions in Chapter four.

Besides making decisions, we frequently rate our decisions as good or bad and, similarly, our ability to make decisions. In the Prolegomenon, the author noted that, in her opinion, you had made a good decision by choosing to read this book. How do you rate your decision-making ability? It may depend on what you are having to decide and the time available to make your choice(s). The author's belief in her good decision-making ability is often defeated by menus in cafés or restaurants! However we rate our decision-making ability, as adults, we don't always make good or wise decisions, but perhaps we learn from making unwise choices. The wisdom of a decision is a subjective judgement; what is wise for one person may not be the appropriate choice for someone else. This raises the matter of children and young people making what those supporting them may feel is an unwise decision – does the education or associated professional intervene to 'help' the young person make what in their view is the right decision? This is a thorny issue; undoubtedly any restriction of the choices offered by the education or associated professional to ensure only those considered 'right' are available is well intentioned, but is it ethical? Surely, making wrong decisions is a learning experience; why is a young person with SEN not having the same opportunity to make mistakes as those without SEN? When making decisions, the author often asks herself: what is the worst thing that could happen if I make the wrong choice? Perhaps education or associated professionals could think about this question if they are considering limiting the options offered, but wish to present a choice or choices they feel would not be the right one for that young person. Although the education and associated professionals' role in relation to developing, supporting and enabling children's and young people's decision-making is considered throughout the book, it possibly does not resolve this dilemma.

Decision-making framework

The discussion above provides a definition and general overview of the decision-making process, as well as introducing some of the associated language. The challenge for education and associated professionals is turning theory into practice. Hopefully, the systematic framework presented below, which both explains the decision-making process and provides a step-by-step guide, will facilitate this; it is intended to be used for 'important' (MCA COP 'more serious or significant') decisions.

At the beginning of the chapter you were invited to write down your decision-making process, which presumably closely follows the usual way of thinking described here. It begins with identifying the decision that needs to be made; the next step is to establish what options there are to choose from, then what information is needed to enable the choice to be made, and having obtained the information work out the pros and cons of each of the options to make the decision. This is the model that is encapsulated in the Mental Capacity Act 2005 and therefore is the recognised decision-making process in England and Wales; the Mental Capacity Act (Northern Ireland) 2016 enshrines the same process. As noted earlier in the chapter, the MCA model is made up of four components (SEND COP Annex 1, MCA COP 4.14), which are to:

- understand the information relevant to the decision
- retain the information long enough to make the decision
- use and weigh the information to arrive at a choice
- communicate the decision in any way, verbally or non-verbally

It is interesting to note that the decision-making process models enshrined in legislation in different European countries also follow a similar model. For example, Dutch medical professionals Grootens-Wiegers et al. (2017) set out the four standards to assess children's and young people's ability to make decisions about their medical care – being able to:

- understand the information
- communicate their choice
- reason about risks, benefits and possible consequences
- appreciate the relevance of the choices to their own situation

Decision-making framework for 'important' decisions

This is a systematic decision-making framework with clearly identified steps, which takes time to work through, emphasising that decision-making is a considered process. Table 1.1 presents the framework, with visual symbols representing each stage. When working with a child or young person, it is important to work through each step, using the symbols and language of decision-making, as this provides both a model and language for independent decision-making. Whilst education or associated professionals can replace the symbols with

Making decisions

those that are consistently used within the education institution to represent the ideas, the key is consistency and as far as possible using widely recognised symbolic representations such as emojis. For example, the author has used smiley and sad faces to indicate like and dislike – she could have chosen thumbs up/thumbs down emojis.

Table 1.1 Decision-making framework for 'important' (more serious or significant) decisions

Framework	Explanatory notes
Teaching, supporting and enabling decision-making is an interactive process based on knowing how to communicate with the child or young person and understanding their communication.	
1. What is the actual decision that needs to be made? • Why is this decision needed? • What happens if the child or young person or their parent does not make the decision? • Is there a time-frame in which the decision needs to be made?	This needs to be framed as straightforwardly as possible, including considering the best way to communicate the decision that has to be made to the child or young person. There is usually a reason a decision needs to be made; helping the child or young person to understand why they are being asked to make a choice may be helpful. If there is a decision to be made, then there is usually a consequence of not making the decision, such as not being considered for something or someone else choosing for you. Some decisions, such as choosing a new education institution, need to be made by a set date.

2. Information about the choices
• What are the options?
   A⊙ B⊙ C⊙
• Need to gather relevant information
  ○ How will the child or young person be helped to do this?
  ○ Who could assist?
• What format should the information be presented in?
  ○ photos, pictures, videos
  ○ objects of reference
  ○ easy written materials
  ○ audio
  ○ via signing
  ○ by experiencing the options
	To consider the choices, the child or young person, or their parent need to know about the options. These need to be presented in a way the child or young person can understand.
	
	Relevant information is information specific to the particular choices. For example, if the decision is choosing an education institution, then the relevant information will be about the institutions under consideration. Presenting the information in the most accessible format for the child or young person is very important to support, develop and enable their decision-making ability. It may be appropriate to consider involving the young person's parents. However, bear in mind that if the young person is aged over 18 years their consent will be needed to involve their parents.

Teaching, supporting and enabling decision-making is an interactive process based on knowing how to communicate with the child or young person and understanding their communication.

Framework	Explanatory notes
⚖️ 3. **Using and weighing the information** 🙂☹️💡 • The child or young person needs to be helped to show what they like or dislike or the advantages or disadvantages of the options. • Having set out what the child or young person likes and dislikes about the options, use this information to make their choice.	This is about analysing the pros and cons of the choice, the things the child or young person likes or dislikes about the options. For many children and young people with SEN, this is probably best done visually, using a Talking Mats style approach or similar, or using technology, such as putting pictures or symbols under a smiley/thumbs up or sad face/thumbs down emoji. It is important to keep a record so the child or young person can revisit their thoughts. Keeping these as a paper file or electronically is essential as a record of the child or young person's decision-making ability and the extent of their participation in the decision-making process. It can be presented to others or included in reports as the child or young person's views. The child or young person now has to look at how they have rated each choice in terms of likes/dislikes, positives/negatives or advantages/disadvantages, and use the information to make a choice based on this consideration. This may be challenging for some children and young people. Generally, if there are more things under the 'likes' it would be expected this would be the child or young person's choice. If the more liked option is chosen it suggests the child or young person has understood the decision-making process for this particular choice. If they choose the option with the more 'dislikes', this may indicate they have not understood the process for this particular decision. However, good practice would suggest trying again on another day.
💬 4. **Communicate the decision** The child or young person can use any verbal or non-verbal means of communication to indicate their choice.	The child or young person can communicate their choice verbally or non-verbally. It is essential the person working with them can understand their preferred means of communication. Equally, those supporting children and young people to enable, or teaching, decision-making should know how to communicate with them.

Making decisions

SEND COP (1.1–1.10) sets out the obligation that children and young people participate as fully as possible in decision-making. Using the framework may assist in demonstrating the child's or young person's participation in the decision-making process for the particular decision. Appendix 1 presents completed decision-making frameworks to show the child's or young person's participation in the decision-making process for the 'important' decision of choosing a new education institution at different phases of education: secondary transfer, post 16 transfer when the choice is being made in Year 11, then when the young person is aged 16–17 years 11 months in Y12 and aged 18–25 years. Appendix 2 provides a child/young person version of the framework which has been completed as if Marvin had used it for his high school choice.

Identifying the decision

The first step is to identify the actual 'important' decision that needs to be made; the example used in Appendix 1, choosing a new education institution is a clear decision, which can be framed straightforwardly. Decision-making is a life skill, an integral part of preparation for adulthood, therefore it is important to include the steps in the process which help the child or young person understand the context of the decision. If there is a decision to be made, generally, there is a particular reason for this and there may be an adverse impact on the child or young person if the decision is not made. Helping children and young people understand the context may facilitate them participating in making the decision. Frequently there is a time-frame for a decision to be made in; this is likely to be the case for many 'important' decisions in education. Thus, teaching children and young people the decision-making process includes ensuring they are taught about time constraints. This is likely to be challenging for children and young people with a limited understanding of the concept of time. However, it may prompt thinking about how to recognisably differentiate days of the week, such as using different scents for each day of the week; this is discussed further in Chapter five (Decision-making syllabus).

Choices

Having established the 'important' decision that needs to be made, the next step is to identify the choices. The number is likely to vary depending on the decision. Earlier in the chapter the number of options to be offered was discussed in terms of whether a child or young person with SEN may be overwhelmed considering all the available options and should only be offered a limited number. Another factor to consider in relation to decisions relating to education is how realistic it is to consider some of the possible options. For example, all children of compulsory school age (see glossary), attending state-funded schools, can make choices about which school they wish to attend, but the actual allocation of a school place is made by the local authority or school. For post 16 education, if the young person is reliant on local authority funding then the same constraints apply as for compulsory schooling, the local authority have to agree the placement. Therefore, is it wise to consider options that are unlikely to be agreed by the local authority, or should only choices that are realistic, from the local authority's perspective, be considered? This is difficult, because decision-making as a life skill and preparation for adulthood suggests the child or young person may need to experience not getting their choice. However, it needs to be considered in what circumstances, when making an 'important' decision as an adult, it does not result in being given one of the choices. In health, doctors and healthcare professionals, generally, only offer choices that are available: the one selected is what happens. Similarly, social care professionals are only likely to offer options that are really available, therefore the one chosen is likely to happen. However, having applied for a job, or an educational or training place, including traineeships, apprenticeships and supported internships, this may not lead to success. Leisure activities are another area where there may be a limited number of places available for any particular activity, and despite choosing to do the activity, the child or young person is not selected or is the 51st person when there are only 50 places. This suggests that, in preparation for adulthood, children and young people may benefit from some experience of not getting their choice.

Information

Many children and young people will require some guidance and support gathering the necessary information about each of the options to assist them in making the decision. This part of the decision-making process will take time, thus, it is essential to ensure that the decision-making process is begun some time before the decision actually needs to be made. For children of compulsory school age, they may receive help and support from their parents, as well as school staff and associated professionals. Depending on the decision, school staff, parents and the child working together may be the most beneficial in terms of promoting the child's participation in the decision-making. Advice and support may be needed from other education or associated professionals to support this. Young people over compulsory school age but under 18 years old may wish their parents to be involved in supporting them. Again, a partnership between parents, education institution staff and the young person may facilitate the young person's participation in decision-making. Furthermore, it may be that advice and support from other education or associated professionals is required to maximise the young person's participation. When the young person has turned 18 years old, they are an adult and should be treated as such. For example, if the decision is an education institution-based decision, such as choosing an option, work experience placement or going on a residential trip, education institution staff can only involve the young person's parents with the young person's consent, if they have capacity to give their consent.

Information must be presented in a format(s) the child or young person understands; this may be visual such as photos, videos, pictures, easy read materials, symbols, signs, or auditory such as recordings, podcasts, etc. What is relevant will depend on the decision being made. For example, when choosing a new education institution, the child or young person will need to know the names of the establishments, ideally to visit each, meeting relevant staff. Preparation for the visit will assist in ensuring the relevant information is gathered, enabling the child or young person to decide what it is they wish to find out about, and plan how to record the information during the visit. The information will need to be retained, if it is on a tablet computer or mobile phone, then backing it up is essential. Chapter four provides a detailed exploration of how to support children and young people to choose a new educational or training placement.

Using and weighing the information

Having gathered all the information necessary to make the decision, the child or young person must evaluate the choices. In reality, for many children and young people with SEN, this process will be identifying what they like or do not like about aspects of the choices. If the child or young person has in some way experienced the options, then their direct experience may assist the process; hopefully there is a video recording or photos, to remind the child or young person what they did and how they felt about it. Additionally, there may have been observations by others about the child's or young person's responses to the options, which may be helpful. Both videos and observations will be particularly useful for parents if they are making the decision.

At the simplest, identifying likes and dislikes will be through using smiley and sad faces, thumbs up, thumbs down, for example a Talking Mats style approach (see Prolegomenon and Appendix 7). Making a visual record, which is retained in some way, such as by photographing it, will be important so the child or young person's views are known and can be reported to others.

Returning to Marvin choosing his secondary placement, he has a decision-making outcome in his EHC Plan:

> By the end of the Y6 Autumn term, Marvin will have been able to follow the decision-making framework with support, to help his parents make the 'important' decision of choosing his high school, to ensure he has participated in the decision-making.

Following his visits to Clipper High, The Willow Centre and Trillian Academy, Mrs Joseph, his TA, takes this as an opportunity to see if Marvin can use the decision-making framework child form (see Appendix 2) to work through the process to make his choice.

Marvin's high school choice (part 2)

Prior to visiting the two schools Mrs Joseph had supported Marvin to decide what information he felt he needed to help him make the decision. Marvin had decided that he wanted his parents to take photographs with his iPad of key areas in the school, and he had listed what these were; also he had some questions for the SENCos of each school. Attendance at Clipper High would be part-time with either home-schooling or attendance at The Willow Centre, the offsite specialist provision for children with medical needs, therefore he also visited this provision. Marvin's parents had informed Mrs Joseph of his reaction to Trillian Academy; nevertheless, Mrs Joseph wanted Marvin to give this school proper consideration under the decision-making framework. She explained that there would be times when one of the choices being offered was not at all to his liking, but it was important to learn to always fully consider all the options. Mrs Joseph and Marvin had been completing the decision-making framework form for each step. Now the time had come to 'use and weigh the information'. Marvin's parents had photographed and videoed the visits on the iPad. Marvin and Mrs Joseph had a checklist of the things he had wanted to find out as well as looking at the different areas. Mrs Joseph had made three columns, one for each school (see Appendix 2 for Marvin's completed form); watching the video she asked Marvin what he thought about each item, like or dislike, and she recorded a smiley or sad face; Marvin could see the smiley or sad faces being drawn on the checklist. At the end of this process, Mrs Joseph showed Marvin his responses, asking him to count the smiley faces for each choice. He had recorded the same number of smiley faces for Clipper High and Trillian Academy. Interestingly, he had fewer smiley faces for The Willow Centre than for the other two schools. Mrs Joseph discussed this with Marvin and then asked him to think about what it would be like attending two schools, Clipper High and The Willow Centre. Marvin was clear he wanted to attend Clipper High. Although he had not really liked The Willow Centre, he thought it would be better going there for some of the week rather than being at home as he felt he would be lonely at home and miss being with other children.

Mrs Joseph copied the child decision-making framework form and the checklist for Marvin's parents for them to consider. Marvin's parents did choose Clipper High and The Willow Centre.

Communicate the decision

Communicate is used here in the broadest sense, verbally or non-verbally. A child or young person's difficulties with verbal communication are not a barrier to being able to participate in decision-making or express their choice. It is important that all those supporting a child or young person with decision-making are very familiar with their means of communicating and can understand it. Equally important is the education or associated professional knowing how to communicate effectively with the child or young person; this may include being familiar with assistive technology or signing.

Conclusion

In summary, although decision-making is a learned developmental process that begins in early childhood continuing into young adulthood, it does not have specific ages by which a typically developing child will have acquired aspects of the skill; they acquire particular reasoning abilities and use particular heuristics at different ages. Research seems to suggest that a child's developing reasoning ability is a better indicator of decision-making ability. There is a pattern of development which relates to increasing normative reasoning ability alongside acquiring and using more heuristics. However, children use these approaches variably in relation to characteristics of the task, motivation, their beliefs and social context factors.

The research consensus indicates that children and young people's experiences play an important part in the development of the reasoning abilities that underpin decision-making skills. As noted above, decision-making is aligned with the prefrontal cortex. Belsky and de Haan (2011) indicate that post-natal childhood brain development may be shaped by children's experiences including parenting. They cite research which demonstrated qualitative differences in brain development between rats raised in enriched environments and those in impoverished ones. This highlights the importance of those first choices offered to a child by their care-givers – milk or water, apple or banana, red or blue jumper – in the development of decision-making skills. The theoretical underpinning for this is provided by Bruner's hypothesis that children can be taught to do things if the task is presented in the right way for them in relation to their developmental level. Lanciono et al. (1996, cited in Beresford and Sloper 2008) reviewed the research literature relating to people with severe and profound developmental disabilities and their ability to make choices and express preferences. The choices were familiar and concrete items, such as food, drink, music, and when presented in an accessible way Lanciono et al. found that most individuals with severe or profound developmental disabilities can make choices and show preferences. A later review of similar literature by Canella et al. (2005) also showed that individuals with severe and profound developmental disabilities are able to make choices, as well as demonstrating that care-givers learn to appropriately provide opportunities for choices on a daily basis, and that being given choices has a positive impact on behaviour.

The importance of the role of experience in developing children and young people's decision-making also gives guidance for education and associated professionals for activities, and potentially developing a syllabus to foster decision-making abilities. Whittaker (2014) focuses on early years practices, advocating education professionals try to offer interesting and challenging experiences, alongside facilitating children's play, helping children understand the differences between guessing and knowing, and assisting children to explore different solutions to a problem. As noted earlier, children and young people with SEN are less likely to acquire decision-making skills through incidental learning and will probably benefit from direct teaching. Returning to Bruner's hypothesis cited earlier in the chapter suggests that Whittaker's guidance is applicable to all children and young people with SEN and any syllabus developed to foster decision-making skills would perhaps be best constructed as a 'spiral curriculum' (see Chapter five).

Summary

- Decision-making is
    - the process of making choices
    - a cognitive developmental process that is learned and is reliant on experiences
    - a life skill.
- Research suggests people use the same processes to make decisions suggesting there is a common set of cognitive skills.
- Rich experiences play an important role in the development of decision-making abilities.
- A developmental perspective demonstrates that it is a child's cognitive (reasoning) abilities that are more important than age in the development of decision-making abilities.
- Consideration should be given to the number of options, whether this should be a restricted number or all the available options.
- The language of decision-making for this book is adopted from the Mental Capacity Act 2005.
- Decisions are classified as 'everyday' or 'more serious or significant', the latter referred to as 'important' decisions in this book.
- A systematic decision-making framework based on the Mental Capacity Act 2005 decision-making model is proposed, which accords with the nationally and internationally recognised models of the decision-making process.
- The decision-making framework and emphasis on providing opportunities for making decisions are supported by Bruner's hypothesis that any subject can be taught effectively in some intellectually honest form to any child at any stage of development. If the task is

presented to a child or young person in the right way in relation to their developmental level, they can be taught to do things.

- Many individuals with severe or profound developmental disabilities are able to make choices, or show preferences, if the items are familiar and concrete such as food and drink, and being given such choices has a positive impact on behaviour.

Notes

1 Online *Cambridge Dictionary.* Available from: https://dictionary.cambridge.org/dictionary/english/decision-making, accessed 10 March 2018.
2 Online *Oxford Living Dictionaries.* Available from: https://en.oxforddictionaries.com/definition/process, accessed 10 March 2018.
3 Online *Oxford Living Dictionaries.* Available from: https://en.oxforddictionaries.com/definition/choice, accessed 12 March 2018.
4 Online *Automotive News*, 16 June 2003. Available from: www.autonews.com/article/20030616/SUB/306160713/model-t-had-many-shades;-black-dried-fastest, accessed 12 March 2018.
5 Online *Cambridge Dictionary.* Available from: https://dictionary.cambridge.org/dictionary/english/hobson-s-choice, accessed 12 March 2018.
6 The American Psychological Association website, www.apa.org/pubs/highlights/peeps/issue-105.aspx, accessed 1 April 2018.
7 Online *Oxford Living Dictionaries.* Available from: https://en.oxforddictionaries.com/definition/heuristic, accessed 1 April 2018.

Chapter two

MENTAL HEALTH PERSPECTIVE

As noted earlier, being able to make decisions enables a child or young person to have some control in their life which in turn has a beneficial effect on mental well-being. The author believes that the education and associated professional's approach to supporting and developing children and young people's decision-making ability, thereby enabling them to make as many of their own decisions as possible, should be embedded in everyday practice. This is both from the perspective of children's and young people's rights, as well as part of the wider agenda of fostering positive mental well-being. This chapter and the next explore the evidence from research, legislation, policy, national and international, and case law, to support the contention that developing decision-making should be part of an education and associated professional's everyday practice.

Children's and young people's mental health has recently become a focus for the government and is seen as a significant social challenge (DfE 2017a), leading to the publication of a Green Paper in December 2017 to consult on transforming children and young people's mental health provision in England. The proposals link to and build on what is already being done by schools and colleges. The consultation outcome was published in July 2018[1] and the government agreed to train Designated Senior Leads for mental health in schools and colleges for a fifth of schools from September 2019, as well as fund new Mental Health Support Teams, supervised by NHS children and young people's mental health staff. The government proposed a range of delivery models for these teams, including those led by a group of schools, others by voluntary or community sector organisations or further education colleges, with the expectation that schools, colleges and other local partners will have a central role in designing and leading delivery. It is expected that the first Mental Health Support Teams will be operational from the end of 2019. Additionally, children will learn about mental health through the curriculum; by September 2020 health education will become a compulsory subject in all schools. Children will be taught about healthier lifestyles, including physical health, as well as how to build mental resilience and well-being; however there is no reference to supporting children to develop their decision-making ability. From July 2019 the government hoped there would be

Mental health perspective

a trained Mental Health First Aid practitioner in over 2,000 secondary schools; in July 2018 there was one in about a third of the 3,448 (DfE statistics)[2] state secondary schools in England.

Mental health

The exploration begins with establishing a definition of mental health in terms that are understood by education and associated professionals. The Royal College of Psychiatrists website[3] defines mental health as 'a state of well-being in which the individual realises his or her own abilities, can cope with normal stresses of life, can work productively and fruitfully and is able to make a contribution to his or her community'. It also provides a definition for the associated term 'emotional well-being' which it recognises is favoured by schools as a synonym for mental health: 'emotional well-being is a positive state of mind and body, feeling safe and able to cope, with a sense of connection with people, communities and the wider environment'. Combining the two definitions, with further information in terms familiar to education professionals, may create a more accessible explanation of mental health to assist thinking about the child's or young person's functioning in the education institution context.

> Mental health: a state of well-being in which the individual realises his or her own abilities (self-esteem or self-belief, confidence), can cope with normal stresses of life (feels safe and able to cope), can work productively and fruitfully (achieves academically and/or in other areas such as sports, creativity, music, dance) and feels a sense of connection with people (friends, family, education institution staff), communities and the wider environment, and is able to make a contribution to his or her community (school, college and/or home community).

DfE (2018) provides a functional guideline indicating a child or young person may be described as experiencing mental health problems or disorders when their emotional and behavioural responses are outside the normal range for their age. This publication also lists the range of mental health issues experienced by children and young people.

This book uses the term 'mental health' and 'mental well-being' interchangeably, with the meaning of the combined definition set out above. The Royal College of Psychiatrists website notes the most common mental health issues relevant to children and young people – these are set out in Table 2.1 below.

Table 2.1

Mental health issue	Prevalence: Public Health England (2016) unless otherwise stated
Conduct disorders – defiance, e.g. physical and verbal aggression, vandalism	5.8% children aged 5–16 years
Emotional disorders, for example:	
• anxiety	2.2% children aged 5–10 years
	4.4% children aged 11–16 years
• depression	0.2% children aged 5–10 years
	1.4% children aged 11–16 years
• obsessive compulsive disorders	0.25% children aged 5–15 years
	However, it is rare in young children and increases towards adult prevalence at puberty (Heyman et al. 2001)
Neurodevelopmental disorders, for example:	
• attention deficit hyperactivity disorder (ADHD)	1.5% children aged 5–16 years
• autism spectrum disorder	1 in 100 children and young people (National Autistic Society website)[1]
Attachment disorders, for example children who are markedly distressed or socially impaired as a result of an abnormal pattern of attachment to parents or major caregivers	
Eating disorders – can develop at any age, although the majority start in adolescence or young adulthood; however these can begin at a younger age (NICE 2017)[2]	Beat eating disorders website[4] presents prevalence data for unspecified eating disorders:
	0.2% girls aged 5–10 years
	2.3% females aged 11–24 years
	0.5% boys aged 5–10 years
	0.79% males aged 11–24 years
• anorexia	16–17 years average age of onset
• nervosa and bulimia nervosa	18–19 years average age of onset
• avoidant or restrictive food intake disorder (ARFID), an anxiety related disorder. It differs from anorexia and bulimia as the food restriction or avoidance behaviours are not related to concerns about body image. It can be caused by a lack of interest in food, such as not being aware of appetite, or sensory aversion, such as look or texture, or a phobia based on the consequence of eating, such as choking or vomiting[3]	Can begin at a very young age

(*Continued*)

Table 2.1 (Continued)

Mental health issue	Prevalence: Public Health England (2016) unless otherwise stated
psychosis, e.g. schizophrenia	Less than 1% children aged 5–16 years
	Rarely seen before 14 years of age, after that an increasing incidence
emerging borderline personality disorder	Presents in adolescence

1 www.autism.org.uk/about/what-is/myths-facts-stats.aspx, accessed 22 April 2018.
2 www.nice.org.uk/guidance/gid-qs10026/documents/briefing-paper, accessed 14 July 2019.
3 www.acamh.org/blog/avoidant-restrictive-food-intake-disorder-arfid/?gclid=EAIaIQobChMIwMXq_LTy4QIVGLLtCh29EgeDEAAYASAAEgKs1vD_BwE, accessed 28 April 2019.
4 www.beateatingdisorders.org.uk/how-many-people-eating-disorder-uk, accessed 16 July 2019.

Prevalence of children and young people's mental health problems

The Department of Health (2015) considers mental health issues as relatively common, indicating that at least one in four people experience mental health problems at some point in their lives, and states that over half of mental health problems in adult life (excluding dementia) have begun by the age of 14, and three-quarters by 18 years old. According to the Young Minds website[4] (a child and adolescent mental health charity), in April 2018, children and young people's mental health is in crisis. This is echoed by the Royal College of Psychiatrists in a briefing paper published on 30 January 2019, citing that about 1.25 million children and young people in England aged between 5 and 19 had a mental disorder in 2017. Education staff in England surveyed by the DfE (2017a, 2017b) commented that they feel there is an increasing number of children and young people presenting with complex needs. This perception is supported by statistics. CentreForum (2016) data analysis suggests there was a significant rise in children's mental health problems between 2010 and 2015. During this time the numbers of young people attending Accident and Emergency departments for mental health conditions almost doubled. Referrals to specialist mental health services between 2013 and 2015 increased by about two-thirds.

The DfE (2017b) indicate that one in ten children (5–16 years) have a diagnosable mental disorder. CentreForum (2016) suggests this equates to around 720,000 children and young people. Fazel et al. (2014) stated that other children (4–17 years old) experience psychological distress at a lower level (that is, not meeting diagnostic criteria), but this still has an adverse effect on well-being. The Young Minds website indicates one in five adolescents may experience a mental health problem in any twelve-month period. The government's mental health of children and young people prevalence survey (England) conducted in 2017, published in November 2018,[5] shows that one in six 17–19 year olds experienced a mental disorder, with one in sixteen experiencing more than one. Females aged 17 to 19 were twice as likely as males of the same age group to have a mental disorder. In the 5 to 15 year old age group there has been a slight increase in the overall prevalence of mental disorders from 9.7% in 1999 to 11.2% in 2017. The prevalence of identified mental disorders in pre-school children was one in eighteen.

In 2016, a quarter of a million children and young people in England were in contact with mental health services (DfE 2017b), however figures cited by the Children's Commissioner (2017) indicate this represents only between 20% and 25% of children with a mental health condition who are receiving treatment. CentreForum (2016) suggests 75% of children and young people needing help may not have been able to access it, drawing attention to the fact that over 50% of headteachers responding to a survey indicated that they had struggled to get mental health support for their pupils. The Royal College of Psychiatrists noted in January 2019 that NHS data released in January 2019 showed there was a decrease in the number of CAMHS[6] (see glossary) psychiatrists between October 2013 and October 2018.

Patalay and Gage's (2018) analysis of two UK birth cohorts – Avon Longitudinal Study of Parents and Children (ALSPAC), following those born in 1991–1992, and the Millennium Cohort Study (MCS), following those born in 2000–2002 – concurs with other statistical analyses showing an increase in mental health problems in adolescents, providing more detailed information about particular mental health issues for children aged 14 in 2005 and 2015. This study's findings are important as poor mental health at 14 years old is known to be predictive of poorer long-term health, social and economic outcomes. During the ten-year period the incidence of depressive symptoms meeting the threshold for a diagnosis of depression rose from 9% to 14.9%; this represents an increase in both males (5.65% to 9.19%) and females (12.4% to 24%). There was also an increase in self-harming behaviours in both genders over the decade – males from 6.86% to 8.49% and females from 16.9% to 22.8%. During the same time period there was also an increase in some parent-reported difficulties from the Strengths and Difficulties Questionnaire (see glossary) for both sons and daughters. Significant emotional symptoms were reported by 4.7% of parents for their sons in 2005, which rose to 10.5% in 2015; daughters showed an increase from 6.67% to 17.4%. Conduct problems rose from 6.42% to 13.7% for males and 5.55% to 9.89% for females. Parental reports of significant hyperactivity in males rose from 8.81% to 13.4% and for females from 3.69% to 6.41%. Significant peer problems also showed an increase for both males (11.2% to 18.5%) and females (6.71% to 14.9%) over the decade. Additionally, the study indicated that in 2015 adolescents had less sleep, their BMI (Body Mass Index) was higher and there were increased perceptions of being overweight. In 2015 other factors that have been associated with poorer mental health such as smoking, drug use and drinking alcohol in fact had declined in young people since 2005.

The study concluded that the link between health-related factors (sleeping, weight and perceptions of being overweight) and mental health appears to have changed, suggesting that the relationship may be more complex and dynamic than has previously been considered. The researchers introduced the idea that the trend in what they term risky health behaviours, such as decreased sleep, higher weight and perceptions of being overweight, might provide an explanation for the increasing mental health issues experienced by adolescents, both males and females. This study found that the increase in depressive symptoms and self-harming behaviours was not greater in females than males, even though the females had a higher baseline level. However, it is important there is more research to find the causal risk factors linked to poor outcomes for young people's mental health.

Mental health problems and children and young people with SEN

When the statistics are examined for children and young people with SEN, the incidence of mental health problems is higher. The Office for National Statistics[7] (2008) found that children with SEN were sixteen times more likely to have a persistent mental health problem and four times more likely to develop mental health issues than children without SEN. Emerson and Hatton (2007) found a prevalence of mental health problems of 36 per 100 in children and young people with intellectual disabilities compared to 8 per 100 for children and young people without intellectual disabilities. The Royal College of Psychiatrists' website (see note 3) indicates that children with learning disabilities are six times more likely than other children to experience mental health problems, one in a hundred children and young people have autism and around seven in ten children or young people with autism have an additional mental health problem.

Deaf children and young people are another group with a higher prevalence of mental health issues, 40% experiencing mental health problems compared to 25% for their hearing counterparts (Department of Health 2002).[8] The Sign Health (a deaf health charity) website[9] indicates that deaf children are 30–50% more likely to experience mental health problems than hearing children.

Children and young people's mental health and education

There is an increasing awareness of the importance of children and young people having good mental health (Department of Health 2015). Public Health England (2016) summarises the impact of poor mental well-being in childhood and adolescence as likely to have an adverse and long-term effect on life chances, leading to low academic attainment, and difficulties with physical health, employment and social relationships. Children and young people with mental health issues are more likely to smoke and abuse alcohol and drugs. CentreForum (2016) indicates that children and young people with mental health problems are more likely to have time off school and fall behind with their education.

In recent years the government has focused on offering schools support for children and young people's mental well-being, publishing two advice documents for schools, *Mental Health and Behaviour in Schools* (DfE 2018) and *Counselling in Schools* (DfE 2015). In the summer term of 2016 the Department for Education (DfE) commissioned research to understand what schools, colleges and other education institutions, in England, currently do to identify mental health issues and support and promote positive mental health and well-being (DfE 2017a, 2017b). The outcome, as noted above, led to the publication of a Green Paper and some staff in education institutions being trained to promote and support children and young people's mental health.

The DfE believe schools and colleges play an important part in a wider systems approach to promoting positive mental well-being and helping prevent mental illness in children and young people (DfE 2017a, 2017b). The research findings suggest this view is shared by the education professionals surveyed; they consider they have a unique position because of the amount of time children and young people spend in their care, enabling relationships to be built that support them as well as their families. However, exactly how this role was viewed differed between different phases of education and between mainstream and special. Mainstream primary school staff felt their roles supporting children's mental health and as educators were equally important. Mainstream secondary school and FE college staff viewed their part in supporting mental health in the context of enabling academic achievement. Special school and pupil referral unit staff believed supporting children and young people's mental health was integral to their work as educators, trying to embed this into everything they did. Fazel, a child and adolescent psychiatrist, and her colleagues (Fazel et al. 2014) highlight the importance of the role of schools in supporting not only cognitive and academic progress but also children's social and emotional development. They promote the idea of child and adolescent mental health services being embedded within schools to improve both mental health and academic attainment.

Mental health perspective

Despite the DfE research (DfE 2017a, 2017b) only receiving responses from about a fifth of the 13,105 education institutions surveyed – schools (mainstream and special), alternative provision, pupil referral units, academies and FE colleges – the results show an impressive understanding and wide range of support for children and young people's mental health issues. Approaches included creating a supportive ethos which seeks to normalise mental health issues, likewise raising awareness of how and where pupils can access support. Therapeutic interventions are offered through counselling, art, music, play and Lego therapy, as well as having a dedicated calm space for use as a break from the classroom. Peer mentoring, buddy systems, and group interventions are noted. Mental health issues form part of the PSHE or similar curricula and are addressed in assemblies and tutor time. Education institutions accessed external support and made referrals to children and young people's mental health services. Education staff identified the barriers and challenges to supporting children and young people's mental health issues as the increasing numbers of those presenting with problems, a lack of financial and other resources, limits to staff capacity to offer support alongside teaching commitments and inability to provide enough counselling or therapy.

The DfE survey (DfE 2017b) showed that education institutions do teach specific skills to enhance children's and young people's mental health and likewise to enable them to manage it. There were some attributes that were considered as essential for good mental health, in effect the underpinnings, including resilience, self-esteem and confidence. Education institutions promote the development of these through providing supporting structures and activities, such as teaching meditation and relaxation techniques to all students. Support, at what could be considered particularly stressful times, is offered, such as in Year 6 around secondary transfer or Year 10 and Year 11 for exam anxiety. Additionally, education institutions offer targeted support to specific groups of children and young people through group and individual interventions, such as anger management, confidence boosting, resilience programmes, addressing loss and bereavement, well-being courses for anxiety and low self-esteem, and support groups for victims of bullying, or looked after children and young people. However, there was no specific mention relating to teaching or supporting the development of decision-making. The absence of decision- or choice-making outcomes in EHC Plans suggests that the importance of enabling children and young people to make as many of their own decisions as possible is not yet recognised as being supportive to mental well-being, as well as the preparation for adulthood required by the SEND COP. Although education institutions do address decision-making in some curriculum areas, such as PSHE and extra-curricular activities, this takes the form of practising decision-making skills rather than being tutored about how to make decisions. There is an implication that children and young people will learn to make decisions by incidental learning or osmosis.

This is reflected in the plethora of resources to practise decision-making skills, in contrast to the dearth aimed at developing children's decision-making ability. At the time of writing the only resource that seemed to include any teaching of the decision-making process has been produced by SEMH (social, emotional and mental health) teachers Shay and Margaret McConnon.[10] Their practical materials are intended to be used as part of PSHE lessons, assisting in recognising and practising decision-making to make informed choices about smoking, alcohol and drugs as well as choosing school subjects and thinking about a career.

Conclusion

The statistics cited suggest that every education and associated professional, during the course of any academic year, will work with children and young people with some degree of mental health problems; this is more likely for those working with children and young people with SEN. Research referred to in previous chapters reports positive benefits to mental well-being when individuals with significant learning disabilities are enabled to make some choices. Canella et al. (2005) reported that when individuals with severe to profound learning disabilities were given choices, this led to, in the majority of cases, a decrease in inappropriate behaviours and an increase in appropriate behaviours. Implicit in this is a benefit to the individual's carers and educators if the young person's behaviour becomes less difficult. This is illustrated by a case from the author's experience.

Arthur's choice-making

Arthur is 20 years old. He is the subject of an EHC Plan recording his barriers to learning as autism and severe learning difficulties, with associated delays in receptive and expressive language skills and social communication, difficulties with sensory regulation and anxiety. Having left his special school at the end of the summer term, he transferred to Willemstad College, a residential specialist college, three days per week, staying two nights, for 38 weeks per year. He follows a life skills programme with some opportunities to practise skills in the community; in the residential accommodation he learns how to prepare simple meals. Additionally, for two days per week throughout the year, he attends Jesska House, a social services provision for adults with autism and learning difficulties. Here he has a bespoke individual learning plan designed to develop his practical life skills, including communication, social interaction, thinking skills and social tolerance, which are targeted in all sessions, and much of his programme is undertaken in a range of community settings. Like Willemstad College, preparing meals is part of his curriculum, including shopping for the ingredients.

> When Arthur is attending Jesska House, he stays with his mother. At the weekends he stays with his stepfather. Initially Arthur found the transition to the two new placements stressful, resulting in a significant deterioration in his behaviour at home, which his mother found very challenging. By the end of the spring term he had settled well into both settings and his behaviour at home had significantly improved. Reflecting on his two terms in the placements, his mother and stepfather commented that he had become more independent in his choice-making and was asking for specific foods, which they were very pleased about, and they generally agreed to his choice. They also considered it showed that he was able to generalise his learning.

The DfE survey highlights that education professionals understand the importance of certain attributes as being factors promoting good mental health; the author believes the evidence supports that the ability to make decisions should be included among these. This would then lead to structures and activities to promote the development of children's and young people's decision-making ability from the earliest age. Lanciono et al. (1996, cited in Beresford and Sloper 2008) noted the importance of the environment and access to assistive technologies to facilitate indicating choices; this is discussed further in Chapter five. As already noted, children and young people with SEN are likely to need direct teaching and guidance to develop their decision-making abilities, as they are far less likely to acquire this knowledge through incidental learning. Therefore, it is imperative that education and associated professionals actively promote the inclusion of a developmentally or age-appropriate decision-making outcome as part of person-centred planning and in EHC Plans to ensure there is a focus on developing this important life skill, which promotes independence and mental well-being.

Notes

1 Available from: https://assets.publishing.service.gov.uk/government/uploads/system/uploads/attachment_data/file/728892/government-response-to-consultation-on-transforming-children-and-young-peoples-mental-health.pdf, accessed 1 July 2019.
2 DfE schools, pupils and their characteristics: January 2019. Available from: https://assets.publishing.service.gov.uk/government/uploads/system/uploads/attachment_data/file/812539/Schools_Pupils_and_their_Characteristics_2019_Main_Text.pdf?_ga=2.168719777.1430611029.1566807840-1194259298.1566807840, accessed 26 August 2019.
3 www.rcpsych.ac.uk/pdf/Bettermentalhealthoutcomesforchildrenandyoungpeo.pdf, accessed 22 April 2018.
4 Available from: https://youngminds.org.uk/about-us/who-we-are/, accessed 15 April 2018.

5 Available from: https://digital.nhs.uk/data-and-information/publications/statistical/mental-health-of-children-and-young-people-in-england/2017/2017, accessed 1 July 2019.
6 In some health authorities CAMHS is known as Healthy Young Minds.
7 http://webarchive.nationalarchives.gov.uk/20160105160709/http://www.ons.gov.uk/ons/about-ons/business-transparency/freedom-of-information/what-can-i-request/previous-foi-requests/people-and-places/mental-health-of-children-from-separated-parents/follow-up-report-on-mental-health-of-children.pdf, accessed 16 April 2018.
8 http://webarchive.nationalarchives.gov.uk/20130124065527/http://www.dh.gov.uk/prod_consum_dh/groups/dh_digitalassets/@dh/@en/documents/digitalasset/dh_4104005.pdf, accessed 15 April 2018.
9 Available from: www.signhealth.org.uk/what-to-do-if-your-ddeaf-child-needs-mental-health-support/, accessed 15 April 2018.
10 S. McConnon and M. McConnon, *Your Choice Decision Making*. Northampton: incentiveplus.co.uk.

Chapter three

LEGISLATIVE CONTEXT

In my view, it is axiomatic that people with disabilities, both mental and physical, have the same human rights as the rest of the human race . . . This flows inexorably from the universal character of human rights, founded on the inherent dignity of all human beings and is confirmed in the United Nations Convention on the Rights of Persons with Disabilities. Far from disability entitling the state to deny such people human rights: rather it places upon the state (and upon others) the duty to make reasonable accommodation to cater for the special needs of those with disabilities.

Lady Hale (2014)[1]

The Prolegomenon introduced the main legislation, relevant to education, that supports children's and young people's rights to make their own decisions; this chapter explores these and other legislative structures that promote this.

The importance of children and young people making their own decisions is recognised internationally; this is supported by UK government legislation and case law. As already noted, in England and Wales the right to autonomy, in relation to decision-making, is enshrined in the Mental Capacity Act 2005, but this only comes into effect after the young person's 16th birthday. Northern Ireland has similar legislation.

A driving force for the UK to incorporate children's and young people's participation in decision-making about their education into the Children and Families Act 2014 derives from the UK becoming, like most countries in the world, a signatory of the UN Convention on the Rights of the Child[2] (UNCRC) in April 1990, ratified by Parliament in December 1991.[3] The fifty-four Articles set out children's rights to life, identity, education, care, protection, and how adults and governments must work together to ensure all children can enjoy their rights. In March 2010 a Department for Education publication documented its implementation programme to show how the rights and obligations of the UNCRC were being incorporated into education legislation, including increased pupil participation. This explains the emphasis in the Children and Families Act 2014, the accompanying SEND COP, and equivalent Welsh and Northern Irish legislation, on children and young people participating in making decisions about their education and the inclusion of a core principle that children will be encouraged to participate in decision-making about their education before their 16th birthday. The Children and Families Act and SEND COP assimilate the relevant Articles of the United Nations (UN) Convention on the Rights of the Child, including:

- Article 5: Governments must respect the rights and responsibilities of parents to provide guidance and direction to their child as they grow up. This must be done in a way that recognises the child's increasing capacity to make their own decision.

- Article 12: Every child has the right to express their views, feelings and wishes in all matters affecting them, and to have their views considered and taken seriously. This right applies at all times. The views of the child to be given due weight in accordance with the age and maturity of the child.

- Article 13: Every child must be free to express their thoughts and opinions and to access all kinds of information, as long as it is within the law. This right shall include freedom to seek, receive and impart information and ideas of all kinds, either orally, in writing or in print, in the form of art, or through any other media of the child's choice.

- Article 14: Every child has the right to think and believe what they choose and also to practise their religion, as long as they are not stopping other people from enjoying their rights. Governments must respect the rights and responsibilities of parents to provide direction to the child in the exercise of his or her rights in a manner consistent with the evolving capacities of the child.

- Article 17: Every child has the right to reliable information from a variety of sources and governments should encourage the media to provide information that children can understand. Governments must help protect children from materials that could harm them.

- Article 28 1d: Make educational and vocational information and guidance available and accessible to all children.

SEND COP paragraphs 1.1–1.12 set out the requirements that children's and young people's voices are heard, they are provided with information, and they participate in decision-making as far as they are able to do so. Thus, the onus is on education and associated professionals to ensure children and young people receive appropriate information to facilitate them being able to make a particular decision. SEND COP 1.39–1.41 address successful preparation for adulthood; decision-making is referred to in relation to independent living – 1.40 specifically states the duty on education and associated professionals to enable children and young people to make their own decisions from an early age. The requirement to provide information about SEN, disability, health and social care is supported through the stipulation that local authorities have impartial information, advice and support services (SEND COP Chapter 2), as well as the Local Offer (SEND COP Chapter 3; see glossary), generally

Legislative context

online information about local support services for children and young people with SEN or disabilities across education, health and social care. SEND COP Chapter 6 sets out schools' obligations, including publishing information in an easily accessible form for children and young people (6.81). These provisions are further supported by education institutions' duties under the Equality Act 2010 to make reasonable adjustments for disabled children and young people, including the way information is made accessible.

SEND COP: children and young people making their own decisions

As noted above, in SEND COP Chapter 1 (Principles) paragraph 1.40 is the statement that '**all professionals** working with families should look to enable children and young people to make choices for themselves from an early age . . .' (p28). Following this, the guidance offered specifically relating to children and young people making their own decisions is in SEND COP Chapter 8 'Preparing for adulthood from the earliest years', essential reading for all education and associated professionals working with children and young people with SEN. As already noted, decision-making is subsumed in the 'independent living' preparing for adulthood outcome (SEND COP 1.39). Therefore, when this phrase is used in relation to preparing nursery and school-aged children for 'independent living', implicitly this includes developing, supporting and enabling decision-making. More explicit information is offered regarding children and young people aged 14 and over with an EHC Plan in terms of the requirements for preparation for adulthood reviews as part of the annual review process (SEND COP 8.9–8.12). SEND COP 8.10 sets out the expectation that, under the auspices of reviewing support to prepare for independent living, the young person's decision-making is addressed and there is a plan for their role in decision-making, implying there will be a decision-making outcome and provision to develop and enable the young person's decision-making. However, at the time of writing (August 2019) the author has rarely seen a decision-making outcome in an EHC Plan (Section E).

For young people over compulsory school age, the Children and Families Act 2014 gives them the right to make decisions about matters relating to EHC Plans rather than their parents; the specific decisions are set out in SEND COP 8.14 and will be discussed further in Chapter four of this book.

Overall there is limited guidance for education and associated professionals about enabling children and young people to make their own decisions from an early age, but there is a clear expectation that this will happen. Any information provided tends to focus on children aged 14 and over, leaving education and associated professionals working with children below this age with little direction, despite the emphasis that children from an early age will be enabled to make their own choices. The author reiterates her concern that there is no explicit advice to consider including a decision-making outcome in person-centred planning and EHC Plans from the earliest age. SEND COP 9.69 sets out the statutory requirements for the content of each section of the EHC Plan: outcomes are recorded in Section E. The only stipulations concerning outcomes related to preparing for adulthood are that they prepare the child or young person well for adulthood and that they are linked to achieving the aspirations set out in Section A. This does not necessarily promote the inclusion of a decision-making outcome. The author believes that education professionals should proactively consider the need for a decision-making outcome, explicitly discussing this with children, young people and parents; likewise with associated professionals supporting the child or young person's education.

Equality Act 2010

The SEND COP (xix) states that the Equality Act 'sets out the legal obligations that schools, early years providers, post 16 institutions, local authorities and others have towards disabled children and young people' (p16). This is further supported by the Department for Education's (2014) non-statutory advice for school leaders, school staff, governing bodies and local authorities, *The Equality Act 2010 and Schools.* Essentially, schools must not discriminate against pupils based on their gender, disability, race, religion or beliefs, or sexual orientation. They must make reasonable adjustments to ensure disabled children and young people are not at a substantial disadvantage compared with their non-disabled peers (SEND COP xix). In relation to developing and empowering children and young people to make their own decisions, this means not making assumptions about decision-making capacity based on disability, and ensuring all reasonable adjustments, including assistive technology, are employed to support children and young people in acquiring decision-making skills and using them. Consider the two scenarios below regarding whether the approaches are in keeping with the Equality Act 2010 requirements.

Rodney cooks his lunch

Rodney is in Year 8 attending a mainstream high school resource for pupils with learning difficulties. He is the subject of an EHC Plan recording he has learning difficulties associated with Down's syndrome, including significantly delayed receptive and expressive language skills, he sometimes uses Makaton signs, and has fine motor difficulties due to low muscle tone. He has some lessons, such as practical subjects, as part of a small mainstream class and others in the resource. The Food Technology

Legislative context

department has one room with a fully adapted cooking station for use by a pupil who is a wheelchair user, and a range of food preparation aids, such as special chopping and spreading boards, adapted chopping knives, graters, can openers and peelers, kettle tippers, cooking baskets and non-slip mats, to facilitate independence for disabled pupils and those with SEN.

Rodney takes part in cookery lessons with ten pupils from the school's 'nurture' provision. He is the only pupil in the group with an EHC Plan; other pupils have their special educational needs met through SEN support. The class is staffed with a teacher and two teaching assistants (Ms Felix and Mr Singh). Rodney likes cooking; his task is usually differentiated for him to use the adapted cooking aids and photo instructions, enabling him to work as independently as possible, though he usually needs some adult prompting and supervision for safety reasons.

As it is the end of term, the group are being given a choice of simple pasta dishes to cook, using either white or wholemeal pasta, which they will eat for lunch. The choices are penne pasta tuna Bolognese, spaghetti Bolognese with mince, macaroni cheese, or macaroni cheese with either bacon or mushrooms. The class was given the same choices at the end of last term. The pupils are shown both photos of the dishes and pre-prepared ones. Rodney usually chooses from the pre-prepared dishes; he likes both macaroni cheese and tuna Bolognese with white pasta.

Scenario A: Mr Singh asks Rodney verbally, supported with Makaton signs, which dish he wishes to cook; he points to the macaroni cheese. Mr Singh puts up the photo sequence to show Rodney the ingredients and the adapted pans and utensils he will need, leaving him to collect these. Mr Singh will help Rodney weigh and measure, and, for safety reasons, he will supervise him using the hob and serving the hot food. He does not do it for Rodney but ensures that he does these safely.

Scenario B: Ms Felix feels Rodney's learning difficulties are more significant than those of the other pupils in the group, therefore he will find it difficult to make a choice. Ms Felix recalls that last term he made tuna Bolognese, and she decides this is what he will probably choose again. She puts up the photo sequence for this dish in Rodney's work area while he, sitting with the rest of the group at the front table, listens to the teacher explaining what they will be doing. Ms Felix goes to Rodney, indicating he should accompany her to his work area, where she shows him the photos for the tuna Bolognese. She asks him to stay in his work area whilst she collects the ingredients. Making the dish involves cutting up an onion and part of a green pepper, opening cans of

> tuna fish and tomatoes, as well as heating the sauce ingredients and cooking the pasta in boiling water. Ms Felix feels this is all too dangerous for Rodney, particularly as he has some difficulties with fine motor skills. She decides he can watch her make the dish, and she will ask him to pass her ingredients and utensils as she needs them.

Scenario A demonstrates that Rodney has the same choices as his classmates, and reasonable adjustments are made so he can complete the task in a similar way to his peers. In Scenario B, the teaching assistant has made assumptions based on his learning difficulties, so he is being treated significantly differently from his classmates; this could be considered discrimination. Additionally, the teaching assistant does not seem to consider there are reasonable adjustments to the activity that would enable Rodney's participation in a similar way to his peers.

Other relevant legislative structures

Cheshire West

Education and associated professionals working in residential special schools or residential specialist colleges will be aware of the guidance from the Law Society (2015) about deprivation of liberty arising from the March 2014 Supreme Court case, commonly known as Cheshire West, applying to the residential section of the school or college. Deprivation of Liberty Safeguards are part of the Mental Capacity Act 2005 and this case addressed whether the residential arrangements made for the appellants, which they lacked capacity to consent to, had deprived them of or restricted their liberty. Understandably, it is not immediately apparent how this has any relevance to developing children and young people's decision-making ability and non-residential education institutions. However, it is some of the issues raised during the case and in the subsequent Law Society guidance that are pertinent to enabling children and young people's decision-making in both residential and day educational provision. Although this guidance applies to those aged 16 years and over, living in some form of publicly funded residential placement, again the ideas can be extrapolated to those younger, in terms of facilitating their preparation for making their own decisions, and thereby to day education institutions.

As noted in the Prolegomenon, the deprivation of liberty element of the MCA has been amended by the Mental Capacity (Amendment) Act 2019 (Act), which is likely to come into force during 2020. At the time of writing, the accompanying Code of Practice, which sets out how the law will work in day-to-day practice, and regulations, have yet to be written. This

Legislative context

Act changes the process by which someone aged 16 years and over can be deprived of their liberty in a publicly funded residential placement and mandates that the views and feelings of the person being deprived of their liberty must be ascertained regarding the proposed arrangements. It also seems to extend the remit to day centre placements and travel arrangements to and from there. Consequently, there will need to be some amendments to the Law Society (2015) guidance, but the substance, which is predicated on Cheshire West, remains relevant.

The Law Society guidance (2015) advocates that young people's 'welfare must be safeguarded and promoted. But equally, they must have the physical and emotional freedom to develop and make, and learn from, their own mistakes' (9.12 p97). Although not specifically mentioning decisions or choices, it is implicit, as mistakes can only be made if the young person has made a choice. Thus, this clearly sets out the expectation that young people should be making choices within the context of a well-supported safe situation. Whilst the quote really refers to living arrangements, it is equally applicable to a day education institution and has implications for the way in which children and young people are supported to enable them to do as much for themselves as possible, even if this means making mistakes. In many ways this document offers more guidance to education and associated professionals working with children and young people with SEN to develop and enable their ability to make decisions than the SEND COP.

The Law Society guidance stems from the Cheshire West case in which the two young people's (MIG and MEG) carers made all the decisions for them about every aspect of their life; they were not allowed to do anything their carers did not wish them to do. MIG was 16 years old; she had a learning disability which was considered to be on the borderline between moderate and severe. She had been placed with a foster mother, whom she loved, who gave her intensive support in most aspects of daily living and took her on trips and holidays. However, if MIG had attempted to leave the house by herself her foster mother would have restrained her. It was accepted that MIG enjoyed a relatively normal life and did not seem to have any objection to her placement, however the restrictions placed on her led Lady Hale (Supreme Court judge) to comment, 'a gilded cage is still a cage' (para 46 Cheshire West).

Information in the Law Society guidance provides an insight into the overarching ethos to support children and young people's decision-making, noting there should be a certain degree of freedom alongside sensible precautions, protection from avoidable risks but avoiding excessive caution. It recommends that children and young people are offered reasonable choices, when there is choice, indicating that children and young people cannot always have what they want; some choices may contravene the law or the education institution's rules or policies. This raises the issue of defining 'reasonable choices', who decides what is reasonable and which choices are offered. However nebulous this advice may seem, it clearly signals the expectation that children and young people with SEN will be offered choices and supported to be able to make a choice. There was some discussion of this issue in Chapter one, and it is revisited again in Chapters four, five and the Epilogue.

The Law Society guidance discusses the supervision element in terms of deprivation of or liberty restricting measures related to living arrangements. However, the issues raised in terms of supervision and intensive support can be extrapolated to classroom or non-classroom activities, be it in a day or residential education institution, to examine how children and young people are supported to promote and facilitate their ability to make decisions. This includes how those assisting the child or young person's learning provide the support. Consider the way in which support is offered in the two case studies below. Which is more likely to develop and enable the child's decision-making ability?

Jill makes a sandwich

Jill is in Year 8 in a special school for pupils with learning difficulties. She has significantly delayed receptive and expressive language skills, and sometimes uses Makaton signs. She has some fine motor difficulties due to low muscle tone. Jill can follow photo instructions to make a sandwich with adult support. She likes ham sandwiches on white bread with margarine, cut into four; sometimes she will choose a cheese sandwich on brown bread. The class are making a sandwich to eat as a mid-morning snack.

Scenario A: Jill is being supported by Mrs Dent, who often works with her. Jill is shown the pre-prepared sandwiches, ham, ham and cheese, or cheese, on either brown or white bread, so she can choose which sandwich she wishes to make; she points to the white bread ham sandwich. Mrs Dent puts up the photos on the Velcro strip to show Jill in what order to do things. Mrs Dent points to the first photo showing the ingredients and asks Jill to get these, supporting her verbal language with Makaton signs. Jill points to the ham, indicating this is what she is going to get first. She repeats this until she has collected all the ingredients and then takes down the photo. Mrs Dent points to the next photograph showing the margarine being spread on the bread. Jill points to Mrs Dent indicating she wants her to spread the margarine. Mrs Dent encourages Jill to do this herself by taking the lid off the margarine tub as Jill finds this very difficult.

Legislative context

> Again Jill points to Mrs Dent, who responds by loading the knife with margarine and giving it to Jill to spread, which she can do and does. Mrs Dent asks Jill what she needs to do next, supporting her verbal question with Makaton signs. Jill points to the ham, and with Mrs Dent's verbal encouragement, supported with Makaton signing, she puts the ham on the bread. Unprompted, Jill puts the slice of bread on the top and points to Mrs Dent, indicating she wants her to cut the sandwich. Mrs Dent shows Jill a picture of a sandwich cut in half and one cut into four. Jill points to the sandwich cut into four. Mrs Dent puts knife marks on the sandwich to help Jill cut it, encouraging her to do this. Jill makes a good attempt but needs Mrs Dent's help to properly cut through all the layers.
>
> Scenario B: Jill is being supported by Mrs Gaborsky, who often works with her. There are pre-prepared sandwiches for the support staff to show the pupils, so they can choose which to make. However, Mrs Gaborsky knows Jill will choose a white bread ham sandwich, therefore she puts up the white ham sandwich sequence photos on the Velcro strip to show Jill how to make her sandwich. Mrs Gaborsky has already collected the ingredients for Jill. Mrs Gaborsky points to the photograph showing the margarine being spread on the bread. Jill points to Mrs Gaborsky indicating she wants her to spread the margarine, which she does as she knows Jill finds this difficult. Mrs Gaborsky points to the ham telling Jill to put this on the bread, supporting the verbal instruction with a gesture. Mrs Gaborsky then points to the slice of bread, gesturing to show this should be put on top of the ham, which Jill does. Mrs Gaborsky then cuts the sandwich into quarters.

Scenario A describes a way of supporting which is more likely to enable the child's decision-making ability as Jill was given choices, albeit limited ones. Most importantly, the teaching assistant did not make any decisions for Jill, she supported her to make all the choices, thereby giving her some control over the making of her sandwich. Equally essential, the teaching assistant communicated with Jill in a way that is known to facilitate her understanding, verbal language supported with Makaton signing. This approach may have taken longer overall to complete the task, but it enabled Jill to make choices and prepare the sandwich she wished to eat. These are the same choices the teaching assistant herself would expect to be allowed to make in the same situation. In scenario B, the teaching assistant is well-intentioned; Jill does have a sandwich, but not one she chose, although it may have been what she would have chosen. Additionally, although the teaching assistant accompanied some verbal language with informal gesture, there was no clear intention to communicate with Jill in the way that facilitates her understanding. This process does not show Jill that she can make choices that give her some control over things that affect her. The main decision, which type of sandwich, was made for Jill, denying her the option to choose a different sandwich that day, despite there being a choice available.

Gillick Competency

Gillick Competency (see glossary), as noted in Chapter one, is a way of determining a child's capacity to make an important decision. The term arises from a legal case, Gillick v West Norfolk & Wisbech AHA & DHSS [1985], in which Mrs Gillick challenged her local health authority and the Department of Health regarding guidance to doctors allowing them to provide contraception to girls under 16 years old without their parents' knowledge. Gillick Competency was set out in the judgment as:

> whether or not a child is capable of giving the necessary consent will depend on the child's maturity and understanding and the nature of the consent required. The child must be capable of making a reasonable assessment of the advantages and disadvantages of the treatment proposed, so the consent, if given, can be properly and fairly described as true consent.

It is generally used by social workers, health professionals and lawyers, probably less often by most education professionals, with educational psychologists being the most likely to consider whether a child is Gillick competent. The author can only recall one case where she formally used Gillick Competency to agree to see a Year 11 pupil, Alice, who had a late July birthday so was not yet 16 years old, without her mother's consent. Alice spent time caring for her mother, who seemed to have some mental health issues, and her younger siblings. On the evening before Alice's art GCSE her mother destroyed Alice's art portfolio and threw her out of the home. Alice was very distressed by these events and found the exams stressful. The author was asked to see her, to enable her to write a letter for the exam boards explaining Alice's emotional state, as she was now being physically sick in exams. The school assured the author that Alice understood the purpose of the meeting and had agreed to it. When the author met Alice, she agreed with the school's opinion that Alice understood the purpose of the meeting and the implications.

Conclusion

Overall children and young people's rights to have a say in things that affect them are protected through a range of legislative structures (see Figures 3.1–3.3 below); not just

Legislative context

protection, but also an expectation that children and young people will make decisions and that there will be a shift from parents making the decisions for young people to the young people doing it themselves. Interestingly, the Gillick case (1985) pre-dates both the United Nations Convention on the Rights of the Child and the various Mental Capacity Acts, yet Lord Scarman, a judge in the case, commented in the judgment that 'parental right yields to the child's right to make his own decisions when he reaches a sufficient understanding and intelligence to be capable of making up his own mind on the matter requiring decision' (Gillick v West Norfolk 1985). Nevertheless, if children and young people lack the skills and experience to make their own decisions, they are unable to exercise and enjoy these rights. The SEND COP supports developing children's decision-making ability from the earliest age with an expectation that education and associated professionals will enable and support children and young people's decision-making skills. However, as already noted, children and young people with SEN are less likely to acquire decision-making ability through incidental learning than those without SEN; they are more likely to need direct teaching and guidance from the earliest age. Ideally, education and associated professionals should be working towards the aspiration that for every child or young person with SEN there will be 'no decision about my education without a contribution from me'.

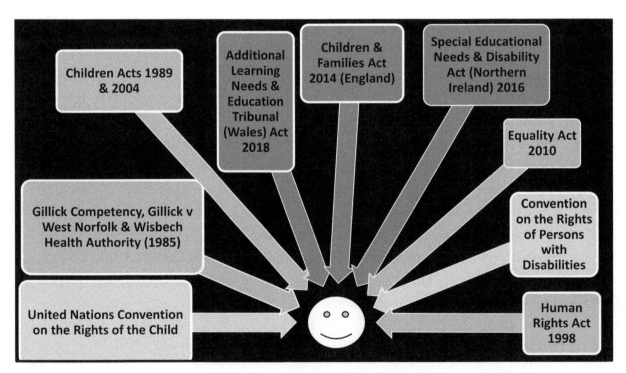

Figure 3.1 UK legislative structures that protect and support children's rights to have a say in things that affect them

Legislative context

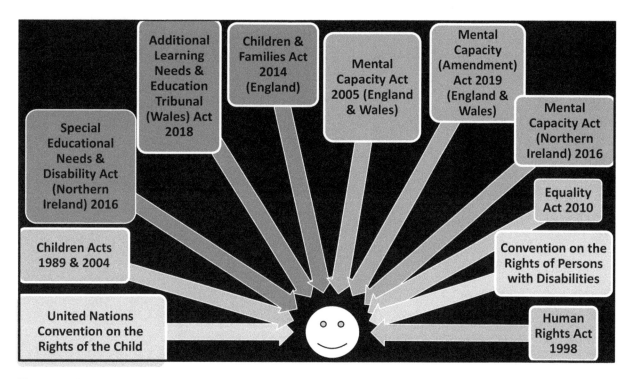

Figure 3.2 UK legislative structures that protect and support young people aged 16 years–17 years 11 months to make their own decisions

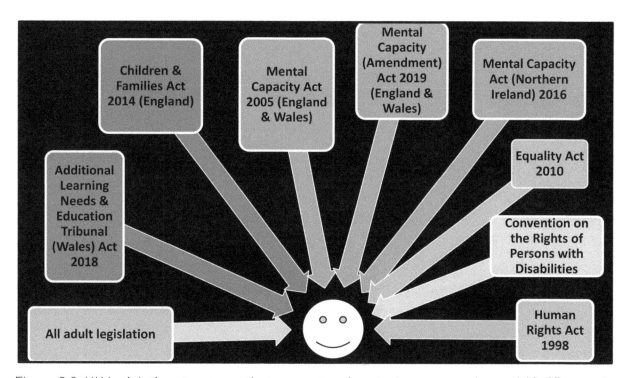

Figure 3.3 UK legislative structures that support and protect young people aged 18–25 years to make their own decisions

Notes

1 Para 45 [2014] UKSC 19 P v Cheshire West & Chester Council & P & Q v Surrey County Council (Cheshire West).
2 Available from: www.unicef.org.uk/wp-content/uploads/2010/05/UNCRC_summary-1.pdf, accessed 28 April 2019.
3 https://treaties.un.org/Pages/ViewDetails.aspx?src=IND&mtdsg_no=IV-11&chapter=4&lang=en, accessed 13 April 2018.

Chapter four
MAKING DECISIONS ABOUT EDUCATIONAL MATTERS

This chapter explores decisions children and young people are likely to make during the course of their education, introducing the education professional's role in developing, supporting and enabling children and young people's decision-making. It also focuses on how education professionals can demonstrate the extent of the child or young person's participation in decision-making. However, for many children and young people, education professionals can be most effective if they work collaboratively with associated professionals.

This chapter should be read in conjunction with Chapter five which presents a decision-making syllabus, probably better conceptualised as a scaffolding to support the development of children and young people's decision-making.

Educational decisions

Essentially, decisions about educational matters fall into two categories, those that are set out in the SEND COP relating to EHC Plans (SEND COP 8.14), and all other decisions a child or young person makes about their education. Education, in this instance, refers to all activities that take place within an education institution, in and outside the classroom, at structured and unstructured (break) times. Most decisions children and young people will make during their education are likely to be everyday decisions. However, there are some 'important' decisions that children and young people will make at certain points in their education, such as choosing:

- outcomes for person-centred planning or an EHC Plan
- a new education institution or training placement
- how to receive support
- how to describe their special educational needs
- options or courses to follow
- work experience

- to take part in an education institution day trip
- to take part in the education institution's residential trip
- to take part in outdoor pursuits, e.g. abseiling, rock climbing
- what to do after leaving education

Child or young person participating in decision-making: 'no decision about my education without a contribution from me'

The SEND COP (1.1–1.10) sets out the obligations around children and young people 'participating as fully as possible in decisions . . .' (p19). This expectation encompasses both everyday and 'important' decisions. Putting this into practice may present a challenge for education and associated professionals, raising questions about what 'participating as fully as possible in decisions' looks like; how will it be shown that the child or young person has participated in making a particular decision? Perhaps the first step is having a developmentally or age-appropriate decision-making outcome as part of person-centred planning or written into an EHC Plan, ensuring there is a focus on developing, supporting and enabling a child or young person's ability to make a decision, thereby prompting thinking about activities and experiences that will facilitate working towards achieving the outcome. This, in turn, should lead to education and associated professionals' heightened awareness of children and young people's responses which may provide information about their views, wishes and feelings, or at the very least their preferences, even if they are unable to make the decision. Considering these helps those making the decision on the child or young person's behalf to choose the option that, hopefully, is the one the child or young person would have chosen.

It is a legal requirement that those making a decision on behalf of a young person, who lacks capacity to do so, take account of their views, wishes, feelings, beliefs and values (MCA COP chapter 5). For decisions about educational matters, it is the young person's parents who make the decision if the young person lacks capacity to do so (SEND COP Annex 1). There was a change to the Mental Capacity Act 2005, via a Statutory Instrument,[1] when it was incorporated into the Children and Families Act 2014, to make parents the decision-makers if the young person lacks capacity to make the particular educational decision, rather than professionals as it is for decisions relating to health and social care matters. This means that the Mental Capacity Act 2005 works differently in education, compared to health and social care, in relation to who makes decisions on behalf of the young person when they lack capacity. Thus, it is good practice for education professionals to support parents in understanding the importance of being aware of their son's or daughter's responses to choices from the earliest age, to assist them in making decisions that reflect their child's preferences as far as is practicable or appropriate. From 16 years old, young people are entitled to make their own decisions; and only if the young person lacks capacity to make the particular educational decision would the choice be made by their parents. In this instance, the MCA COP (chapter 5) sets out the matters that need to be considered by the young person's parents to make the decision on their behalf; this includes the young person's views, wishes and feelings. However, this raises the issue of how much weight should be given to the young person's views, wishes and feelings if they lack capacity to make the decision. All the supporting legal structures, including the SEND COP, have a caveat about the weight that should be given to the child or young person's views, wishes and feelings, by the person making the decision on their behalf when the child or young person is unable to make the decision themselves.

Mr Justice Munby[2] (High Court (Family Division) 2009), hearing a Mental Capacity Act 2005 case, discussed the issue of giving weight to the views, wishes and feelings of a vulnerable adult, who lacked capacity regarding making a Will and managing their financial affairs, and when these may be determinative. Although the subject matter is not relevant to a discussion about decisions about educational matters, the Judge's thoughts are pertinent to any consideration about the weight to be given to a child or young person's views, wishes and feelings, and he offers some helpful guidance. From the outset there can be no pre-determined view about the weight to be given to a child or young person's views, wishes and feelings, it will depend on the topic. For some matters the child or young person's views, wishes and feelings may carry great weight; for another topic, for the same child or young person, they may carry less weight. Equally, the Judge considered the strength and consistency of views or responses being demonstrated as an important factor. For example, a young person may clearly demonstrate a consistent preference for cookery sessions, and their dislike of art is evident, therefore their views, wishes and feelings about making a choice of options between art and cookery should be given great weight. On the other hand, the same young person may show an inconsistent response to swimming and badminton sessions. Some weeks they clearly enjoy swimming or badminton, another week they show distress in one, or both activities, for no apparent reason. When shown the objects of reference/photographs representing the two activities and asked to choose, the young person always selects the object of reference/photograph on the right, regardless of whether it denotes badminton or swimming. In this case the child or young person's views, wishes and feelings can be given little weight.

Additionally, the Judge raised the issue of the possible impact on the vulnerable adult if their views, wishes and feelings are not being given any weight. Chapter 2 notes the benefits and importance to mental well-being of being able to make some choices. It is essential that education and associated professionals are alert to indications that a child or young person is distressed by any education institution activity and take the appropriate action. Consistently noting the child or young person's responses to activities is good practice as it may provide useful information in assisting them or their parent when making a decision about educational matters or when parents, education or associated professionals are considering limiting the choices being offered.

The role of the education professional

Perhaps the biggest challenge for education professionals will be enabling children and young people with severe or profound and multiple learning difficulties to participate in making decisions about their education, especially 'important' decisions. The scenario below imagines what 'participating as fully as possible in decisions' may look like for an everyday decision, how it could be shown that the child or young person has taken part in making this decision, and, if they are unable to make the decision, that their views, wishes and feelings have been considered. The key features are that preparation to make the decision has taken place over time, including experiencing the choices, consistency from all school staff in how the choices are represented, and noting behavioural responses, particularly looking for consistent reactions. These factors would also form the foundation for helping children and young people to participate in making 'important' decisions. This will be revisited in Chapter five in relation to developing a decision-making curriculum.

Friday afternoon choice (part 1)

Victorine is in Year 12 at Seraphine Special School which she has attended since Year 7. She is the subject of an EHC Plan recording her barriers to learning as profound and multiple learning difficulties; she vocalises but has no recognisable speech. She is unsteadily ambulant over very short distances indoors, using a wheelchair for moving around school and outdoors. On Friday afternoons, students in Victorine's class can choose between time in the ball pool or the sensory room. Over the years Victorine has done both activities, but now she is in the post 16 department staff like the students to make their own choice. Throughout the school all staff use the same objects of reference for each activity: the ball pool is represented by one of the balls and the sensory room by a scented cushion. Therefore, Victorine has become familiar with the activities and associated objects of reference over the past six years. In Year 12, from the beginning of the school year to October half-term the students experience both activities on alternate weeks. On Friday afternoons the classroom is scented mandarin to help

> distinguish it from the rest of the week. After half-term, the students choose their Friday afternoon activity. At the beginning of the afternoon session, the teacher or teaching assistant works with each student individually supporting them making their choice. The student is given both the ball and cushion to touch and smell and is then asked to choose. The school staff are aware that Victorine likes both activities, but possibly prefers the ball pool. She seems to be willing to stay longer in the ball pool than in the sensory room, using more vocalisations, which the staff know indicates she is happy. When she is asked to choose, the staff observe which object of reference she reaches for first. To confirm whether she is making a real choice or just choosing the item on the right, the staff swap the objects of reference. If she selects the one on the right again, the staff consider she is not making a choice, but if she chooses the object of reference that is now on the left, the staff consider she has made a decision. If she does not make the decision, the staff have already ascertained from her parents, via the home school book, which activity they believe she would like to do. Whether she makes the decision, or her parents do, Victorine is then given the object of reference for the chosen activity and it is explained to her this is what she is going to do, and she is then taken to the activity.

Equally important are education institution structures and policies that support education professionals embedding developing, supporting and enabling children's and young people's decision-making into everyday practice. The KidsMatter website,[3] an Australian government-funded initiative to support children's mental health and well-being, provides some guidance to education professionals to support developing children's decision-making ability. It highlights the importance of the adult's interaction with the child in helping to develop problem-solving and decision-making skills, including adults modelling the decision-making process. Likewise, it advocates the need to provide children with opportunities to make decisions as part of their everyday school life, as well as teaching the steps of decision-making.

Everyday decisions

There is a myriad of everyday decisions that children and young people may make whilst attending their education institution, from the earliest age. For very young children this may be choices about what activity to do, who to sit or play with, what colour to use, or what to choose for a snack or lunch. To make a decision, children and young people need both to be aware of and to have experienced the choices. For example, they can only choose what to eat at lunchtime if they have had the opportunity to taste the foods to know what they like.

Therefore, a key role for education professionals is enabling children and young people to have a wide range of experiences to build up their knowledge of the world, thereby facilitating their ability to make everyday decisions from the earliest age. This can be achieved by providing a curriculum, opportunities and activities which are embedded within the education institution's ethos, organisation and environment, supported by all education and associated professionals working in that establishment. Equally important is education and associated professionals encouraging parents to give their child or young person opportunities to make everyday decisions, including the experiences necessary to enable choices to be made.

Returning to the 'Jill makes a sandwich' scenario (Chapter three, p. 51), Jill preferred white bread ham sandwiches cut into quarters. The case study below shows how Jill was supported, from the earliest age, to develop her ability to make this everyday decision, at home, in nursery and at school.

Developing Jill's decision-making ability

Jill has been the subject of an EHC Plan since she was in Reception, recording her barriers to learning as severe learning difficulties, with associated delays in expressive and receptive language as well as some fine motor difficulties due to low muscle tone. From the age of 2 years old until she started full-time schooling Jill received Portage on a fortnightly basis. It was Ms Robinson, Portage Home Visitor, who first encouraged Jill's mother, Ms Wilson, to give Jill some choices. Ms Robinson explained that any options offered had to be for things Jill liked, as it was important she was being offered real choices. Therefore, it was essential Jill was given a range of experiences to enable her to learn what she likes and dislikes. As Ms Wilson wanted Jill to eat the same meals as the rest of the family she began by introducing Jill to different foods. Choosing between a piece of banana and a quarter of apple then became a Portage target. To prepare for this Jill was introduced to apples, bananas and satsumas over a few weeks, as these are available all year round. Jill had the opportunity to touch, smell and taste them. She seemed to consistently like bananas and satsumas, but not apples. To help Jill understand about making a choice, the options had to be real choices, thus she was offered a piece of banana and half a satsuma. Jill was able to choose and varied her choice. Ms Wilson offered these at a morning or afternoon snack time. About once a week she offered a piece of apple and a piece of banana or half a satsuma. Jill did not choose the apple. When Jill was about to start nursery, Ms Wilson was asked by nursery staff whether Jill liked water or milk to drink; Jill drank both. Ms Wilson's preference was for Jill to make that choice herself; she prepared Jill for making this

> choice by offering her these options at home whenever the opportunity arose. Jill would sometimes choose milk, at other times water.
>
> In school, Ms Wilson was keen for Jill to have a range of experiences that would enable her to make her own choices. Ms Wilson wanted a developmentally appropriate decision-making outcome in the EHC Plan from the outset. The very first was 'Jill will be able to choose whether to have pasta or potatoes with her school lunch.' She liked both. This progressed to choosing between the main courses on offer as well as pasta or potatoes. In class she was given the opportunity to choose between activities when there was a choice. From Year 5, when the group did cookery lessons, there was often a choice of what to make, such as chocolate or plain buns, or different fillings and breads for sandwiches. Since transferring to the secondary department, Jill has a choice of break and lunchtime activities, and where and with whom she sits in the dining room. Her current decision-making outcome is 'Jill will choose which lunchtime activity she wishes to do from a choice of two.' At home, Ms Wilson is working with Jill to choose which clothes she wishes to wear at the weekends. To let Jill know it is the weekend, Ms Wilson uses two different essential oils to scent the house, one for school days, another for weekends and school holidays. Ms Wilson is helping Jill understand the need to wear a jumper when it is cold in the autumn or winter.

'Important' decisions

Some of the 'important' decisions a child or young person may have to make during their education are listed earlier in the chapter, such as choosing an educational outcome or a new education institution. Chapter one introduced a decision-making framework, which guides the steps involved in making the particular decision; this can be used by education and associated professionals to assist in supporting and enabling a child or young person to make their own decision or to support parents in facilitating their son's or daughter's participation in decision-making.

To illustrate the ways in which education professionals can support and enable children and young people to participate in decision making, the discussion will focus on choosing a new education institution. This is a decision that most children and young people will make at least once during their education. Appendix 1 is a set of completed decision-making frameworks for children and young people at different ages and phases of education, demonstrating the decision-making process for choosing a new education institution. Even though the case studies are fictitious, they provide a possible model for each part of the decision-making process, although it is acknowledged that all that is proposed may not be appropriate for every child or young person. Overall, the aim is to realise the SEND COP aspiration that no child or young person will have a decision made about their education without a contribution from them. Contribution in this context is in the broadest sense, which may range from participation at every stage to an expression of preference by way of behavioural responses which provide an indication of the child or young person's views and feelings about the choices. Depending on the decision, a child or young person's ability to contribute to the decision-making process may vary. For some decisions the child or young person may participate fully, for others their participation may be more limited.

It is good practice for education and associated professionals to record the extent to which the child has participated in making a particular decision. For young people it is essential there is an accurate record of their participation in the decision-making process, especially if they are unable to make the decision and the choice is being made on their behalf by their parents.

Choosing an education institution
Secondary transfer

A child's level of participation in making this decision may be related to both their functional ability in relation to the elements of the decision-making process and the nature of the decision. Actually, it is parents who choose their child's education institutions until their child has completed Year 11. However, at secondary transfer stage, many parents do involve their child in the decision. Although Appendix 1A is a fictional case study, the author is aware of real examples of children's participation in choosing their secondary educational placement. For example, the two case studies below.

Peter and Zsofia choose their secondary schools
Case study A

Peter is in Year 6 and the subject of an EHC Plan recording his special educational needs as Asperger syndrome and significant sensory issues, including sensitivities to sound and smells. He was described as keen to learn but has barriers to learning associated with his autism. Peter had attended his local mainstream primary since Reception, but over the past couple of years had become increasingly aware of his differences from his classmates. Despite significant adjustments by the primary school to facilitate attendance, this was below 85%. His attainments were below age-related expectations, but within the range expected in a mainstream Year 6 class. Peter was aware that he was in the last year of his primary school and would have to move schools. When choosing the secondary school, Peter's parents took him to the two mainstream secondary schools suggested by the local authority. The visits were conducted after school to minimise the noise and other sensory issues. In these two schools Peter demonstrated very distressed behaviours, which caused concern to the secondary school teachers conducting the visits. Peter's parents also took him to visit an independent special school catering for pupils with social and emotional difficulties and challenging behaviours, offering personalised learning and therapeutic support. Peter's response to this school was very different, even stating he wished to attend this school, having never previously wanted to attend a school. On returning to his primary school, Peter happily told his teachers about his visit to this school. His parents requested the independent special school as Peter's high school choice.

Case study B

Zsofia is of Year 6 age but she is being educated in Year 5 as it was felt the Year 6 focus on SATs was not appropriate for her. She is the subject of an EHC Plan recording her special educational needs as microcephaly and developmental delay. She has severe difficulties with understanding, word finding and social communication. She has problems retaining learning and needs to overlearn. She has attended her mainstream primary since Reception supported by a full-time 1:1 teaching assistant. Zsofia is not aware that she is in the final year of her primary schooling. When choosing her secondary school, her parents visited a range of mainstream and special schools without her. Her parents chose an academy special school, which they then took Zsofia to visit. Her parents reported that she talked very positively about the school.

These two case studies highlight the reality of involving a child in decision-making and whether it is appropriate to offer the full range of choices. It is evident from the description of their respective special educational needs that Peter and Zsofia function differently in relation to understanding the decision to be made. Peter is aware he has to leave his current school, Zsofia is unaware. Peter's parents showed him all the possible schools he could attend, using his response to guide their choice. Zsofia's parents probably felt her lack of understanding about the need to choose a new school meant she would be overwhelmed by visiting all the possible schools. Thus, she only visited the school her parents had chosen for her, they hoped her response would be positive, which it was. It would have been interesting to know what Zsofia's parents would have done if she had not responded positively to their school choice. This raises the issue of the weight her parents may have given to Zsofia's negative reaction to the school visit. What advice would you have offered her parents?

As secondary school choice is a parents' decision, education professionals may be wondering what their role may be in relation to this, particularly as parents express a preference for a school, but the actual decision is made by the local authority. In this case, the education professional's role is likely to be limited, unless parents request support or advice. Appendix 1A provides a model that can be shared with parents if they seek support. For children who are the subject of an EHC Plan, secondary transfer is usually discussed during the Year 5 annual review, which may be an opportunity for the education or associated professional to offer some advice and support, such as signposting parents to the Local Offer website, which sets out the secondary provision available. The Year 5 annual review may be a time to explore the child's participation in choosing the secondary school and help parents plan for this.

Post 16 transfer: Year 11 to Year 12

Choosing a Year 12 (Y12) placement may have to be undertaken before the young person's 16th birthday, but as they are approaching the age when they are entitled to make their own decision, participation in the decision-making process should be encouraged as far as possible. However, if the young person is the subject of an EHC Plan, then their choice for Y12 has to be presented to the local authority by their parents, as the Children and Families Act 2014 and SEND COP stipulate that young people only have the right to request an education institution to be named in their EHC Plan after they have completed compulsory schooling (end of Year 11).

For many young people with SEN, choosing a Y12 placement may be a similar decision to choosing a secondary placement – it is likely to be their parents' choice. This highlights the difference between the young person's right to make their own decisions from the age of 16 and their right to directly ask for changes to their EHC Plan. Like secondary transfer, a young person's level of participation in the decision-making process is likely to be related to their functional ability in relation to the elements of the process and the nature of the decision. Therefore, it is probable the role of the education or associated professional is to support the young person's parents to enable the young person to participate in the decision as far as possible. Thus, the education or associated professional could be considered as the young person's advocate, ensuring that their parents are aware of the reasons their son or daughter should be facilitated to participate in the decision-making as far as possible. However, if developing decision-making has been an integral part of the curriculum from the earliest age, parents will be familiar with empowering their young person to make choices.

The education professionals' advocacy role, supported by associated professionals, may include facilitating parents to enable the young person's participation in choosing their Y12 education institution. This could take the form of encouraging

- a shared language to refer to the choices being considered, such as objects of reference, pictures, symbols or simple verbal labels or signs
- thinking about the things that are important to the young person to find out about or see during a visit to the education institution, possibly writing a checklist, including one the young person can understand such as using pictures, emojis or symbols
- the young person or their parents to take photos or videos of key areas in the education institution (e.g. canteen, toilets, classrooms, specialist rooms) and things on the checklist, as well as the young person taking part in an activity during the visit
- parents to
    - observe and record their young person's reactions when visiting each education institution
    - talk with their young person about the choices, showing the photos/videos

Post 16 transfer: young person aged 18+ years

At this juncture the options in relation to education include leaving education or continuing education via an apprenticeship or supported internship, as well as attending an education institution or transferring to social care day provision. The range of post 16 or post 18 educational, training or social care provision is set out in each local authority's Local Offer website.

Once a young person has had their 18th birthday, they are an adult, which means the expectation is that they will make their own choices. Education and associated professionals have an important role in supporting parents to understand it is their young person's decision, unless it can be formally demonstrated that the young person lacks capacity to make the particular decision at the time the decision is needed. The author can hear the clamour of education professionals telling her that it is fine in theory that all 18+ year olds should be making their own decisions, but what about the reality of the young person with profound and multiple learning difficulties or severe learning difficulties in their class, how will they make their own decision about their next educational or other placement? Education professionals would, undoubtedly, continue lecturing the author about how their students are likely to have significant difficulties with the process of making 'important' decisions such as understanding even the most basic of information. Whilst the author understands the reality, young people's rights must be respected; therefore, part of the education or associated professional's role is as a young person's advocate to ensure their right to self-determination is upheld as far as practicable, and that assumptions about the young person's decision-making ability are not based on their SEN. As noted in the Prolegomenon, the author's experience is that some parents believe their 18+ year old young person is unable to make a decision due to their SEN. Perhaps reality and the education professional's role can be illustrated by returning to Zsofia in case study B, who is now 18 years old in Year 14 at Bonaire Academy Special School, which she has attended since Year 7. She needs to choose her next education institution or a social care placement.

Zsofia's post 18 placement

Since attending Bonaire Academy Special School Zsofia has made progress with her self-care skills. She can dress and undress herself, but she needs assistance with buttons, zips and shoe laces. She can drink independently from a glass and feed herself with a spoon. She is toilet trained but is unable to manage her sanitary products and needs reminding to wash her hands after using the toilet. She is unable to travel independently but she is learning to use a pelican crossing. Measures of adaptive functioning suggest she is functioning at the level of the average 3–5 year old. Zsofia's parents feel her next education institution should focus on developing her life skills. They would like her to move to an independent living project in the next few years as they know they are getting older and wish to see her settled in an appropriate setting before they are no longer able to care for her.

Zsofia does not understand she has to leave her current school. She has been attending White Crest FE college, with her current classmates, one day a week supported by school staff – teaching assistants Mr Kovacs and Ms Charles. This college has an independent living skills course.

When choosing her secondary school, Zsofia's parents chose the school, Zsofia only visiting the school after her parents had made the decision. Zsofia's parents discussed using this same approach to choose the new education institution with Mrs Roman, Zsofia's class teacher. During the discussion Mrs Roman explained that, as Zsofia is now an adult, she needs to participate in making this decision. Mrs Roman agreed with Zsofia's parents that Zsofia is unlikely to be able to make this decision herself as she has significant difficulties understanding even the most basic concepts relating to the decision. Nevertheless, Zsofia clearly demonstrates when she likes or dislikes something. Mrs Roman advised Zsofia's parents that it is important to be aware of

Zsofia's reactions during visits to the establishments and to visit each two or three times to see if these are consistent. Mrs Roman indicated Zsofia's parents should use the MCA 'best interests' checklist to guide their decision-making, which she gave them along with a 'best interests' balance sheet (Appendix 3). She explained that in choosing the next placement Zsofia's parents needed to stand in Zsofia's shoes to try and work out what decision she would make if she was able to do so. To this end, Mrs Roman proposed working together with Zsofia's parents to make a list of the things that Zsofia would wish for in her next placement to help her parents make the decision.

Jointly, Zsofia's parents and Mrs Roman identified things Zsofia likes and dislikes. Mrs Roman reported that Zsofia enjoys the cooking sessions at college but does not like going to the gym area. The process showed that Zsofia likes cooking, art and craft, horse riding, going out into the community, animals and a quiet calm environment. She prefers to go to school than be at home – she likes to be occupied and being among other young people. Zsofia's parents noted that her behaviour can be more difficult to manage during school holidays. She does not like swimming, gym-type activities, sports centres, horticulture or noisy and/or crowded places.

Mrs Roman suggested that Zsofia's parents look at the local authority's Local Offer website to see the range of post 18 provision available, including social care provision, to help identify suitable placements to visit with Zsofia. She recommended that Zsofia's parents take photos and/or videos during visits to the placements of key areas and Zsofia taking part in activities, as well as choosing an object of reference to represent each of the choices.

Having reviewed all the options in the Local Offer, Zsofia's parents decided that they would visit Zsofia's current college (White Crest), Blue Wave House, a social care provision for adults with learning difficulties, and Portside Road FE college, in the neighbouring local authority, which is much smaller than White Crest. The two college placements offer three-day per week provision for thirty-eight weeks a year and Blue Wave House offers 1–3 days' provision throughout the year. (See Appendix 3 for Zsofia's parents' completed 'best interests' checklist and balance sheet, and Sinson (2016) for further information about MCA 'best interests'.)

Zsofia visited all three establishments with her parents. Her parents noted that Zsofia seemed relaxed at Blue Wave House, happily accompanying a member of staff to the kitchen to make a drink and snack. At Portside Road there was an emphasis on music

> and physical activity. Zsofia joined a music session during which her reaction suggested was too noisy for her. She was shown the gym, which she was reluctant to enter; college staff encouraged her to join a game of catch with other students, but Zsofia would not. Her facial expression indicated she did not like being in the gym. Her parents concluded, whilst the staff at Portside Road were very caring, the environment and curriculum emphasis did not suit Zsofia. They chose White Crest College and a two-day per week placement at Blue Wave House throughout the year.

The case study illustrates the education professional's role when there is a consensus that the young person is unlikely to be able to make the decision. It highlights how to support parents to understand the need to consider their young person's views, wishes and feelings, including helping parents to recognise the need to take note of their young person's responses to the choices. Education professionals need to be confident in their knowledge of young people's rights, advocating for these even when the young person is unable to make the decision. Equally important is the education professional's knowledge of where to find information such as via the Local Offer.

The education professional's role when the young person is more able to participate in the decision-making process and may be able to make the decision can be illustrated by returning to Jill who we met in the case study above (p. 62) and in Chapter three. Jill is now in Year 14 aged 18, and she needs to choose her next placement. Appendix 1C–D sets out the decision-making process when the options to be considered have been selected, raising the issue of the education professional's role in supporting a young person to find and choose the options to be considered. Jill is an adult, and her permission needs to be sought to involve her parents in the process of choosing a new placement. The SEND COP (1.8) sets out that from the end of Year 11, the local authority should communicate directly with the young person rather than their parent, although it suggests most young people 'will continue to want, or need, their parents and other family members to remain involved in discussions and decisions about their future' (p21). Thus, education professionals cannot assume that they can contact parents or involve them in matters without first checking with the young person. For the purposes of this case study, Jill has indicated she would like her parents to assist her in choosing her next placement. Nevertheless, school staff should always check with Jill that she agrees for her parents to be contacted and given information. The role of the education professional is to ensure Jill is aware that a new education, social care or supported internship placement needs to be chosen and that she can make this choice. The education professional should also explain to Jill that the decision has to be made by a set date and assist her in finding information about the post 18 provision available via the Local Offer. As Jill has agreed for her parents to help her, it would probably be good practice for education professionals to meet with Jill and her parents to establish how to work together to enable Jill to make this decision. This is illustrated by the case study below.

Jill chooses her post 18 placement

Jill is 18 years old, in Year 14, final year, at her local special school for pupils with learning difficulties, therefore she needs to find a placement for the next academic year. She uses both her iPad and Makaton to help her communicate. She can dress and undress herself, sometimes needing assistance with buttons, and is independent in the toilet except when having her period, when she needs prompting to manage sanitary towels. She can feed herself using a knife, fork and spoon, follow photo instructions to make a simple snack such as a sandwich or beans on toast, and find items in the supermarket. Jill can cross a road using a pelican crossing, nevertheless she continues to require supervision. Although her concept of money is basic, she can recognise almost all the coins, but has a limited understanding of their value. In the EHC Plan Section A, her aspirations are recorded as wanting to work with animals and live in her own flat.

At the start of the academic year, Ms Roberts, Jill's teacher, explains to Jill this is her final year at the school and she will need to find a new education institution or other placement. She explains the new placement needs to be identified by Christmas as the local authority needs to know her choice. Ms Roberts asks Jill if she would like her parents to help her. Jill thinks this is a good idea and agrees. Ms Roberts arranges a meeting with Jill's parents, Jill and herself present to make a plan about how they can all work together to help Jill choose her new placement. Jill already is aware of the local FE college as she attends there a day a week with her class and school staff. The group take part in practical activities: Jill has experienced cooking, horticulture, animal care and hair and beauty.

Both Ms Roberts and Jill's parents agree that Jill has her own views, her likes and dislikes, and she is probably able to decide which placement she would like to attend. Jill's parents do discuss decisions with her as they want her to make as many of her own decisions as possible.

Ms Roberts suggested that it would probably be helpful to find out what Jill would want from a new placement to help her learn and what things she would not like. Jill had made her views known to school staff about her dislike of horticulture and hair and beauty. She liked the animal care experience at the local city farm; her aunt has a cattery which she enjoys visiting and she would like to work there.

Ms Roberts indicated that she felt Jill may find it helpful to complete the young person's decision-making framework form (Appendix 2, available as an eResource) to assist her in understanding the process. Ms Roberts showed Jill and her parents the form, both in paper form and the electronic version, and Jill thought she would like to do this. Ms Roberts asked who she would like to help her. Jill pointed to Ms Roberts.

Ms Roberts's proposed plan for supporting Jill, with steps 1–5 to be completed by October half-term, steps 6 and 7 by the end of November, and step 8, the meeting, scheduled for early December, is:

1. Parents and Ms Roberts finding out from Jill the attributes she would want in her next placement, both from what she is able to tell them and considering her reactions to experiences.

2. Jill and her parents to look at the Local Offer to identify placements that they wish to visit. Ms Roberts emphasised that Jill and her parents should look at education institutions, social care placements and supported internships.

3. Jill and her parents, with Ms Roberts's help if they wish, to make a checklist of things to look for during the visits. Ms Roberts encouraged a pictorial checklist for Jill to use.

4. Ms Roberts suggested that Jill choose an object of reference/picture/emoji/word or sign to represent each of the establishments to be visited, so that school staff, education and associated professionals and parents are using the same language to talk about the choices.

5. Ms Roberts to help Jill complete sections 1 and 2 of the young person's decision-making framework form.

6. Jill and her parents to visit the chosen establishments and take photos/videos of key areas and Jill taking part in activities. Jill's parents were also encouraged to note Jill's reactions during the visits.

7. Ms Roberts suggested that she talk with Jill after the visits to see what she liked and did not like, making a record of this as well as completing section 3 of the young person's decision-making framework form.

> 8. Ms Roberts proposed a meeting with Jill and her parents to make the choice and complete section 4 of the young person's decision-making framework form.
>
> (Appendix 1D details how this plan was operationalised to support Jill making this decision.)

Jill's completed young person's decision-making framework form, below, illustrates the decision-making process from her perspective. It is made accessible to her by using pictures and symbols she is familiar with or chose, such as the pictures to represent herself and the options.[4] Ms Roberts helped Jill record the information, which shows Jill has understood the basic key information she needs to make the decision. It shows the choices to be explored, her likes and dislikes, and demonstrates that she has used this information to make her choice, as her decision is logical from her expressed preferences.

Jill's completed young person's decision-making framework

Name: Jill Date started: 23rd September 2019 Who has supported the decision-making process? Ms Roberts and Jill's parents	Decision-making process
1. What is the decision to be made?	I need to choose a college for next September
Why do I have to make this decision?	I am in Y14 which is the last year of my special school
What happens if I do not make this decision?	? I may not be able to go to college. ✓ I will be able to go to Cottage Road House If I do not choose a college the local authority may choose one for me or they may not let me go to college
When do I have to make this decision?	College choice form has to be sent to the local authority by 15th January 2020

(*Continued*)

(Continued)

Name: Jill Date started: 23rd September 2019 Who has supported the decision-making process? Ms Roberts and Jill's parents	Decision-making process
❶ 2. Information about the choices what are the choices? A ◉ B ◉ C ◉	⛵ White Sails FE College 👧 I go there now. 👧 ☀☀☀ I can go 3 days a week.
	🌼 Tansy Park FE College, Newtown 👧 ☀☀☀ I can go 3 days a week. 🚌 Next town
	🐝 Isidore Specialist College 👧 ☀☀☀ I can go 3 days a week and 🛏 🌙 🌙 sleep there 2 nights. Or 👧 ☀☀☀☀☀ I can go 5 days a week and 🛏 🌙 🌙 🌙 🌙 Sleep there 4 nights.
	🏢 Cottage Road House ❌ Not college 👧 ☀ I can go 1 day a week. 👧 ☀☀ I can go 2 days a week. 👧 ☀☀☀ I can go 3 days a week. 👧 ☀☀☀☀ I can go 4 days a week. 👧 ☀☀☀☀☀ I can go 5 days a week. 👧 🛁 🧺 🚌 It will help me learn how to look after myself in my own flat. 👧 🛏 🌙 📅 I can sleep there 1 night a month. 👧 ⛵ + 🏢 I can go to White Sails FE College and Cottage Road House. 👧 🌼 + 🏢 I can go to Tansy Park FE College and Cottage Road House.

Making decisions about educational matters

Name: Jill 👧 Date started: 23rd September 2019 Who has supported the decision-making process? Ms Roberts and Jill's parents	Decision-making process
ℹ️ What information do I need?	👧 Need to know about if I can learn ☆ 🍲 to cook simple meals ☆ 🧺 to shop for food and household items ☆ 🐱 about animal care ☆ 🚌 to travel independently ☆ 🍴 know where you eat lunch
ℹ️ How will I get this information?	🚌 🌸 ⛵ 🏢 🐝 Visit Tansy Park FE College, White Sails FE College, Cottage Road House and Isidore Specialist College. 🏊 Take part in activities 📷 Photos, videos 👥 Talk to people 🎤 Record people talking 💻 Use the internet to find information
ℹ️ Who can help me get the information? 👪 Family members 👫 Friends 🏫 People in school/college	🐝 🏢 🌸 ⛵ 🚗 👫 👧 I want my parents to take me to visit the colleges and Cottage Road House. 👫 📷 📄 I hope my parents will take photos and videos and make notes as well. 👤 📋 I hope Ms Roberts will help me make a checklist 👥 ????? I hope the Course Leaders will answer my questions
A⬤ B⬤ C⬤ ☺☹ 3. What I like and do not like about each choice?	⛵ White Sails FE College 👧 ☺ 🏃 knows everyone, has friends 🍲 can learn to cook your own lunch 🐱 can do animal care 🚌 help learn to travel independently 👧☹ I did not dislike anything or want to change anything.

(Continued)

75

Making decisions about educational matters

(Continued)

Name: Jill 👧 Date started: 23rd September 2019 Who has supported the decision-making process? Ms Roberts and Jill's parents	Decision-making process
	🌼 Tansy Park FE College 👧☺ 📽 teachers nice 🐈 can do animal care 🍜 can learn to cook her own lunch 🍴 canteen was nice 🍜 🍴 liked the canteen food 👧☹ 🚗 🕐 🕐 The car journey to the college took a long time.
	🐝 Isidore Specialist College 👧☺ 🍜 can learn to cook my own lunch 🐈 can do animal care 👧☹ 🛏 Did not like the student bedroom 🚗 🕐 🕐 The car journey to college took a long time. 👧 🏠 🛏 🌙 ✓ I want to sleep at home.
	🏢 Cottage Road House 👧☺ 🍜 can learn to cook my own lunch 🧺 can learn to shop for food and other household items 🚌 learn to travel independently 👧 🏢 🛏 🌙 ? 👧 🏠 🛏 🌙 ✓ Not sure about the residential accommodation, wants to sleep at home.

76

Making decisions about educational matters

Name: Jill 😊 Date started: 23rd September 2019 Who has supported the decision-making process? Ms Roberts and Jill's parents	Decision-making process
⚖️ A ● B ● C ● 💡 Which choice do I like better? Which choice am I going to choose?	⛵ **White Sails FE College** With some additional help and support Jill understood that she can choose both White Sails and Cottage Road House. It was explained that this would mean she could go somewhere every day during the week. ⛵ ➕ 🏢
💬 4. Who do I need to tell my decision to? What is my decision?	The local authority, White Sails and Cottage Road House. My parents will help me do this. ⛵ ➕ 🏢
Date completed: 17th December 2019	

Overall, the case study suggests that the education professional's role is:

- to be a facilitator for the decision-making process helping to ensure the young person's participation

- to be an advocate for the young person upholding their right to make their own decision

- offering practical suggestions as to how to assist the young person in making their own decision, such as ensuring there is a shared way of referring to the options under consideration, using the young person's decision-making framework form or similar

- ensuring any education or associated professional who is supporting the young person or has an interest in their decision, e.g. LA SEN officers, knows how the young person is referring to the options

- advising about how to collect information such as taking photos/videos during visits and encouraging the noting of the young person's responses and reactions to each option

Conclusion

Decisions about educational matters are not just the 'important' decisions such as choosing a new education institution, options or whether to take part in a residential trip, they include everyday decisions about anything that happens within the education institution, in and out of the classroom. Supporting and enabling children and young people to develop and use their ability to make everyday choices is equally as important as helping them learn how to make 'important' decisions. Having a structured approach to this, such as a decision-making curriculum, is likely to be beneficial to education and associated professionals, children and young people, and their parents. Many everyday decisions a child or young person learns to make within the education institution can be generalised to the wider world. Knowing what you like, and dislike, helps a child or young person have some control over what they are given to eat, drink or do in their leisure time. Therefore, helping children and young people learn about their preferences as well as supporting and encouraging parents to do the same at home is an integral part of the education professional's role and, ideally, should be embedded in everyday practice. As children become young people, the education professional's role develops to include being the young person's advocate, ensuring they participate in decision-making and make their own decisions whenever possible. Following a structured approach for 'important' decisions, such as the decision-making framework, will support education and associated professionals to facilitate the young person's participation in decision-making and help their parents understand the process. Education professionals continue to have a role supporting parents, but now it is to explain that their son or daughter should be making their own choices and be empowered to participate in decision-making.

Notes

1 Statutory Instrument is a form of legislation which allows the provisions of an Act of Parliament to be altered without Parliament having to pass a new Act.
2 IRW v Z [2009] EWHC 2525 (FAM). Available from: www.bailii.org/cgi-bin/format.cgi?doc=/ew/cases/EWHC/Fam/2009/2525.html&query=(2009)+AND+(ewhc)+AND+(2525)+AND+((FAM)), accessed 4 August 2019.
3 www.kidsmatter.edu.au/mental-health-matters/social-and-emotional-learning/making-decisions, accessed 22 June 2018.
4 Generally, the young person's photo would be used to represent them, although some young people may prefer a symbol or picture, like Jill.

PART 2

DECISION-MAKING SYLLABUS

Chapter five
DECISION-MAKING SYLLABUS

This chapter sets out the decision-making syllabus referred to in earlier chapters. Chapter four mooted that this could be conceptualised as scaffolding – not an unusual metaphor in education. However, this may not be a wholly accurate representation as, unlike a conventional syllabus, this document records both the prerequisite structures and organisational elements which need to be in place to promote, enable and support the development of children and young people's ability to make decisions, as well as suggested content. Perhaps it is better considered as a combination of infrastructure and scaffolding, the latter referring to both a structure and proposed teaching approach. The author envisages education professionals using the syllabus to guide building their own curriculum to facilitate embedding the development of decision-making into everyday practice. In previous chapters there has been reference to some of the elements that would be included in a syllabus, drawn together in the mind map below (Figure 5.1), but these need to be put together in a coherent structure.

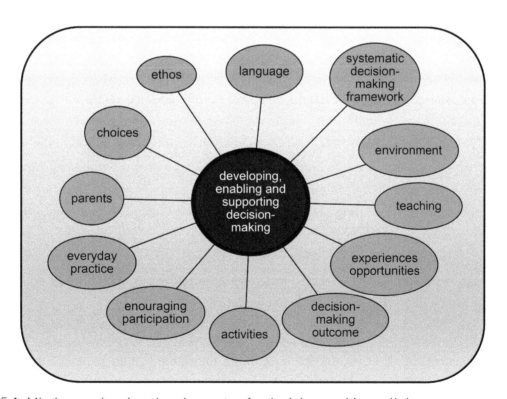

Figure 5.1 Mind map showing the elements of a decision-making syllabus

Theoretical underpinnings

The proposed syllabus is predicated on Bruner's hypothesis, 'any subject can be taught effectively in some intellectually honest form to any child at any stage of development' (cited in Elkind 1975, p245). Here, this is interpreted as every child with SEN should be given the opportunities, experiences, appropriate teaching and support to be enabled to make whatever decisions they can for themselves from the earliest age, or at the very least demonstrate preferences.

Earlier in this chapter it was indicated that the intention is that education professionals will construct their own curriculum from the proposed syllabus. It is envisaged this would be a spiral curriculum, for which the theoretical underpinning is also Bruner's hypothesis (Johnston 2012). Johnston describes the key features of a spiral curriculum as the topic being revisited several times during the child's and young person's education, the complexity of the topic increasing each time, and new learning contextualised by being related to previous learning. For example, a decision-making spiral curriculum developing a child or young person's ability to choose a snack would begin with learning about the options on offer, progressing to choosing between two; the next stage may be increasing the number of options or perhaps introducing different settings for making the choices. Johnston advocates the benefits of this curriculum model as giving the child or young person the opportunity to consolidate learning and it progresses logically. A spiral curriculum enables, and in a sense encourages, overlearning as an integral approach, which is likely to be very beneficial for children and young people with SEN.

The proposed teaching strategy is 'scaffolding' – a frequently used term, but how many education professionals really understand what this means and are aware of the theoretical underpinnings? Frequently 'scaffolding' seems to be used interchangeably to mean 'teaching' or 'support' (Wood and Devereux 2014), without any reference to it being a specific style of support. It was proposed as a teaching approach in a 1976 research paper by Wood, Bruner and Ross, essentially a development of Vygotsky's social learning theory – the zone of proximal development. The zone of proximal development describes the area of a child or young person's learning: the bottom of the zone is what the child or young person can achieve independently, and the top is what can be achieved with the help of the teacher (Fox 1993). Learning is viewed as an interactive process initiated by the teacher; however learning only occurs if the child or young person engages actively.

Wood et al. (1976) presented 'scaffolding' as a process 'whereby an adult or "expert" helps somebody who is less adult or expert' (p89). It aimed to enable a child or novice to undertake a task or reach a goal that would be beyond them without assistance. Wood et al. developed their concept of scaffolding through a problem-solving task with participants aged 3, 4 and

5 years old. Although the research paper makes no mention of whether any participants had learning difficulties, it can be assumed they probably did not. However, the issues raised about the process and the adult's role, particularly in relation to the youngest children, are likely to be relevant to education or associated professionals embarking on teaching or supporting children and young people with SEN to make decisions.

Wood et al. set out the key features of the adult's role in the scaffolding process, beginning with the most important, which they termed 'recruitment', referring to the adult gaining the child's interest in the task and helping them follow the task requirements. They noted the youngest children presented a challenge in terms of getting them interested in the task, with the adult's role to try to enlist their interest by demonstrating the task, providing motivating material, and trying to keep them on task. For this to possibly be successful, the adult needs to know what may motivate the child or young person to become engaged with the task, and provide appropriate materials. The researchers indicated the reality of working with the youngest children, observing that the adult's attempts to engage them were often ignored and that the adult intervened frequently to try to engage the child. For the older children, who were engaged in the task, the researchers describe the adult's role as verbal prodder and corrector, and for the oldest children the adult became a confirmer and checker of the child's completion of the task. This shows the evolution of the adult's role as the child or young person masters the task.

Equally essential is the education or associated professional's ability to simplify the task –differentiation, enabling the child or young person to complete it. In relation to teaching or supporting decision-making, this may be reducing the number of options from which the child or young person chooses or using real objects/objects of reference rather than words or pictures, thereby making the task achievable. Again, this entails the education or associated professional knowing the child or young person in order to modify the task appropriately.

Aligned with differentiation is the education or associated professional's role to highlight the important features of the task, helping the child or young person understand what is required, as well as ensuring they do not become frustrated by the activity. This includes demonstrating or modelling the task, with the child or young person giving their attention to this with the aim that they will, in the first instance, imitate.

Scaffolding can be summarised as a teaching technique whereby the education or associated professional adjusts the level of guidance and support to fit the child's or young person's current level of performance – it is about giving just the right amount of help. As the child or young person becomes more competent, less guidance is given. Its success as a teaching approach is reliant on knowing how to motivate and engage the child or young person, and likewise how to modify the task to enable them to be successful – illustrated, for example, by 'Jill makes a sandwich' (Chapter three, p. 51). Analysing the support offered, scenario A suggests that Jill has been given just the right amount of help as she chooses and successfully makes her own sandwich, with adult prompting and very minimal physical intervention. Yet if Jill had been expected to complete this task independently, it is unlikely she would have been able to do so, especially as parts of it were too physically challenging due to her fine motor difficulties. However, the education professional's knowledge of Jill facilitated her engagement with the activity by presenting and modifying it in such a way that she was enabled to mostly complete it herself. This included communicating the task requirements by using a photo sequence and supporting verbal language with Makaton signing, and likewise prompting Jill at each stage. The education professional flexibly adjusted their support by allowing Jill to complete the task in her own way when she had understood the requirements, thereby enabling her independence, including decision-making, and helping her develop her sandwich-making ability. The adult only intervened physically when what was required was, at the time, beyond Jill's physical abilities.

The decision-making syllabus

Earlier in the chapter it was suggested that the 'syllabus' is perhaps best considered as a combination of infrastructure and scaffolding with the essential elements needing to be organised into a coherent structure. Perhaps the simplest visual representation of this is presented in Figure 5.2, a combination of scaffolding and the building it is enabling to be constructed.

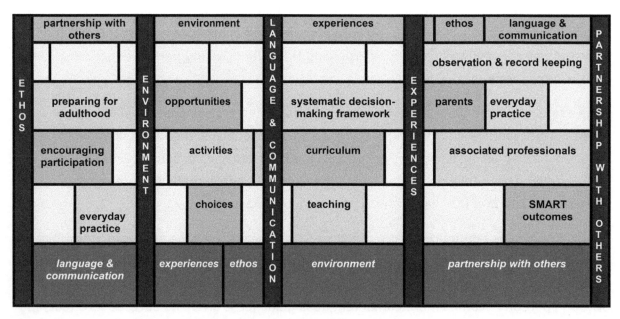

Figure 5.2 Visual representation of the decision-making syllabus

Scaffolding is a temporary structure, but the bricks laid with the help of this are permanent. In this case the five uprights represent the infrastructure that needs to be in place to aid the establishment of the essential components represented by the bricks. As scaffold uprights, they may be considered temporary, removable once the other elements are solidly in place; however, in this case, the upright factors also need to remain in place as part of the permanent structure. These five interconnected supporting uprights form the overarching components needed to develop and operationalise a decision-making curriculum. Each of these will be explored in detail to explain their function in the decision-making syllabus.

Overarching components

Ethos

Oxford Living Dictionaries defines ethos as 'the characteristic spirit of a culture, era, community as manifested in its attitudes and aspirations'.[1] Thus, it is the education professional's attitudes towards, and aspirations for, the children or young people they educate, regarding developing and enabling decision-making, that are fundamental to and underpin the development of an appropriate decision-making curriculum. 'Aspirations' is a key word in the SEND COP – for education and associated professionals as well as children and young people, who are encouraged to have aspirations. Throughout the SEND COP, education professionals are exhorted to have high aspirations for children and young people with SEN. The introduction to chapter 8 ('Preparing for adulthood from the earliest years') states that 'high aspirations are crucial to success' (p120). SEND COP 8.7 refers to high aspirations about independent living, which encompasses the ability to make decisions, as well as community participation and employment, being developed through the curriculum and extra-curricular provision. Therefore, as regards developing children and young people's decision-making, the supportive ethos would be education professionals whose approach is to view the glass as half full and who have a can-do attitude. This includes a belief that decisions about a child or young person's education should be made with some form of contribution from the child or young person. For those working with young people, this extends to supporting young people's right to make their own decisions, ensuring that young people participate in decision-making about their education.

This ethos should be shared by every education or associated professional who comes into contact with a child or young person within the education institution, whether an establishment employee or visiting professional. Thus, all education institution staff should believe that, whether they are a teacher, support assistant, receptionist, caretaker or lunchtime staff, they have a role in contributing to the long-term goal of preparing children and young people for adulthood. The author recalls excellent examples of this from a resourced high school with a very proactive attitude to inclusion. It was notable that the school reception staff felt they could spend time with the children and young people with special needs. The author recollects seeing one receptionist sitting in the reception area with a Year 11 pupil with SEN looking at and talking with her about her school memory book that staff, and pupils, had written messages in. Another receptionist was concerned that a Year 12 student with Asperger syndrome was unable to use a landline telephone (mobile phones were not widely used at the time), deciding to help him as described in the case study below.

> Oscar is in Year 12, and the subject of an EHC Plan recording his special educational needs as barriers to learning associated with Asperger syndrome. Oscar is articulate and can have a conversation if it is something he is interested in, such as his pets. He joined his current mainstream secondary school at the start of Year 12, having been educated for the past three years at a provision for mainstream pupils who have difficulties attending school. Oscar is studying for two science and maths 'A' levels, over three years, with the aim of attending the local university to study for a science or engineering degree; his predicted grades were As and Bs. In lessons his support assistant sat at a discreet distance from him, only intervening if Oscar found the situation stressful, which became less frequent. He mostly coped well in lessons; however study periods were more problematic. Mrs Green, the school receptionist, became aware that Oscar was unable to use the telephone to make calls or speak to someone. She decided to try to help him with this, to which suggestion Oscar was agreeable. Every day, in a free period, Oscar would go to the reception desk. Mrs Green's husband worked from home and had agreed to be the recipient of Oscar's phone calls. First, Mrs Green had to show Oscar how to dial the number, which he mastered quite quickly. The next challenge was for Oscar to speak on the phone and listen to the disembodied voice replying to him. To assist this, Mrs Green gave Oscar a simple short message to give to her husband; this progressed to Mr Green giving Oscar a reply to relay to Mrs Green. As Oscar became more accustomed to using the phone, he and Mr Green began to have short conversations.

Experiences

Children and young people's knowledge of their immediate environments and the wider community is critical to developing their ability to make decisions. Chapter one highlighted the importance of experiences in the acquisition of reasoning abilities and overall brain development. For education professionals to ensure experiences are purposeful and contributing meaningfully to the child or young person's acquisition of knowledge of their immediate world, they should be linked to a long-term outcome. In terms of this bigger picture, the SEND COP indicates the long-term goal is successful preparation for adulthood, with the outcomes (SEND COP 1.39) focusing on employment, independent living, community participation and maintaining good health. Thus, experiences provided by education institutions should be building towards this long-term objective; however, this needs to be analysed to explore what are developmentally or age-appropriate experiences to build into the curriculum for a particular individual, class, key stage, or educational phase.

Considering experiences raises questions about the nature of these, whether there are key features, and how they should be selected. If the end goal is preparation for adulthood, which can be interpreted as acquiring life skills, this probably should be the foundation or overarching characteristic for experiences being offered to an individual, class, key stage or phase of education. This book is concerned with the life skill of making decisions, consequently children and young people must have had experiences that enable them to make choices. Thus, the experiences offered should be purposeful and grounded in real life, thereby adding to a child or young person's understanding of the world around them, developing the necessary knowledge to enable them to make choices and decisions, or at the very least demonstrate preferences.

In January 2019 the DfE launched the 'My Activity Passport'[2] aimed at primary aged pupils, based on the National Trust's '50 things to do before you're 11¾'.[3] The suggested enrichment activities recognise the benefits to children and young people of trying things out and expanding their knowledge of the world around them to enable them to learn what they like, what interests them and what challenges they enjoy. Many of the proposed experiences are relevant and appropriate for all children and young people with SEN to facilitate them building their knowledge of the world around them. For example, experiences include: posting a letter, taking a photograph, making a sandwich, tasting a new fruit, learning to play a game of cards, taking a trip on a train, borrowing a book from the library. The author would add learning to use a mobile phone and/or tablet computer, going on local public transport, learning to play boccia – what would you add?

The DfE have provided editable work books, proposing that a number of activities are identified for each year group to experience. The accompanying guidance recommends adapting the activities to the local area, developing links with the local community and making activities relevant to the curriculum. This is similar to the author's suggestions for building a decision-making curriculum.

The above discussion is somewhat theoretical; perhaps it is not easily seen how this could be operationalised in an education institution, FE college department or social care provision offering support for young people with significant learning difficulties. It is envisaged that the educational or social care establishment would have a view about what lifelong skills are being targeted, what it is hoped a child or young person will be able to do when they leave the establishment. This does not preclude the child or young person having their own outcomes but provides the foundation for a life skills curriculum. For example, in terms of decision-making, it could be that a primary aged SEN provision would like, at minimum, children to be able to make their own choice of:

- snacks
- drinks
- school lunch
- activities at break times
- in-class activities, when a choice is offered

Thus, from the earliest age the child attends the school, experiences building towards this goal would be part of everyday activities; these would be purposeful, grounded in reality and, as far as possible, practical and hands on. Mitchell's (2012), albeit small-scale, research study found that directly experiencing options increased the participation of the young person with SEN in decision-making. For instance, choosing a snack or food offered for school lunch, children and young people should be given the opportunity to explore the food, touching, smelling and tasting it, to enable them to learn if this is something they like. Reality relates to the choices offered – these should be actually what is on offer. School snacks or lunch may be a limited range of food; this does not preclude children or young people experiencing other foods or drinks as part of the wider curriculum, such as when learning about another country, or celebrating a cultural or religious festival. However, when working on choice-making for snacks or school lunch, the options offered must be those that are really on offer.

As the suggested curriculum model is a spiral curriculum, choosing snack or lunch food will be a feature of a child or young person's curriculum at various stages of their education. For example, this may be to extend the number of options provided, introduce foods on offer at a café regularly visited by the child or young person, or that they can cook for their lunch. To maximise the development of a child's or young person's decision-making ability, education institutions, within a local authority, could think about sharing their decision-making curriculum to ensure consistency of approach when the child or young person changes placement as they progress through their education. Post 16 education institutions could consider sharing their decision-making curriculum with social care provision. Whilst exchanging curriculum information between education, FE and social care institutions may be an ambitious aspiration, sharing this within a school should be achievable, however between schools may be a challenge.

Language and communication

In previous chapters the importance of a shared consistent use of verbal or non-verbal language has been emphasised. To promote a child or young person's decision-making ability, it is essential that all staff within an education institution routinely use the same language and/or non-verbal representation of items and activities, which is communicated to both parents and associated professionals such as speech and language therapists, occupational therapists or educational psychologists. This is illustrated by the case study 'Friday afternoon choice (part 1)' (Chapter four, p. 60), where all staff used the same objects of reference throughout the school to denote school activities, for example:

- cooking – wooden spoon and bowl
- swimming – swimming costume smelling of chlorine
- break time – ball
- lunch – knife, fork and plate

Ideally, this language and non-verbal representation system would be shared between schools in a local authority, particularly if the special school system has separate primary and secondary schools, and with post 16 establishments, both education and social care, so all use the same.

Equally essential is that those enabling and supporting children and young people to develop and use their decision-making ability understand their communication, be it spoken, signed or via a picture- or app-based communication system. Lanciono et al.'s (1996) research, cited in Chapter two, highlighted the importance of access to assistive technology to facilitate indicating choices. Since the research was undertaken, the use of personal digital technology has become widespread and readily available. Many children and young people will already be familiar with, and may use, tablet computers or mobile phones. Therefore, the use of digital technology should be considered an integral part of facilitating the development of decision-making, as well as a means for children and young people to communicate their choices or express a preference.

Making decisions entails the child or young person knowing what they like, or dislike, or think is good or bad. The increased use of personal digital technology has given rise to the widespread use of emojis or emoticons – the small digital images used to express an idea or feeling – becoming commonplace in the wider environment beyond the mobile phone or tablet computer. It is probably helpful to utilise these now common representations of emotions and concepts as the symbols used in the education institution to represent basic emotions such as happy (☺), sad (☹), love/like (red heart ♥), like (👍), dislike (👎), likewise adopting the range of pictures representing people, places, foods, animals, transport, etc. At the time of writing an internet search suggested there are a range of child-safe emoji soft toys available; equally there may be staff or even parents who are able to make emoji soft toys.

Environment

The dictionary defines this as the 'surroundings or conditions in which a person lives or operates' or 'the setting or conditions in which a particular activity is carried on'.[4] In this case, environment refers to the education institution setting and its learning environment, comprising both the physical and ambient environment, each of which can be adjusted to support, enable and facilitate a child or young person's decision-making. Children and young people spend most of their time in an education institution in a classroom, and the way the physical environment is organised can support decision-making. Nursery and Early Years settings do this well with clearly defined play or activity areas; this can be emulated to a certain extent in classrooms for older children and young people. It is appreciated that there may be very restricted opportunities for arranging the classroom due to equipment that is needed or space constraints, nevertheless consideration should be given to the physical environment when thinking about promoting and enabling decision-making, and adjustments made whenever practicable. This includes the way resources, equipment or leisure activities are made accessible and displayed to assist children and young people in making independent choices. If things have to be stored in cupboards, having pictures/symbols on the cupboard door of those items that children and young people can choose facilitates choice-making. Developing a decision-making curriculum may be an opportunity to review the use of space in classroom and non-classroom areas.

Adjusting the environmental ambience can be used to help children and young people acquire some understanding of time, such as the consistent use of scents or sounds, or colours or textures, to differentiate one day from another, or to signal just one particular day of the week. As already noted above, consistent means across the education institution, for example if Monday is lemon scent, a particular piece of music or a distinctive sound, then this is used by all teachers or support staff in classrooms and/or non-classroom spaces on Mondays. In 'Friday afternoon choice (part 1)' (Chapter four, p. 60), the teacher scented the classroom on Friday afternoons to distinguish it from the rest of the week, signalling this is when the students choose their afternoon activity.

It is just as important to organise non-classroom spaces to facilitate decision-making, such as the education institution's dining area. In schools the dining area is often used for other activities, frequently it is the school hall. To enable children and young people to choose their lunch they need to be able to see the food on offer, which may present challenges depending on how the meals are served. For example, if the food is on a counter, young children may not be tall enough to see the serving dishes, likewise for children and young people who are wheelchair users. One solution may be to have small samples of the food displayed on an easily accessible separate low table to enable children and young people to make their choices, or, if they recognise photographic representations, then photos of the food on offer could be used.

Partnership with others

Education institutions operate as part of a network of support for children and young people with SEN – a team around the child or young person. Besides staff employed by the education institution, children and young people may receive input during the school or college day from a range of external visiting associated professionals such as speech and language therapists, occupational therapists, physiotherapists, specialist teachers and educational psychologists. These professionals generally provide advice, programmes or recommendations, as well as contributing to person-centred planning and/or EHC Plan reviews. Their support for the education institution's approach to developing, supporting and enabling children and young people's decision-making is very much needed to maximise the education staff's efforts in this area, thereby contributing to both a consistent and holistic approach. It is hoped these external professionals will feel they can work in partnership with the education institution staff. This can be promoted by ensuring that all education and associated professionals are made aware of the education institution's approach and the language used, being given the current decision-making outcome for each child or young person on their caseload.

Local authority (LA) SEN officers managing EHC Plans, as guardians of the content, also have a role to play. It is essential they are made aware of the importance of decision-making outcomes and ensuing provision in the overall aim of preparing children and young people for adulthood. Educational psychologists have a part to play in supporting LA SEN officers' understanding of this issue, which is discussed further in Chapter seven.

Education and associated professionals are probably yelling at the author that she has omitted the most important people in a child or young person's life – their parents, meaning anyone who cares for the child or young person, including grandparents, siblings or other family members, and staff in establishments providing respite care. The SEND Code of Practice places emphasis on education and associated professionals working with parents to enable children and young people to make a successful transition to adulthood. Thus, it is essential that education and associated professionals work in partnership with parents to develop children and young people's ability to make their own decisions, ensuring parents know and understand the education institution's approach to this and are encouraged to consider decision-making outcomes. The education institution's website is probably a good place to set out its aims in this area, likewise including a section in the prospectus and to consider holding parent workshops. Additionally, perhaps the education institution could consider producing a paper leaflet, online video or DVD/USB memory stick for parents to borrow; the latter two have the advantage of providing models of what is meant, enabling the viewer to see what you mean – some parents may find this easier to understand.

Putting this into practice

The discussion above has set out ideas with some exploration of what this looks like in practice, which will be developed further here through a case study. Like most of the case studies it is made up to illustrate the points and is being presented to stimulate reflection and debate.

Decision-making curriculum

Seraphine Special School caters for pupils aged 5–19 years with severe and complex learning needs. The school has placed preparation for adulthood at the heart of its ethos, encapsulating this in the school's mission statement reproduced on the website and in the prospectus. Developing, supporting and enabling children and young people in making their own decisions is highlighted as a focus, alongside other life skills, emphasising that all school staff work towards all pupils being able to make their own choices about matters in school wherever possible, such as choosing their school lunch, snacks, and activities when a choice is offered. School staff actively encourage young people's participation in choosing their next placement. The school's aspiration is that there will be 'no decision about a child or young person's education without a contribution from them'.

Two years ago, the teachers developed a basic decision-making curriculum as a starting point, reviewed annually to consider developing it further, ensuring it is meeting its aim to develop this important life skill. When the staff embarked on this journey, they used two training days to kickstart it, as well as consultation with teaching assistants and other school staff. As language and communication is central to teaching, they began by examining the consistency of their use of language and communication across the school. An audit of objects of reference, signs, symbols and pictures was undertaken, revealing differences between staff. For example, the object of reference for lunch in Key Stage 1 was a plate, in Key Stage 2 a bowl and spoon and in Key Stages 3, 4 and 5 a knife and fork. The teachers decided the object of reference would be a plate, knife and fork, either as real objects, photo or emoji (📷), depending on the pupil's understanding, and the Makaton sign for eating. They reviewed all school-based activities, agreeing a common object of reference, photo, symbol (emoji where possible) and Makaton sign for each, recording this on the school's intranet and in a paper version in a file kept in the staffroom.

Before being able to consider experiences and the environment, the teachers needed to decide the basic choices they wished the pupils to be able to make, focusing on those that are life skills, such as being able to choose what you wish to eat, drink or do as a leisure activity. These formed the core decision-making curriculum, with the associated long-term outcomes. However, this did not preclude other particular decisions that parents hoped their child or young person would be able to make, or those chosen by the child or young person. Therefore, pupils in

- Key Stages 1 and 2 would be introduced to choosing snacks, drinks, lunch food and play activities.

    Long-term outcome: by the end of Key Stage 2 pupils will be able to choose their own snack, drink, lunch food or play activity, when offered a choice of two.

- Key Stage 3 would continue with snacks, school lunch, adding break and lunchtime activities.

    Long-term outcomes: by the end of Key Stage 3 pupils will be able to choose their own

    - snack, drink, and lunch food, when offered a choice of two
    - snack or lunch food when offered a choice of three
    - break time activity when offered a choice of two
    - lunchtime activity when offered a choice of two.

- Key Stage 4 would continue with Key Stage 3 choices, and long-term outcomes, adding sport and leisure activities, and/or choosing a new educational placement.

    Long-term outcome: by the end of Key Stage 4 students will be able to choose their own sport or leisure activity when offered a choice of two.

    Long-term outcome: by the end of Key Stage 4 students moving to a new education or training institution will participate in choosing their placement.

- Key Stage 5 would extend choosing food and drink to places outside school such as the college canteen, also focusing on helping young people to participate in choosing their next placement. Additionally, it introduced choosing the Friday afternoon activity.

Long-term outcome: by the end of Key Stage 5 students will be able to choose their own

- food when offered a choice of two in the college canteen
- drink when offered a choice of two in the college canteen
- food when offered a choice of two in the community, e.g. café, community centre
- drink when offered a choice of two in the community, e.g. café, community centre.

Long-term outcome: by the end of Key Stage 5 students will be able to choose their own

- leisure activity when offered a choice of two in school, e.g. Friday afternoon choice
- leisure activity in the community when offered a choice of two.

Long-term outcome: by the end of Key Stage 5 students will have participated in choosing their next education or training institution or social care provision.

This led to analysing the experiences that would need to be provided to enable the pupils to make these choices. For example, the teachers considered the range of lunchtime and break time activities that would be offered to the Key Stage 3–5 pupils. Taking into account the interests of the current cohort, it was decided that activities involving arts and crafts, ICT, playing indoor ball games, snooker, indoor card or board games such as snap, bingo/lotto, going for a walk outdoors, and watching cartoons would be organised either at lunchtime and/or break time. Consideration was given as to whether there should perhaps be more outdoor activities offered in the summer term.

Key Stage 3–5 pupils were offered a variety of break and lunchtime activities on different days for the duration of a school year. For instance, on Monday there was a choice of arts and craft activities or music at lunchtime; on a fine day there was also a walk in the grounds. Tuesday was music or table-top games, and a walk in the school grounds, weather permitting.

The teachers were also keen for each pupil to have a 'My Activity Passport' which would be shared with parents, ensuring pupils are receiving a wide range of experiences; each Key Stage identified ten activities for the Key Stage Activity Passport, plus two more which would be tailored for each pupil.

The teachers and teaching assistants reviewed the use of classroom and non-classroom spaces, particularly the dining room, to consider adjustments to support the pupils making choices. To ensure food could be easily seen by all pupils, a table was placed near the dining room entrance displaying small portions of the day's food so pupils could choose from this. Additionally, photos of the food were displayed in the dining room and picture menus were produced for those pupils who could understand these.

The use of space review showed that the Key Stage 2 classrooms are variable sizes; one class has several pupils who are wheelchair users which impacts on how space can be used. Although Key Stage 2 staff wished to have a more leisure type (play) activity area of the classroom to distinguish it from the 'work' area, this was not possible. Nevertheless, the Key Stage 2 staff wished to introduce choices for leisure (play) activities, identifying that the room known as the 'library' was a suitable space to be converted into a leisure/play area that the whole school could use, but with timetabled sessions for Key Stage 2 pupils. Currently the room was used for a range of purposes, including, at times, an equipment store. Agreement for this change was sought from the headteacher and the rest of the staff and granted. The room was divided into three distinctly different areas, one for arts and crafts activities, another with bean bags and cushions to listen to music, stories or for relaxation, the third was for table-top games/activities.

Additionally, staff were concerned that room doors gave no indication of whether the room was a classroom, office area or specialist room, although classroom doors displayed the name of the class with a picture. They decided that a photo and symbol should be placed on each door to show the room type as well as class names for classrooms.

To help pupils understand time, across the school, it was decided that on the regular day the class goes swimming, or to riding for the disabled, or on other excursions, the classroom would be scented lemon, unless it was a Friday, as this would always be mandarin to link into Key Stage 5 'Friday afternoon choice'. Key Stages 4 and 5 were considering using additional scents for other days of the week. Consideration was also being given to having a scent for the last day of term, which is usually a Friday, which would mean Key Stage 5 could not have 'Friday afternoon choice' that day as there would be no mandarin scent. It was decided that it was important to signal the end of term, so patchouli was chosen to denote this day.

To maximise the efficacy of the decision-making curriculum the teachers were aware that the ethos and approach had to be shared effectively with all school staff; for new staff this would be included in the induction process. School staff believe that the consistency of approach is essential to help children and young people develop their abilities, and actively seek to work in partnership with all external professionals and parents. To this end the headteacher

Decision-making syllabus

- met with the lunchtime staff, both those that serve the lunch and those supervising the pupils, to introduce the shared language, objects of reference, signs and symbols relating to meal times and lunchtime activities.

- put information in the staff handbook and included it as part of the oral information given during the induction process.

- produced an information leaflet for visiting associated professionals, e.g. speech therapists, occupational therapists, physiotherapists, specialist teachers and educational psychologists, so they are aware of the school's efforts to develop and support pupils' decision-making ability.

- met with the school reception staff and caretaker to introduce the common language, objects of reference, signs and symbols that had now been adopted across the school.

- organised a training afternoon for teaching assistants.

To promote parents' understanding of the school's ethos and approach to developing and enabling decision-making, the parents' section of the school website had further information, including practical ideas to support their son or daughter making their own choices, likewise the objects of reference, words, pictures, sign and symbols that had been adopted. There are two parent workshops each school year, one after October half-term, the other early in the summer term, focusing on encouraging and enabling decision-making, providing practical advice and support. Actually, each time the workshops run, there are two, one for parents of children in Reception to Year 10, the second for parents of young people in Years 11–14, as the legal requirement changes when pupils become 16 years old. For the older pupils, there is an emphasis on participation in decision-making about choosing a new educational, training or other placement. In these workshops, parents are introduced to the decision-making model, the Mental Capacity Act 2005 and the MCA 'best interests' checklist. Parents are encouraged to read the NatSIP[5] parent information booklet about understanding the Mental Capacity Act, which they can download free from the school's website or borrow the paper copy from the school receptionist. Additionally, the school has produced a range of leaflets, online videos and a DVD or USB memory stick parents can borrow.

Parents and young people are encouraged to consider a decision-making outcome as part of person-centred planning or EHC Plan annual reviews. Prospective pupils' parents are made aware of the school's approach during visits to the school. The school has developed good links with foster carers and respite providers, who are encouraged to support the school's efforts to develop and enable children and young people's decision-making.

> The headteacher has also worked with the LA SEN officers managing EHC Plans to ensure they are aware of the importance of decision-making outcomes and these are included in each pupil's EHC Plan.
>
> Developing the decision-making curriculum process highlighted some areas where the teachers felt they were not as adept as they would like to be. They wished to be able to write better outcomes, which would help to develop the provision they need to make in terms of teaching and practical experiences. They also felt the choice of activities offered to Key Stages 3–5 was not broad enough; they wished to extend these to be more representative of the leisure type activities that young people would be able to access in supported living or other community placements. To this end they contacted both the local authority's respite care providers and supported living placements to explore the leisure activities offered within these establishments.

Essential components

Choices

Choices are at the heart of decision-making. The number of choices offered for any decision was a matter of debate in Chapter one, including exploring the issues around restricting the number of choices to reduce the likelihood that the child or young person was overwhelmed by the task, but it did not resolve the dilemmas, only raised more. It highlighted that any choices offered should be real, suggesting that a criterion for selecting options should be to see the situation from the child or young person's perspective, considering the choices they would wish to be given. This applies equally to everyday and 'important' decisions. However, within an education institution, the food or activity options will be limited to those available therein and are likely to have been chosen by the establishment for specific reasons such as curriculum requirements, cost, space for the activity, staff availability or experience, etc. Thus, for food or activities where there is a choice, this may be just two options, thereby negating the need to consider the criteria by which to limit the choices offered. Nevertheless, education institution staff should always be alert to the attributes of the choices being offered, particularly when developing the overall curriculum offer or introducing new activities or foods. Perhaps the following guidelines for offering choices are helpful. The choices offered should be:

- real, ideally aligned to what is available in the wider community
- likely to be desirable

- culturally appropriate, that is careful consideration of the wider community experiences of the education institution's attendees such as those from different heritages or if the establishment is located in an area with a distinctive characteristic such as rural or seaside areas. This lifelong city-dwelling author recalls undertaking an EP training placement in a rural area where many of the children on her caseload lived on sheep farms and having to quickly learn about sheep to enable her to talk with the children!
- only limited when not to do so would overwhelm the child or young person, hindering their ability to make the choice. In this instance, the education professional should consider carefully the criteria used to restrict the options offered, avoiding only giving what the education professional believes are the right choices for this child or young person.

There is further discussion about choices in the Epilogue.

Curriculum

UNESCO[6] (2010) defines an education institution's formal curriculum as the planned programme of objectives, content, learning experiences, resources and assessment offered by the institution. Additionally, UNESCO terms the 'hidden curriculum' as the incidental learning pupils acquire, such as an understanding of socially acceptable behaviour, personal relationships and motivation. In relation to developing a specific decision-making curriculum, the incidental learning achieved through the direct teaching of decision-making is, hopefully, that making choices enables children and young people to have some control over what happens for them.

The discussion above made some references to a specific decision-making curriculum, envisaging that education institution staff will build their own decision-making curriculum around the key aims for its pupils or students. Above it was suggested that a spiral curriculum would be an appropriate model for children and young people with SEN. Overall, the purpose of a decision-making curriculum is fourfold. Most importantly, it ensures that there is a focus on developing and supporting the child or young person's decision-making ability. Secondly, it assists the education institution staff to understand the importance of promoting the development of this life skill and communicates the school's ethos in relation to it. This in turn assists education institution staff collaborating with associated professionals to ensure the curriculum is effective, and children and young people achieve their decision-making outcomes. Likewise, it helps parents appreciate the need to empower their son or daughter to make their own decisions.

The 'Decision-making curriculum' (p. 92) explored the multi-pronged hypothetical process by which a special school developed a decision-making curriculum, endeavouring to optimise the likelihood of achieving its goal. This enterprise highlighted issues to be considered. The starting point was deciding which choices the teachers would like their pupils to be able to make for themselves by the time they leave the education institution. Analysing these choices shows that these are mostly everyday ones, enabling the children and young people to make choices which will give them some control in their life, not just in school, but at home and in the wider world. The school staff's decision is supported by the research cited in Chapters one and two, demonstrating that assisting individuals with severe to profound learning disabilities to make everyday choices, or at least demonstrate preferences, had a positive impact on their behaviour. Thus, indicating that focusing on choices that enable children and young people to decide what they wish to eat or drink or choose as their leisure activities should be foundation content for a decision-making curriculum. What decisions would you like the children or young people you teach or support to be able to make by the time they leave your education or training institution?

Having decided which choices and outcomes to target, the next consideration is how to structure the curriculum. Seraphine Special School chose to divide the curriculum by Key Stages. However, tailoring the curriculum for Victorine (Year 12) ('Friday afternoon choice (part 1)', p. 60) highlighted that, for some students, the artificial divide of Key Stages may not be appropriate. To demonstrate this, Seraphine Special School's Key Stage 3 decision-making curriculum content for choosing snack or lunch food is detailed below (Table 5.1), followed by Victorine's bespoke decision-making curriculum (Table 5.2). She continues to have outcomes relating to Key Stage 3 activities as well as a Key Stage 5 outcome relating to choosing food in the college canteen. This suggests the long-term outcomes Seraphine Special School staff formulated for each Key Stage are aspirational, in keeping with an ethos that believes children and young people can be supported to make their own decisions. Actually, perhaps a pick and mix approach is more appropriate for some students, that is continuing with selected outcomes, associated experiences and activities from earlier Key Stages as well as some from their own Key Stage. Equally, dividing the decision-making curriculum by individual Key Stages may not actually be helpful; for instance, it may be better for a primary special school to express long-term decision-making outcomes as 'By the time the pupil leaves the school they will be able to . . .'; this may also be more appropriate for some all-age special schools. Thus, it may have been better if Seraphine Special School had developed their decision-making curriculum across three Key Stages aligned to primary, secondary and post 16 educational phases, or two, compulsory education and post 16; with hindsight, this may have been the school's view. The argument for having some Key Stage-specific decision-making outcomes, particularly for post 16 students, is that it ensures that children and young people are supported to participate in 'important' decisions about their education, such as choosing their next educational or training placement.

Decision-making syllabus

Table 5.1 Sample decision-making curriculum

Essential components	Content: Being able to choose food to eat	Notes/guidance – including learning environment and partnership with others including parents
Outcomes	Long term: By the end of Key Stage 3 pupils will be able to choose their own • break time snack • lunchtime food **Short term**: tailored to the needs of each pupil, one outcome for break time snack, one for lunchtime food, as appropriate. For example, in the first term of Y7 it may be that a pupil only has one outcome either for break time snack or lunchtime food.	The long-term outcome should be written into the EHC Plan with the planned small steps to achieve this outcome. These will need to be updated at the annual review. To be chosen in discussion with parents and the pupil, recorded in person-centred planning with a copy given to parents and pupil, as well as recorded in the EHC Plan as part of the annual review process.
Language and communication	All staff to use the agreed objects of reference, Makaton signs, symbols, emojis and words for activities, experiences and foodstuffs. Staff to be aware of the pupil's way of referring to foodstuffs.	All staff, including lunch supervisors and lunch servers, to ensure they are fully familiar with the agreed communication and this is shared with parents, visiting professionals and university students on placement.
Experiences	All pupils to experience seeing, smelling, touching and eating the foodstuffs either at snack time, lunchtime, cookery lessons or celebration events. Foods experienced will depend on those being provided at lunchtime and snack times. **Enrichment experience**: tasting a new fruit – pupils are introduced to a seasonal fresh, canned or frozen fruit each term to be tasted in snack time or cookery lessons: Y7 autumn term: plums; spring term: rhubarb; summer term: gooseberries Y8 autumn term: blackberries; spring term: tinned pears; summer term: apricots	Teachers to ensure that their pupils can see the foods on offer in the dining room. To liaise with the kitchen staff to discuss any changes to the food on offer each half-term. Teachers to agree at the start of each academic year exactly which fruits will be experienced, dependent on any availability/allergy issues.

Essential components	Content: Being able to choose food to eat	Notes/guidance – including learning environment and partnership with others including parents
	Y9: autumn term: fresh pears; spring term: tinned mandarin oranges; summer term: strawberries (fresh or frozen)	
Activities and opportunities	The main learning opportunities for this activity are at snack time, lunchtime and in the weekly cookery lesson. This involves seeing the food, touching, smelling and tasting it to enable the pupil to learn if they like the food, progressing to choosing foods at snack and lunchtime. Pupils should be introduced to choosing their own snack or lunch food at the earliest opportunity. Additional opportunities to taste fruit will need to be created by introducing an afternoon snack time during two afternoons per week or replacing the usual morning snack with the fruit twice a week.	Activities are to be undertaken in the appropriate context, that is when food is usually eaten or prepared. Ensure the pupils can always see the food when it is presented to them in the dining room or at snack time or fruit tasting time. For choosing lunch food ensure that there is a low table at the dining room entrance with small samples of the day's menu displayed for pupils to see and smell, also photographs of the food available daily in the dining room and classroom.
Teaching	1:1 basis at snack time, fruit time and in the dining room. Ideally, the same member of staff works with the pupil each snack time, fruit time and lunchtime. Alternatively, one member of staff works with the pupil each snack time and fruit time and another member of staff each lunchtime. Familiarising the pupil with the food: present the food to the pupil, encourage them to smell, touch and taste the food. Give the name and sign for the food. If the pupil understands photos or pictorial representations such as emojis, introduce these as well.	It is important there is daily liaison between members of staff and clear observational records, ideally using a set format or checklist.

(*Continued*)

Table 5.1 (Continued)

Essential components	Content: Being able to choose food to eat	Notes/guidance – including learning environment and partnership with others including parents
	Choosing lunchtime food: in the dining room encourage choice-making initially between two options. Snack time: encourage choice-making initially between two options.	Observe the pupil's non-verbal and any verbal responses to ascertain which may be their choice if they are not appearing to make a discernible choice.
Observations and record keeping	Record the pupil's non-verbal and verbal responses to different foodstuffs, and choices made, to establish consistency of responses which may indicate like or dislike. Also record the way the pupil refers to the foodstuff.	Observations to be shared with parents through the home-school communication system, e.g. home-school book.
Parents	Staff to encourage parents to give their son or daughter opportunities to choose what they eat, whenever possible, and to provide experiences of different foods. Parents or respite carers may be willing to try the enrichment activity with their child. Staff to ensure the school's information about the decision-making curriculum is kept up to date and there is information about activities and experiences to support the development of children and young people's decision-making ability. Parents or respite carers may be interested in the teaching approaches being used.	Regular communication with parents through the home-school communication system to provide information about their child's progress.

Table 5.2 Victorine's decision-making curriculum

Essential components	Content: Being able to choose food to eat	Victorine's decision-making curriculum
Outcomes	**Long term**: By the end of Key Stage 5 Victorine will be able to choose her own • break time snack • lunchtime food • sandwich in the college canteen	***Short-term outcomes:*** ***By the end of Y12 Victorine will be able to choose between*** • *toast or yogurt for her break time snack*

Essential components	Content: Being able to choose food to eat	Victorine's decision-making curriculum
	Short term: tailored to the needs of each pupil	• the pudding of the day or fruit for her dessert at lunchtime • a brown bread tuna or ham sandwich in the college canteen ***without support on each occasion so she experiences some independence.***
Language and communication	All staff to use the agreed objects of reference, Makaton signs, symbols, emojis and words for activities, experiences and foodstuffs. Staff to be aware of Victorine's way of referring to the foodstuffs. College staff need to be made aware of how Victorine understands communication and how she communicates so there is a shared language. The communication strategy also needs to be shared with Victorine's parents and respite carers.	*Victorine understands the staff's communication with the support of objects of reference or real items. She tends to use vocalisation to indicate pleasure, and pulls a face without vocalisations to show displeasure. She recognises thumbs up for good, but cannot sign this herself without help.*
Experiences	All pupils to experience seeing, smelling, touching and eating the foodstuffs either at snack time, lunchtime, cookery lessons or celebration events. Foods experienced will depend on those being provided at lunchtime and snack times. **KS 5 enrichment experience**: Making a sandwich, Victorine is being introduced to ham, cheese, tuna, and egg sandwiches to help her choose from a wider range of sandwiches at college.	*Victorine can recognise snack and lunchtime foodstuffs.* • *When new foods are introduced she needs the opportunity to see, touch, smell and taste these.* *She needs to experience choosing her own* • *snack – yogurt or toast* • *dessert at lunchtime – pudding of the day or fruit* *Victorine recognises ham and tuna in sandwiches, but not the way egg and cheese are presented in sandwiches. Victorine needs to experience:* • *seeing, smelling, touching, tasting grated cheese*

(*Continued*)

Table 5.2 (Continued)

Essential components	Content: Being able to choose food to eat	Victorine's decision-making curriculum
		• *seeing, smelling, touching, tasting, mashed-up egg with mayonnaise* • *making sandwiches with the four fillings over the school year, beginning with ham and tuna*
Activities and opportunities	The main learning opportunities for these activities are at snack time, lunchtime, in the weekly cookery lesson and the weekly visit to the FE college. Other opportunities may arise for sandwiches when the class group go out into the community such as to cafés or coffee mornings in the local community centre.	*Victorine will have a daily opportunity to* • *choose between toast or yogurt at school or at college* • *choose her dessert – pudding of the day or fruit for school lunch four days per week* *Victorine will also have the opportunity to* • *choose a ham or tuna sandwich in the college canteen one day per week* • *choose sandwiches in other venues such as the community centre or cafés* • *try other foods as part of celebrations held in school or college or other venues*
Teaching	1:1 basis at snack time, in the school dining room and college canteen. Ideally, the same person should support Victorine for each college session. Staff should use the actual item, word and sign to let Victorine know her choices and what she chooses. Staff need to be aware of how Victorine refers to the foodstuffs. College staff need to be made aware of how Victorine understands communication and how she communicates. Staff need to ensure that Victorine can see the foods on offer, particularly in the college canteen.	*Victorine will always be shown the two options she has to choose between.* • *Staff will ask her to choose verbally and supported with Makaton signing.* • *If she does not seem to choose, staff will model choosing.* • *If staff have modelled choosing, Victorine will be asked again to choose verbally and with Makaton signing.*

Decision-making syllabus

Essential components	Content: Being able to choose food to eat	Victorine's decision-making curriculum
	Victorine's respite carers wish to be informed of the teaching strategies being used to develop her decision-making ability.	- *If she makes a discernible choice she is given her choice.* - *Staff will observe her to discern her choice if she does not appear to clearly indicate her choice.* - *In this instance, staff will give her the choice they think she has made.* - *If staff are uncertain of her choice they will give her the choice her parents have made on her behalf which should already be noted.*
Observations and record keeping	Record the pupil's non-verbal and verbal responses to different foodstuffs, and choices made, to establish consistency of responses which may indicate like or dislike. Also record the way the pupil refers to the foodstuff.	*Staff to record the choices Victorine makes each day and any verbal or non-verbal behaviours. Victorine is over 16 years old so her permission to share information with her parents is needed. Victorine is deemed to lack capacity to give her consent for this, therefore, as her parents are the decision-makers for educational matters, staff can share this information with them.*
Parents	Staff to encourage parents to give their son or daughter opportunities to choose what they eat when possible and to provide experiences of different foods. Parents may be willing to try the enrichment activity with their child. Staff to ensure the school's information about the decision-making curriculum is kept up to date and there is information about activities and experiences to support the development of children and young people's decision-making ability	*Victorine's parents are very supportive of the school's approach to decision-making and, whenever possible, they provide a range of experiences for Victorine, including trying new foods. About once a month, Victorine's parents take her to a local café so she can experience choosing her sandwich.* *Victorine has respite care twice a month and her carers are also trying to give her a range of experiences, they are using the 'My Activity Passport' for ideas. The carers also take Victorine to a café once a month.*

Decision-making framework

Whilst education professionals will mostly be enabling and supporting children and young people to make everyday decisions, there are some 'important' decisions, such as choosing a new education or training institution, which will entail teaching more about the decision-making process. Having a structured decision-making framework, such as the one presented in Chapter one, will support education and associated professionals in this endeavour, likewise assisting parents in understanding what making an 'important' decision involves and how to help their son or daughter participate in making the decision.

Outcomes

Outcomes are at the heart of the Children and Families Act 2014 and the SEND COP; that is, the overall outcomes and setting outcomes to achieve the overall aim of the legislation which is to help children and young people to 'achieve the best possible educational and other outcomes, preparing them effectively for adulthood' (SEND COP 1.1 p19). Outcomes, long- and short-term, are the linchpin for the approaches, intervention and support offered to a child or young person to assist them in achieving their goal on their journey to effective preparation for adulthood, as well as being an essential part of monitoring progress and guiding the next step. For young people aged over 18 years, the decision to maintain or cease an EHC Plan is based solely on whether the young person has achieved the education or training outcomes set out in the EHC Plan. Thus, individual outcomes need to be clearly written and achievable; the author has lost count of the number of times she has seen unachievable, vaguely worded outcomes. For example, George, a Year 6 pupil, of average ability, but who was not reaching age-related expectations due to behavioural issues, had an outcome relating to emotional regulation, entailing recognising ten feelings on an emotion regulation chart showing twelve faces expressing different emotions. He had to point to the one which reflected how he was feeling. This was unrealistic as it can be difficult for a child with emotional regulation issues to make such fine distinctions between emotions – many adults would find it challenging to distinguish between frustrated and angry or scared and anxious. In the first instance, the author advised only four feelings faces should be used – happy, sad, angry and bored.

The overall aim of the SEND Code of Practice is about preparation for adulthood and the very broad outcomes, set out at 1.39, covering helping children and young people to realise their ambitions in relation to higher education or employment, independent living, participating in society and being as healthy as possible (see Appendix 4). Information and guidance about 'outcomes' is set out in various places in the SEND COP, with most general guidance located in Chapter 9 (9.61 and 9.64–9.69). SEND COP 9.66 defines an outcome as 'the benefit or difference made to an individual as a result of an intervention. It should be personal and not expressed from a service perspective' (p163). This section reiterates the 9.61 stipulation that outcomes in EHC Plans should be SMART (specific, measurable, achievable, realistic, time-bound). Although not indicated in SEND COP Chapters 5, 6, 7 or 8, by implication all outcomes, whether for SEN Support or an EHC Plan, should be SMART. The SEND COP offers no guidance about writing, or examples of, SMART outcomes, which is a skill addressed in Chapter six of this book.

The advice about 'outcomes' for Early Years practitioners is recorded in SEND COP Chapter 5, supplemented by the DfE (2013) publication 'Early Years outcomes: a non-statutory guide for practitioners and inspectors to help inform understanding of child development through the early years'.[7] This document assists Early Years practitioners to understand the outcomes they should be working towards; these are aligned to the Early Years Foundation Stage (EYFS) curriculum. It is based on recognised developmental checklists (e.g. Sheridan 1975), which are all predicated on the work of the American paediatrician Dr Arnold Gessell in the 1920s and 1930s; his final version was published in 1947. To date this has not been updated to take account of changes in health and other factors. Thus, whilst the EYFS curriculum focuses on developing the prerequisite skills needed for a child or young person to begin to be able to learn to make choices, there is no specific decision-making objective within the curriculum. In the Early Years, 'outcomes' need to be considered at the point it is decided the child requires SEN support, and these should be agreed in consultation with parents, with the support and intervention provided chosen to meet the identified outcomes (SEND COP 5.40).

For pupils of compulsory school age, SEND COP Chapter 6 provides information about outcomes. Like the Early Years phase, consideration of special educational provision should begin with the outcomes sought, in consultation with parents, and the support and intervention provided chosen to meet the specified outcomes (SEND COP 6.40 & 6.50). To support this, SEND COP 6.49 sets out that all teachers and support staff should be aware of a pupil's outcomes, support to be provided and any teaching approaches or strategies. More specific guidance about the focus of outcomes is given; SEND COP 6.42 stipulates that 'the outcomes considered should include those needed to make successful transitions between phases of education and to prepare for adult life' (p100). From Year 9, the SEND COP states that outcomes will be focused on ensuring young people are preparing for adulthood (SEND COP 6.41).

SEND COP Chapter 7 covers further education – post 16 education provision – but has little specific information about outcomes, it would seem; for this age group, this is contained in SEND COP Chapter 8. The SEN support in College section indicates that support should be aimed at promoting the young person's independence and enabling progress towards the preparing for adulthood outcomes (SEND COP 7.13). The guidance in SEND COP Chapter 6 noted above would also seem to be appropriate for education professionals working in the post 16 sector, some of which is reiterated in SEND COP Chapter 8.

SEND COP 8.9–8.10 sets out the requirements for preparing for adulthood reviews – the EHC Plan annual review. Transition planning must be built into the EHC Plan; this should lead to clear outcomes to prepare young people for adulthood. In 8.10 the emphasis is on support to prepare young people to meet their preparation for adult outcomes. As noted above, outcomes determine the interventions and support needed, therefore, by implication, young people will have identified outcomes in the four preparing for adulthood outcome areas.

In SEND COP 8.15, which relates to young people making their own decisions, all agencies, including parents, are urged to support the young person to help them make decisions that will lead to 'good outcomes' for them, but it is acknowledged that the final decision rests with the young person. The notion of 'good outcomes' is subjective and what those working with the young person may feel is a good aim, may not be shared by the young person. For example, the author recalls a young person (Dylan), aged 19 years with high functioning autism, supported at college through SEN support. His views on remaining at college differed from his parent's: he wished to leave and get a job or possibly an apprenticeship; his mother wanted him to continue at college to gain some qualifications. Dylan was very clear he did not want to do any more studying. He was interested in animals; he and his family had a number of pets and he wished to work in a pet shop. College staff knew that Dylan's wish was to leave college and get a job; he variously engaged with college work. If you were the education professional working with Dylan, how would you help him resolve this?

Post 16 institutions are advised to provide a coherent study programme that provides progression, enabling young people with SEN to achieve the best possible outcomes in adult life (SEND COP 8.30). The 'best possible outcomes' can be interpreted as referring to the preparing for adulthood outcomes, but not exclusively.

Outcomes, outcomes everywhere – but what is the optimum number?

The author reads EHC Plans from lots of local authorities and is struck by the large number of outcomes listed, sometimes at least five short-term outcomes, which are usually referred to as the steps to meeting the long-term outcome, for each of the four broad areas of SEN: cognition and learning, communication and interaction, social, emotional and mental health difficulties and sensory and/or physical needs. Sometimes there is an overlap between the steps for cognition and learning and communication and interaction. Invariably these outcomes are not always SMART. As already noted, it is very rare for the author to see a decision-making outcome. Where does it fit in the categories used in EHC Plans? For EHC Plans organised with sections covering the four broad areas of need (SEND COP 6.28–6.35), a decision-making outcome may be best placed in the social, emotional and mental health section; consideration could be given to placing it in communication and interaction. Some EHC Plans have an independence skills section, which may be the appropriate section for a decision-making outcome. If post 16 EHC Plans use the preparing for adulthood outcome areas, then independent living may be the appropriate section. The lack of a seemingly suitable place in an EHC Plan for a decision-making outcome should not be a barrier to ensuring one is included – if necessary be creative about where it fits best.

How many outcomes, long- or short-term, is the right number? Key factors to consider are how the child or young person learns and that both the long-term and short-term outcomes need to be workable and manageable for both the education professionals and the child or young person within the education institution working day. For example, for a child or young person with profound and multiple learning difficulties one long-term outcome per SEND COP area of special need may be appropriate, broken down into no more than three short-term outcomes per long-term outcome. Ideally, at least some short-term outcomes could be linked to the normal pattern of behaviour for the child or young person within the education institution, in particular those relating to making everyday decisions and independence.

Key points about outcomes

The discussion above demonstrated that outcomes are central to making provision for children and young people with SEN, therefore it is essential that these are clearly written and achievable. The SEND COP emphasises that outcomes are the starting point to think about planning support and interventions; for young people in the post 16 sector, outcomes inform the curriculum offered to a young person. Figure 5.3 (overleaf) summarises the key points that education professionals need to know and remember about outcomes in relation to the SEND Code of Practice. Chapter six in this book addresses the art of formulating outcomes and associated issues.

Teaching

As noted earlier in the book, children and young people with SEN are very likely to need direct teaching about how to make decisions. This process entails developing a decision-making curriculum from the decision-making syllabus guidance, perhaps for a Key Stage or class group, differentiated for each child or young person, writing SMART outcomes and selecting the appropriate interventions and support to assist achieving the outcomes, as well as ensuring that all those working with the pupil or student are aware of the outcomes and strategies. Fundamentally, there needs to be consistency in all aspects of communication, as well as the teaching and learning approaches employed with the pupils/students. Equally essential is the education professional's ability to communicate with the child or young person and to understand their communication.

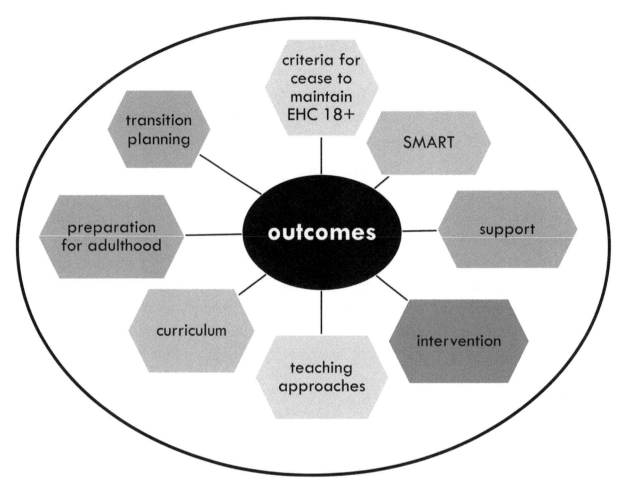

Figure 5.3 Key points relating to outcomes from the SEND Code of Practice

Scaffolding was introduced earlier as a teaching approach to support and enable children and young people to develop their decision-making ability. Successfully scaffolded support depends on the education professional knowing the child or young person in order to engage them in the task; particularly important is being aware of what motivates them. Equally important is the ability to appropriately differentiate (adapt) the task to facilitate the child or young person making choices. There are several ways this can be achieved, such as considering the content of the lesson, the process by which the child or young person is assisted to acquire the skill or desired outcome, as well as ensuring the learning or education institution environment enables the learner to be successful; the latter is discussed above.

Returning to the case study 'Friday afternoon choice (part 1)' (Chapter four, p. 60), consider the teaching involved in preparing Victorine to be offered this choice. The scenario indicated preparation for choosing her own activity in Year 12 started in Year 7. The continuation of this case study below shows the teaching she received in the early stages to enable her to make this choice.

Friday afternoon choice (part 2)

The decision-making curriculum has a long-term decision-making outcome for all pupils that they will be able to choose their own Friday afternoon activity in Year 12. This is broken down into small steps which are progressive, beginning in Year 7.

Decision-making curriculum

Year 7

Outcomes: Long-term outcome: In Year 12 students will be able to choose their own Friday afternoon activity from a choice of two with support.

Short-term outcome: Year 7: pupils will recognise the object of reference or sign or symbol for the ball pool (ball pool ball), sensory room (scented cushion), art (paint brush) and music (triangle).

This short-term outcome will need to be individually personalised for each pupil, in discussion with their parents, taking into account factors such as how they learn.

Language and communication: use the agreed objects of reference, Makaton signs, symbols and words for each activity. These are available on the school intranet and in the folder in the staff room.

Activities: Year 7 classes use the ball pool and sensory room twice a week, music and art sessions are once a week.

Teaching: Teaching approach to introduce the objects of reference and Makaton sign and/or symbol will be on a 1:1 basis so pupils can touch, feel and smell the object of reference as well as hearing the name of the activity, seeing the sign, and then being taken to the activity holding the object of reference. The object or reference will be used before the timetabled activity, so the pupil makes the link between the object of reference and the activity it denotes.

The staff member will hold the object of reference so the pupil can see it and say the agreed name for the activity. The staff member will give the object of reference to the pupil, say and sign the name of the activity. The pupil will be encouraged to feel the object of reference and smell those that have a smell. Taking the time to engage the pupil in the process is important; this may mean hand over hand to help the pupil feel the object of reference, and encouragement to smell scented ones as well as feeling them. Sighted pupils should be encouraged to look at the object of reference as well as touching it. At the same time the staff member working with the pupil should also repeat the name of the activity.

Experiences: every pupil will experience each activity on each occasion it is timetabled. Pupils will be supported 1:1 for some of the time in each activity on each occasion.

Observations and record keeping: Pupils' responses to the activity will be recorded each time to establish which activities they like or dislike, ensuring pupils' views, wishes and feelings are known, and can be recorded formally in the person-centred planning or annual review meeting. Observations should be shared regularly with parents in the home-school communication book, at parents' evenings and review meetings.

Parents: The outcome is written into person-centred planning; parents are given a copy through the home-school communication book, at parents' evenings and review meetings. The school website also has written information as well as podcasts, online videos and there is a DVD or USB memory stick parents can borrow.

Year 8

Outcomes: Long-term outcome: In Year 12 students will be able to choose their own Friday afternoon activity from a choice of two without support.

Short-term outcome: Year 8: pupils will recognise the object of reference, sign and/or symbol for the ball pool (ball pool ball), sensory room (scented cushion), art (paint brush), music (triangle), trike (bicycle bell), card games (playing card), listening to music (headphones), watching cartoons (picture of cartoon character), playing pool (small pool cue), Velcro darts (Velcro dart), tablet computer (tablet computer).

Short-term outcome: Year 8: pupils will be able to indicate if they like or dislike:

- being in the ball pool
- activities in the sensory room
- activities in music sessions
- art sessions
- activities at break time

These short-term outcomes will need to be individually personalised for each pupil, in discussion with their parents, taking into account factors such as how they learn.

Language and communication: Introduce the pupils to a range of ways to indicate their like or dislike, such as thumbs up, thumbs down, smiley and sad faces emojis, words, Makaton signs and other symbols or facial expressions. Equally important is the staff recognising the child or young person's way of communicating like and dislike. All adults use the agreed objects of reference, signs, symbols/emojis and words for each activity. These are available on the school intranet and in the folder in the staff room.

Activities: Year 8 classes use the ball pool and sensory room twice a week, music and art are once a week. Break time activities include the outside play 'adventure playground', the trike, ball games; inside activities include board games, card games, listening to music, watching cartoons, playing pool and Velcro darts and tablet computer-based games.

Teaching: The teaching for introducing objects of reference, signs and symbols is the same as for Year 7. Use the objects of reference, signs and symbols with the class group as well as individually. Teaching the pupil to begin to communicate like or dislike will be undertaken 1:1. It begins with facilitating the pupil's understanding of the concept of like or dislike, which is done by linking the relevant sign, emoji soft toy or emoji/symbol or word to the pupil's behaviour, using the most appropriate means of communicating for the particular pupil. For instance, when the pupil shows obvious pleasure, use the most appropriate sign, emoji/symbol or word for like and link it to the activity. For example, when a pupil is showing pleasure in the ball pool, the adult shows the pupil the thumbs up sign, also using hand over hand as appropriate to help the child make the thumbs up sign. Alternatively, the smiley face emoji soft toy or symbol can be shown and then given to the pupil. The next step would be for the pupil to be able to sign good/like or select the good/like emoji soft toy or symbol from two, like and dislike.

Experiences: The pupils should be able to experience the range of activities offered at break time, being encouraged to try those they may not have experienced. During a term, every pupil tries each activity, particularly unfamiliar ones, at least ten times, that is about once a week. Wet break activities may occur less frequently, but it is equally important that pupils experience each activity so they learn what they like.

Observations and record keeping: Pupils' responses to the activity will be recorded each time to establish which activities they like or dislike, ensuring pupils' views, wishes and feelings are known, and can be recorded formally in the person-centred planning or annual review meeting. Observations should be shared regularly with parents in the home-school communication book, at parents' evenings and review meetings.

> **Parents:** The outcome is written into person-centred planning, and parents are given a copy through the home-school communication book, at parents' evenings or review meetings. Parents are introduced to the signs, words and emojis being used, so they can use these at home to facilitate consistency between home and the education institution. For the break time activities parents are encouraged to give their child or young person similar experiences, such as going to the park or playing games at home. The school has a library of games for parents to borrow. The school website also has written information as well as podcasts, online videos and there is a DVD parents can borrow.

Observations and record keeping

The SEND COP emphasises the child or young person's participation in decision-making; good records enable it to be shown the extent to which the child or young person participated in making the particular decision. In Chapter four it was noted that it is good practice to record the child or young person's responses to activities, as this may provide useful information to assist the child or young person's decision-making or help a parent make a decision on behalf of their son or daughter. Additionally, the Mental Capacity (Amendment Act) 2019 has made it mandatory that the views and wishes of the young person are ascertained in relation to the proposed arrangements, which are considered to be a deprivation of liberty. For young people unable to indicate these in any way directly, it is essential that their views and wishes are determined through observations of their responses. Thus, education institution staff's noted observations are likely to facilitate a young person's views, wishes and feelings being known about educational matters. For example, returning to 'Friday afternoon choice (part 1)', the staff's observations indicated that Victorine probably preferred the ball pool to the sensory room, suggesting that if she was not able to make the choice, this information would assist her parents choosing, on her behalf, the activity she would have chosen herself. In Chapter four, case study A (p. 64), Peter's parents observed his responses during the visits to prospective secondary schools, using this to inform their choice. It is likely that they chose the school Peter himself would have chosen.

The above discussion highlights the importance of noting observations about the child or young person's responses to experiences and activities. This becomes essential when young people reach the age at which they are legally entitled to make their own decision; it is expected they will do so (see Appendix 5 for further information about undertaking observations and guidance for observing by videoing). Chapter four proposed that the role of the education professional, in relation to young people making their own decisions, could be considered as the young person's advocate, ensuring their right to participate in decisions about their education. Education professionals' observations would be especially important in instances when the young person is considered to lack capacity to make the particular decision, as these would facilitate the young person's views, wishes and feelings being made known so they can be considered by parents making the decision on behalf of their son or daughter. Thus, it should be a fundamental part of an education professional's everyday practice to make and record observations of children's and young people's responses to activities and experiences. Good records can show patterns of behaviour such as whether the child or young person

- demonstrates consistent responses
- is affected by different factors such as noise levels, the presence or absence of particular adults or peers, time of day, day of the week, activity, etc.

However, there needs to be consistency in the way in which children and young people's reactions are recorded by education institution staff, enabling patterns of behaviour to be discerned. Thus, it may be helpful for education institution staff to use a set format for observational record keeping. For instance, returning to 'Friday afternoon choice (part 1)', school staff noting the same information enabled them to identify Victorine's behaviour pattern and to be fairly confident that she preferred the ball pool to the sensory room. An example of an observational recording format is presented overleaf (see Appendix 5 for a completed observational recording). It is not necessarily intended to be used as a form, but to ensure the relevant information is noted – it could be considered as a checklist. Hopefully, the emphasis on observations about a child's or young person's decision-making ability is not viewed as burdensome and its important role in highlighting reactions, thereby providing an insight into the pupil's or student's views, wishes and feelings, is understood.

Activities

There are references to activities, often linked with experiences, in the discussion above and in other chapters, as well as an indication that education professionals should consider activities both in and out of class time. However, activities cannot, and should not, be envisaged without also contemplating opportunities. The discussion above highlighted that activities need to be purposeful, relevant, realistic and in context. For example, when the child or young person is still learning about the choices on offer, it may be necessary to create opportunities to experience the activity. For example, if ball games are a Key Stage 2 break or lunchtime activity, then pupils must experience the range of possible games. Therefore, ball game activity opportunities will probably need to be created at other times of the school day, such as perhaps in PE. It is important that activities are done in context, even when opportunities are having to be created, for instance, ball games played in the appropriate place, outside or in the designated indoor area, not in the classroom.

Table 5.3 Observation recording format/checklist

Name of pupil/student:	Name of person making the observations:
Date:　　　Time: Location:	Who else was present: Staff: Pupils/students: Visitors:
Activity or experience: Communication: *note how* • *you communicated with the pupil/student, e.g. verbally alone, verbal supported with signing, use of objects of reference, symbols, pictures, photos* • *the pupil/student communicated with you*	
Pupil/student response: *Include comments related to:* verbal – *record the words used by the pupil or student* non-verbal behaviour: *record facial expressions, body movements, vocalisations, signing, or symbols, behaviour, length of time engaged in the activity, behaviours indicating a wish for the activity to continue or to stop*	

Copyright material from Jane L. Sinson (2020) *Developing Decision-making with Children and Young People with SEN: A Practical Guide for Education and Associated Professionals*, Routledge.

Another factor in considering activities is how they are referred to by education institution staff. As noted above, there needs to be consistency within the education institution, which is shared with parents and visiting education and associated professionals.

Opportunities

To reiterate, opportunities should be considered in conjunction with activities and experiences. Ideally, contemplating opportunities to develop, enable and support children and young people's decision-making should become a part of education professionals' everyday thinking. Opportunities, like activities and experiences, need to be purposeful, relevant, realistic and in context, even if being created through activities being undertaken outside their usual time. For example, if the class group need to develop and practise handwashing, it may be that the natural time for this, such as after the toilet, or before lunch, provides insufficient opportunities for learning, therefore additional opportunities may need to be created by doing messy activities necessitating handwashing afterwards.

Considering suitable purposeful, relevant and realistic activities to extend children and young people's knowledge and experience of the world around them may be facilitated using the 'My Activity Passport'. For example, the 'My Activity Passport' posting a letter activity has several opportunities for this experience at different ages. For very young children it may be 'writing' and posting a letter to Santa Claus; as pupils get older it could be posting a birthday card, other occasion card, or postcard to someone in school.

Looking for opportunities to teach children and young people to take a photograph, and, likewise, to practise this, is essential – taking photographs is an integral part of information gathering to assist a young person when they are choosing a new educational or training placement. It is envisaged that, for many children and young people with SEN, they are more likely to be using a mobile phone or tablet computer as the camera. Beginning teaching and practising this from a young age ensures the young person has had ample opportunity to master this skill.

Everyday and every day practice

'Everyday practice', in this chapter and others, refers to education professionals embedding developing, supporting and enabling children and young people's decision-making into their every day practice, which entails considering the experiences, activities and opportunities that each day affords for this, and likewise ensuring this is supported by the organisation of the learning and wider education institution environment. 'Every day practice' relates to education professionals providing daily opportunities enabling children and young people to develop or use their decision-making ability. Returning to the 'Decision-making curriculum' scenario (p. 92), an analysis of how school staff endeavoured to embed supporting the pupils to make their own choice at lunchtime into everyday practice demonstrates the starting point was to ensure that there was consistency across the school in terms of their language and communication with the pupils. Thus, whenever foodstuffs formed part of the curriculum, school staff used the same word, sign, symbol and object of reference to denote these, whether it was for school meals or the foodstuff was being talked about in another context. The pupils were given the experience to see, touch, smell and taste the food on offer daily in the dining room and in the weekly class cookery lessons. This sensory approach is used by education institution staff for all food-related experiences, such as opportunities to try different foods when the class celebrate different festivals, birthdays or other occasions. Staff record observations about how the pupil has responded to the particular food to build up a picture of their likes and dislikes.

Parents

References to involving and supporting parents have been made in this chapter, earlier in the book and will be explored in detail in Chapter eight. This section discusses the main points relating to involving and supporting parents.

The success of the decision-making curriculum is likely to be enhanced if parents understand the education institution's approach in this area and can be encouraged to support their child or young person on their journey to adulthood. Ideally, parental involvement in empowering their child or young person's decision-making ability would entail parents

- using the same words, signs, symbols and, where practicable, objects of reference as the education institution to refer to activities, foods, people, items, etc.
- sharing with education institution staff their son's or daughter's way of referring to an activity, experience or family member and how they show pleasure and displeasure
- enabling
    - a wide range of experiences including having a 'My Activity Passport' to follow at home
    - their son or daughter to make everyday decisions, such as choosing what to eat, wear or leisure activities
    - their son's or daughter's use of personal digital technology to promote making choices and communicating choices, including taking photographs
- considering decision-making outcomes as part of person-centred planning and/or an EHC Plan from the earliest age

- noting observations about their son's or daughter's responses to activities and experiences to be able to use when making decisions on their behalf

. . . and finally

Hopefully this lengthy discussion has provoked reflection, discussion and debate, as well as providing the impetus for the reader to consider their everyday practice in relation to developing, supporting and enabling children and young people's decision-making ability. What will be your first step – what will you do tomorrow? Perhaps the summary of the key points below will assist your thinking.

Summary of key points to help children and young people with SEN learn how to make decisions

- The need for a structured curriculum, or strategy, to develop, support and enable children's and young people's decision-making ability, with clearly formulated SMART outcomes.

- Curriculum content should include making everyday decisions such as choices about food, drink and activities.

- Having a structured decision-making framework, such as the one presented in Chapter one, supports education professionals to teach children and young people how to make 'important' decisions.

- Education professionals should embed developing, supporting and enabling children and young people's decision-making into everyday practice – it becomes a way of thinking.

- The need for consistency in language and communication between education institution staff and children and young people, shared with parents, respite carers and visiting professionals.

- Promoting an ethos where education institution staff hold the belief that decisions about a child or young person's education will not be made without a contribution from the child or young person. This will need to be shared with parents, respite carers, visiting professionals and local authority SEN officers.

- Education institution staff
    - provide children and young people with a wide range of purposeful, relevant and realistic experiences, in context, to enable them to gain a knowledge of the world around them to help them make their own decisions as part of their preparation for adulthood.

- are alert to activities and opportunities, in context, to develop, support and enable decision-making.

- should consider ascertaining which activities and opportunities are available to children and young people provided by social services, for example in respite care placements, so, if possible, these can also be experienced in the education institution, thereby extending choice-making to include community-based activities. For example, if respite care establishments play certain board games, it would be helpful if children and young people also had the opportunity to do this in the education institution.

- organise the learning environment and non-classroom spaces to promote, facilitate and support children and young people making their own decisions.

- Formulating SMART decision-making outcomes, which are purposeful, relevant and realistic, for person-centred planning, and/or written into EHC Plans. Consideration is given to limiting the number of outcomes so they are manageable for education institution staff and achievable for children and young people.

- Working in partnership with parents and associated professionals to promote, encourage, support and enable children and young people to make their own decisions.

- The need for education and associated professionals and parents to observe, and record, children and young people's responses to activities, experiences and decision-making to facilitate children and young people's views, wishes and feelings being known, enabling them to participate in making decisions about their education.

Notes

1 https://en.oxforddictionaries.com/definition/ethos, accessed 31 December 2018.
2 Available from: www.gov.uk/government/publications/my-activity-passport, accessed 19 February 2019.
3 Available from: www.nationaltrust.org.uk/50-things-to-do, accessed 17 February 2019.
4 https://en.oxforddictionaries.com/definition/environment, accessed 4 January 2019.
5 See Sinson (2015).
6 www.unesco.org/education/tlsf/mods/theme_a/popups/mod05t01s01.html, accessed 22 January 2019.
7 Available from: www.foundationyears.org.uk/files/2012/03/Early_Years_Outcomes.pdf, accessed 22 January 2019.

Chapter six

THE ART OF WRITING SMART OUTCOMES

Outcome – the benefit or difference made to an individual as result of an intervention. It should be personal.

(SEND Code of Practice para 9.66)

Chapter five explored the SEND Code of Practice definition of and guidance about outcomes, the linchpin for the special educational provision made for children and young people, emphasising the need for outcomes to be clearly written and achievable. The current chapter specifically addresses the art of formulating and writing SMART outcomes – long- and short-term – with the aim that children and young people have specific, achievable and realistic outcomes that enable and support the development of their decision-making ability, likewise facilitating preparation for adulthood. Outcomes link directly to the provision to be made for the child or young person, therefore, by implication, it will be more challenging to determine approaches and interventions if it is unclear what it is that needs to be achieved, how it can be achieved, and whereby education or associated professionals, or parents, would know it has been. Thus, the formulation of outcomes, and the language used to write them, becomes important; this is addressed later in the chapter, introducing Mager's (1972) notion of 'fuzzies' and 'performance' terms.

The first part of this chapter works through the mechanics of formulating and writing SMART outcomes; points are illustrated using mostly actual, or adapted, EHC Plan outcomes (all names have been changed). Due to the dearth of actual EHC Plan or person-centred planning decision-making outcomes, those selected generally address other issues. Later in the chapter possible decision-making outcomes are discussed to provide inspiration and models of formulated SMART outcomes.

What is an 'outcome'?

The quote at the beginning of the chapter is the SEND Code of Practice's definition of what is meant by 'outcome'. Additionally, the same paragraph indicates that an outcome describes how the individual will benefit from the education or training intervention. By implication this should be steps on the route to preparation for adulthood. Overall, an outcome's aim is to enable the child or young person to do something they cannot currently do, in preparation for adulthood. Outcomes should be personal to the child or young person, addressing something the child or young person wishes to accomplish or what it is considered important for them to achieve as determined by others considering their best interests (SEND COP 9.67). The SEND Code of Practice notes that an outcome should be focused on 'something that those involved have control and influence over' (p163), as well as indicating by when it is anticipated it will have been achieved.

The phrase 'relevant and purposeful' is used in the SEND Code of Practice to describe the actions taken by education institutions in identifying, assessing and meeting children and young people's special educational needs. This phrase could equally be applied to describing the essential characteristics of an 'outcome', to which the author would add 'realistic' in the same way as Chapter five emphasised that experiences and activities should be purposeful, relevant and realistic.

SMART outcomes

The acronym SMART has some slightly different variations for the meaning of 'A', 'R' and 'T', but the ones adopted by the SEND Code of Practice (9.61) are *specific, measurable, achievable, realistic, time-bound*. The National Audit Office[1] offers some helpful guidance to understanding each of the components, which has been incorporated in the explanation below.

Specific: the outcome should be written to target the specific issue and be clearly understood. This means each outcome should address a single issue. The following long-term outcome for physical and sensory skills is taken from a real EHC Plan.

> *By the end of Key Stage 3 Esmeralda will develop her fine motor skills, self-help skills and sensory regulation skills so she is able to become more independent and able to tolerate a variety of sensory experiences for longer periods of time.*

This outcome lacks specificity as it addresses several different issues; it is really three long-term outcomes, one each for fine motor skills, self-help skills and sensory regulation skills. It could be argued that developing fine motor skills will assist with self-help skills, therefore these could be combined in one outcome. However, this may present some challenges when setting the measurable criteria. In the author's view the outcome would have been better formulated as

> *By the end of Key Stage 3:*

- *Esmeralda will have developed her fine motor skills enabling her to be more independent.*
- *Esmeralda will have developed her self-help skills enabling her to be more independent.*
- *Esmeralda will have developed her sensory regulation skills enabling her to tolerate a variety of sensory experiences for longer periods of time.*

Thus, each outcome relates to a single developmental area, and the desired benefit of developing the skill is clearer. Does combining fine motor and self-help skills into a single outcome achieve the same clarity? A possible formulation of the joint outcome could be

By the end of KS3 Esmeralda will have developed her fine motor skills which will have helped improve her self-help skills, so she has been able to become more independent.

In this instance, fusing fine motor and self-help skills into a single outcome does retain clarity; it is considerably clearer than the original formulation which included sensory regulation skills. Development of the latter did relate to independence, but also had an additional aim to increase her tolerance of sensory experiences; this addition seemed to make the original outcome somewhat confused, and possibly more challenging to measure progress. However, separating out the skills does not preclude sensory outcomes supporting developing self-help skills. Given Esmeralda's actual short-term self-help outcome related to hand washing, it would be sensible to ensure her tolerance of the necessary sensory elements is established, such as putting her hands in warm or cold water, having soap on her hands and using a paper towel or hand dryer in school.

Measurable: Outcomes must be expressed in a measurable form to be able to evaluate a change from the starting point. This can be some type of numerical form such as on 3/5 occasions or as a percentage – 50% of the time. For example:

By the end of Year 12 Victorine ('Friday afternoon choice (part 1)') will be able to choose, without support, between

- *toast or yogurt for her morning break time snack on 3/4 days per week*
- *pudding and custard or fruit for her dessert at lunchtime on 2/4 days per week*

or

By the end of Key Stage 2: Imran will be able to communicate, verbally or non-verbally, which object, activity, or food he would like from a choice of two within the school setting on every occasion without support.

or

> *By the end of Key Stage 1: Jamie will be able to engage in an adult-chosen activity, without support, for at least 5 minutes on 2/5 occasions when her visual timetable shows this is followed by an activity she is known to enjoy.*

Likewise, measurable could be expressed as an increase or decrease in the occurrence of something. Returning to Esmeralda's outcome, there is an implication that she will be able to do more following the intervention, in this case more fine motor, self-help or sensory regulation skills, indicating that she has become more independent. For this to be measurable, there has to be a baseline measure of her skills before the intervention, with an aim of what will be achieved by the intervention, so that the increase in skills, and thereby independence, can be measured. For self-help skills, the measure could be the items of clothing she could remove or put on before and after the intervention, or the elements of hand washing, after using the toilet, she is now able to do, with or without support.

> *Short-term SMART outcome: Esmeralda will be able to wash her hands, with support, after using the toilet.*

Whilst it is specific, it omits both how often it is expected she will do this and what behaviours constitute hand washing, both of which are needed to assist measuring progress towards achieving the outcome and to know when it has been achieved. As she is being supported, it is probably assumed this will happen every time she uses the bathroom, however it should have been stated. The outcome would have been better formulated as

> *Short-term SMART outcome: Esmeralda will be able to wash her hands with soap in warm water and dry them with the hand dryer, with support, after using the toilet* **on every occasion**.

The sensory regulation outcome had two measurable elements that would denote progress: tolerating a variety of sensory experiences and the length of time of her tolerance. Esmeralda's EHC Plan short-term outcome for sensory regulation was specific and measurable, however it omits whether this is supported or independent:

> *Short-term SMART outcome: Esmeralda will taste/feel one different food item a week.*

Education institution staff supporting Esmeralda are informed about what they will need to do, how often, and what to record to demonstrate she is making progress towards her long-term outcome. Furthermore, education institution staff will need to record Esmeralda's responses to the food item being tasted or felt to build up a pattern of her behaviour over time. This can be evaluated to ascertain her progress in this area, as well as providing information to consider what the next outcome may be to extend her experiences or skills. Again, there would need to be a baseline measure of which sensory experiences she could tolerate and for how long, any increases in the length of time of her tolerance for existing and any new experiences would need to be recorded, likewise the noting of all new experiences.

Esmeralda's independence-focused outcome combined motor skills, self-help and sensory regulation, however progress in self-help skills may be dependent on developing the associated sensory tolerances. Therefore, it makes sense to have outcomes addressing sensory issues alongside those for self-help skills, thereby assisting progress in both areas. For example, Esmeralda's actual EHC Plan self-help short-term outcome, as noted above, concerned washing her hands after using the toilet. Given her sensory regulation outcome was unrelated to tolerance of the associated sensory experiences it would be assumed that she was able to tolerate her hands in water, soap and drying her hands. However, if Esmeralda experiences any difficulties with these various sensory experiences, it would be logical that her sensory outcomes relate to building her tolerance of these to support her achieving the self-help outcome. Thus, her short-term SMART outcomes for sensory regulation may be:

By the end of the school year in July, Esmeralda will be able to tolerate

- *her hands in warm water for 1 minute, with support, each time she has used the toilet*
- *soap on her hands, with support, for 20 seconds each time she has used the toilet*
- *her hands in cold water for 1 minute, with support, once a day*
- *having her hands dried using the hand drier, with support, each time she has used the toilet.*

Prior to the intervention Esmeralda could tolerate with support	**After the intervention Esmeralda could tolerate with support**
• her hands in warm water for 15 seconds	• her hands in warm water for 1 minute
• unable to tolerate soap on her hands	• soap on her hand for 5 seconds
• unable to tolerate her hands in cold water	• her hands in cold water for 1 minute
• difficulties with having her hands dried with a hand drier, she preferred a towel	• having her hands dried with a hand drier for 10 seconds

This shows measurable progress, both for the self-help and the sensory outcome; furthermore it suggests possible next steps in terms of associated experiences, strategies, approaches, and support, to formulate the next outcome, depending on what Esmeralda and/or her parents feel is important for her to be able to do, bearing in mind the overall aim of preparation for adulthood.

Some outcomes can be harder to measure – this is more likely to apply to those concerning areas related to social, emotional and mental health or social communication, such as 'increase in confidence'. Thus, it is better to formulate the outcome describing behaviours indicating an increase in confidence. For example, an outcome for Kirby, who lacks confidence, presents as very shy and is reluctant to speak to school staff, may be:

> *By the end of the school year:*
> *SMART outcome: Kirby will be able to sign or say hello to his teacher, at the beginning of the school day, without support, on 2/5 days per week, thereby developing his social communication skills and understanding of socially expected behaviour.*

Achievable: This refers to achievable both for the child or young person and those supporting them to achieve the outcome. Setting unachievable outcomes is demotivating for both parties, and counterproductive. Let us return to George (Chapter five, p. 106), a Year 6 pupil, whose outcome concerning recognising his own feelings by pointing to one of the twelve faces on the feelings chart was unlikely to be achievable due to the difficulties of making such fine distinctions between frustrated and angry or scared and anxious, thereby raising the question, how do education professionals work out what may be an achievable outcome? Chapter five introduced Vygotsky's zone of proximal development – the bottom of the zone represents what the child or young person can achieve independently, and the top is what they can achieve with support; Figure 6.1 illustrates this visually. The first step is where the child or young person is at now, the second step is what they could be doing next with support to progress their development.

However, the challenge is to make the next step the right size – how does an education professional know what could be achieved? Firstly, it would be important to establish the components of the task, which will be a guide as to what the child or young person needs to be able to do to have achieved the outcome. For example, hand washing entails hands in water, using soap, rubbing the soap on the hands, rinsing, and drying. This helps create a baseline providing information to decide the next step. However, to formulate what may be an achievable next step, consideration will need to be given to the various factors which may affect achievability, such as whether the child or young person has developed the

The art of writing SMART outcomes

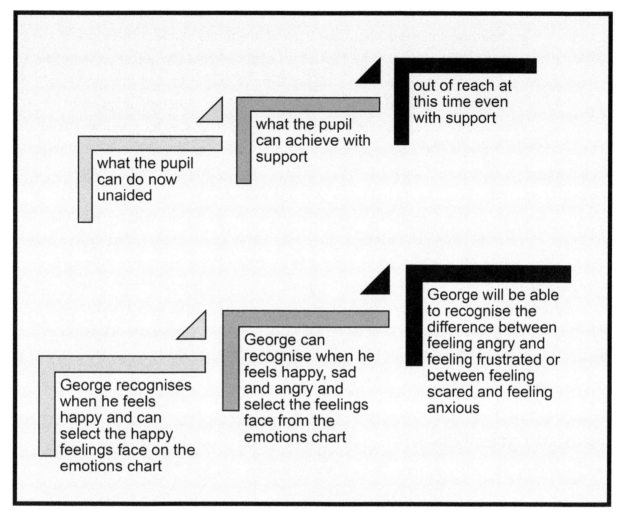

Figure 6.1 Vygotsky's zone of proximal development

necessary associated motor, sensory regulation, or speech, language and communication skills, their rate of learning, opportunities and activities that address the outcome, attention and concentration. For instance, many self-help skills have a sensory element such as tolerating water or textures touching the skin. Therefore, a hand washing outcome would be unachievable if the child or young person cannot tolerate water. Thus, the child or young person would also need an outcome that builds up their tolerance of having their hands in water, supporting the hand washing outcome. This may necessitate creating relevant, purposeful and realistic activities entailing placing hands in water, such as washing up or, for young children, water play.

For instance, this real EHC Plan social communication skills outcome,

By the end of Key Stage 2: Alberto will have learned to use the name of key adults in school

is only likely to be achievable if Alberto can make the required speech sounds enabling him to produce reasonably recognisable approximations of the adults' names. Therefore, his speech and language abilities need to be considered and, if necessary, adjustments made to the desired outcome to make it achievable. Furthermore, it may be that the number of adults whose names he is expected to learn to use is ambitious, although unspecified in the outcome. Additionally, Alberto's rate of learning and opportunities for practising need to be considered in terms of the achievability of the outcome. A key adult in school is likely to be the headteacher, but it may be that Alberto does not see them very often, whereas he sees his class staff daily. It is certainly important that children and young people recognise and know the name of the headteacher or head of department, therefore to achieve this outcome, learning opportunities may need to be created. The case study below demonstrates the process whereby Alberto's social communication skills outcomes were written, using Vygotsky's zone of proximal development as a guide, in a way that increased the likelihood that they may be achieved during the school year. The thinking began with what Alberto could do without support and how that could be extended, initially with support, with a view in the longer term to being without support.

Alberto greets adults

Alberto is in Year 6 at Seraphine Special School. He is the subject of an EHC Plan recording his barriers to learning as severe learning difficulties, speech, language and communication difficulties and delayed motor skills development. Alberto generally communicates using single words or approximations, as he has not acquired all the speech sounds, as well as using a few Makaton and his own made up signs. His speech is mostly intelligible to those that know him, his own signs are recognisable. Staff communicate with him using speech supported with Makaton signing. Alberto recognises photographs of people. He is very sociable and likes to 'talk' to adults and peers. Alberto's parents and class teacher, Ms Large, feel that it is the right time to introduce Alberto to addressing staff by their name or at least his approximation, as his speech sound difficulties mean that he is unlikely to be able to say names accurately. He can say 'dog' but says 'gar' for 'car'. He already says an approximation of Ms Large's name – 'are'. His favourite teaching assistant is Ms Drake, he likes Mrs Miller, one of the ladies who serves the lunches, and Mrs Baker, a lunchtime supervisor. He recognises Ms Hussain, the headteacher, and Mr Hunter, the deputy headteacher. It was decided that staff will focus on Alberto addressing Ms Large, Mrs Drake and Mrs Baker by name, or his approximation, during the autumn term and then review his progress.

> Alberto's outcomes for the autumn term:
>
> *Alberto will be able to address*
>
> - *Ms Large by name, or his approximation, without support, three times each day.*
> - *Mrs Drake by name, or his approximation, with support, three times each day.*
> - *Mrs Baker by name, or his approximation, with support, once each lunchtime.*

Realistic: A dictionary definition is 'having or showing a sensible and practical idea of what can be achieved or expected'.[2] As noted in the SEND Code of Practice (9.66) the outcome should focus on something that those involved have control or influence over; added to this could be that it falls within the remit of an education institution or training provider. For example, Naomi in Year 7 wanted the EHC Plan outcome – to be able to go to the Girl Guide camp and stay overnight in the summer holiday without her sister – as her outcome. Whilst the school staff do not have any control of influence over what happens at the Girl Guide camp or who is able to attend, they did recognise that there are skills that Naomi would benefit from acquiring which could be targeted in school that would assist her to achieve her aspiration. Naomi identified that she needed to be able to

- ask adults for help
- join in small group social activities
- go from one place to another with peers without adult support

These became her outcomes for the school year. As noted above, the author would expand realistic to include that outcomes are purposeful and relevant. Naomi's negotiated outcomes could be considered as realistic, relevant and purposeful to her, fulfilling the overall aim of preparation for adulthood.

Timebound: The outcome should clearly state by when it is anticipated it will be achieved. This could be by the end of a particular school year, Key Stage, educational phase, or by a particular date. For 'important' decisions, the related outcome's achievement date will be set by when the decision has to be made, therefore it is essential education and associated professionals know this information.

Formulating outcomes

The SEND Code of Practice (9.66) indicates that the structure of SMART outcomes should be to state both what it is that the child or young person will be able to do following the intervention, by implication what they cannot do now, **and** the expected benefit from this. Thus, the outcome,

> *By the end of Key Stage 3 Bella will be able to understand her emotions and how to regulate them*

as well as not being SMART, is incomplete as there is no indication of the benefit to Bella of acquiring emotional literacy or whether this is with or without support. The outcome,

> *By the end of Key Stage 3 Bella will be able to understand her emotions and how to regulate them, which will reduce her anxiety*

does indicate the benefit to Bella, but continues to be incomplete as it omits any information about support and the benefit to Bella of reducing her anxiety, although it would be generally acknowledged that being less anxious facilitates more efficient functioning. As a SMART outcome detailing the benefit to the individual, as intended by the SEND COP, the one below probably comes closer to fulfilling the brief, but, ideally, it needs to be much SMARTer e.g. support,

> *By the end of Key Stage 3 Bella will be able to understand her emotions and how to regulate them, which will reduce her anxiety, in turn enabling her to re-engage with learning as well as developing coping strategies to manage herself in different situations.*

As outcomes have to be evaluated to ascertain progress, they need to be stated in a way that is clearly understood, observable and measurable. To reiterate, outcomes are central to the approaches, intervention and support offered – this enables children and young people to achieve their goal. Thus, outcomes have to be formulated in a way that guides the strategies needed. Vaguely worded, imprecise outcomes have less likelihood of being achieved than those that are written in clear terms.

The language of outcomes

Mager (1972) introduced the idea of 'fuzzies' and 'performance' terms to help formulate outcomes where the desired behaviours can be observed and measured. Mager referred to ill-defined, unquantifiable and unobservable terms as 'fuzzies', whereas 'performance' terms are discrete, observable and quantifiable. He introduced the 'Hey Dad' test – 'Hey Dad watch me while I . . .' – which demonstrates if the desired aims of the outcome can be observed and therefore measured. For example,

> *Eva will demonstrate an awareness of her own feelings and those of others.*

Now apply the 'Hey Dad' test to ascertain if those working with Eva will know when she is showing behaviours that indicate she is making progress towards the outcome.

Hey Dad, watch me while I – demonstrate an awareness of my own feelings and those of others.

'Demonstrate an awareness' is not easily observable. It is unclear what behaviours might show that someone is aware of their own or others' feelings, therefore 'awareness' cannot be measured, and by implication the outcome is probably not achievable. Nor is it immediately obvious what provision may be required to support the child or young person in achieving this outcome. Rewording this to describe observable behaviours, Mager's 'performance' terms,

Hey Dad, watch me while I read facial expressions showing happy, sad and angry in other people and show that I am happy, sad or angry by my facial expression

turns it into a SMARTer outcome (it lacks a time-frame, frequency and reference to support) that guides the interventions and approaches to achieve the outcome. It is now clearer what those supporting Eva will need to help her to do and what behaviours will indicate that she is making progress towards achieving the outcome. Essentially, performance terms (e.g. reading, show) are more likely to be verbs rather than nouns (awareness) or adverbs (consistently, frequently). An outcome from a real EHC Plan provides a good example of the pitfalls of using fuzzy words:

By the end of Key Stage 1 Lila will be able to consistently request more of something she enjoys or likes.

Ignoring the fact that the outcome is incomplete as it does not indicate either the benefit to Lila of being able to request more of something she enjoys or if she is expected to achieve the outcome with or without support, the use of the word 'consistently' is ambiguous. Is it referring to the number of times Lila makes the request, or the quality of the request, e.g. using a particular sentence construction? A better formulation would be, depending on the intended meaning of 'consistently', either

By the end of Key Stage 1 Lila will be able to request more of something she enjoys or likes on every occasion.

or

By the end of Key Stage 1 Lila will be able to request more of something she enjoys or likes by saying 'please may I have' on every occasion.

Guidelines for formulating and writing SMART outcomes

The structure of SMART outcomes has to include both what the child or young person will be able to do following the intervention and how this will be of benefit to them; by implication this relates to the overall aim of preparing for adulthood. You will have noticed that all the outcomes above are formulated using the phrase 'X will be able to'; it is suggested education and associated professionals consider using this construction as it accords with the SEND COP aim of an outcome enabling a child or young person to do something following the intervention that they are not able to do now. A proposed formula for writing structured SMART outcomes would be:

Time-frame for the outcome to be achieved

+ X will be able to _____

+ how often, e.g. 2/5 times per day/week

+ with/without support (for U2 fans think of their song 'With or without you')

+ the benefit to the child or young person of being able to do this

Using this model for Lila's outcome above suggests this may be a possible formulation that contains all the elements:

(Time) By the end of Key Stage 1 **(will be able to do)** Lila will be able to request more of something she enjoys or likes **(how often)** on every occasion **(support?)** without support **(benefit)** so she will have fewer temper tantrums.

For those who like mnemonics, perhaps this is a suitable one to assist in ensuring outcomes are written with all the elements:

Time Will Often Support Benefit (TWOSB)

As noted above, another key to formulating and writing effective SMART outcomes is the language used to express the intended outcome. Essentially, an outcome should be written in a way that means exactly what is intended, which can be tested using the 'Hey Dad' test. The author reads EHC Plans on a weekly basis, noting the 'fuzzies' that are frequently used, such as 'consistently', 'regularly', 'frequently', which would be better expressed by the performance equivalent, such as 'on every occasion' or '2/5 times per day/week/month'.

Mager proposed a five-step process for writing outcomes, which the author has adapted as a useful checklist for formulating and writing an outcome.

1. Write down the goal of the outcome – what it is that the child or young person wishes to be able to do or that their parents, education or associated professionals supporting them would like them to be able to do. This can be considered the first draft, the essence of what is intended to be the aim of the outcome, which will be refined by working through the checklist. Remember the outcome must follow the Time Will Often Support Benefit

(TWOSB) formula, clearly setting out what the child or young person will be able to do following the intervention, and how this will benefit them in relation to education or training and, ultimately, preparing them for adulthood.

Returning to Bella's not wholly SMART outcome above, essentially the education professionals formulating this outcome think it would be helpful if Bella was able to understand unspecified emotions and that she could then learn to control them. This, in turn, will reduce the anxiety she experiences, although the manifestation of her anxiety is not indicated, which, hopefully, will then enable her to learn and assist her in developing strategies to cope with her feelings in different settings. However, it does not fully follow the Time Will Often Support Benefit formula, omitting the support and how often elements.

2. Write down the behaviours that you would expect to see that would demonstrate that the child or young person has achieved the outcome – what can they now be observed being able to do.

> Education and associated professionals know Bella's anxiety manifests in various ways, she may say she is feeling sick, shout, scream and/or throw things, and be verbally aggressive. The emotions leading to her anxiety have been identified as feeling angry or frightened; it is these feelings that education and associated professionals would like her to understand and control. In broad terms, the outcome indicates, if the strategies have been successful, that the observable behaviours would be:
>
> - Engaging in learning – Bella
>   - remains in the classroom for at least half the lesson 3/5 lessons per day with support
>   - undertakes one piece of work in 3/5 lessons per day with support
>   - attends home-work club one lunchtime per week with support
>
> - Reduced anxiety – Bella will
>   - reduce the number of times she says she feels sick during a school day to no more than three times
>   - reduce the episodes of shouting or screaming to no more than one per day
>   - use her elastic band round her wrist once a day, rather than throwing things
>   - use her calm box once a day, rather than throwing things

The art of writing SMART outcomes

> - Managing her emotions in different settings
>   - Once a day Bella will use one of her coping strategies, which are
>   - carrying and using her calm box
>   - using her elastic wrist band
>   - seeking an adult
>   - taking herself to the SEN room
>
>   if she is feeling anxious in different areas of the school, without adult prompting.

3. Check that the language used to write the outcome is in 'performance' terms and not 'fuzzies' – use the 'Hey Dad' test. All the behaviours noted above pass the 'Hey Dad' test as they are observable and measurable. However, the formulation of the overall outcome is not as clearly written as it could be. Having established what behaviours would show the outcome had been achieved, the outcome may be better formulated as:

   By the end of Key Stage 3 Bella will

   - *be able to understand her emotions (anger, being frightened)*
   - *be able to regulate her emotions (anger, being frightened) using one of her coping strategies with support on every occasion.*
   - *be having fewer episodes where she shows behaviour indicating she is feeling anxious (stating she feels sick, shouting, screaming, throwing things or being verbally aggressive).*

   This will enable her to

   - *re-engage with learning (stay in the classroom, undertake class work)*
   - *develop and use coping strategies to manage herself in different settings (carry and use her calm box, use the elastic band on her wrist, seek out an adult, take herself to the SEN room).*

4. State clearly what constitutes achieving the outcome in terms of the quality, circumstances (e.g. supported, unsupported) and the amount and/or quality of the desired behaviours.

   Bella will have achieved the outcome when she is able to

- *remain in the classroom for at least half the lesson 3/5 lessons per day with support*
- *undertake one piece of work in 3/5 lessons per day with support*
- *attend home-work club one lunchtime per week with support*
- *reduce the number of times she says she feels sick during a school day to no more than three times*
- *reduce the episodes of shouting or screaming to no more than one per day*
- *use her elastic band round her wrist once a day, rather than throwing things*
- *use her calm box once a day, rather than throwing things*
- *use one of her coping strategies, once a day, without adult prompting, which are*
  - *carrying and using her calm box*
  - *using her elastic wrist band*
  - *seeking an adult*
  - *taking herself to the SEN room*

  if she is feeling anxious in different areas of the school

5. Check that
   a. all the behaviours that constitute achieving the outcome have been noted
   b. the outcome formulated follows the Time Will Often Support Benefit formula and contains all the required elements.

Decision-making outcomes

The discussion above has worked through the mechanics of formulating and writing outcomes, introducing the Time Will Often Support Benefit formula (TWOSB). This will now be applied to decision-making outcomes. As noted earlier in the book, the author rarely sees decision-making outcomes in person-centred planning or EHC Plans. Chapter five set out a decision-making syllabus suggesting some everyday decisions that children and young people may be supported and enabled to make. With these in mind, the Time Will Often Support Benefit formula SMART outcome model could be a good starting point, although the outcomes will need personalising for each child or young person. For example

By the end of the term/school year/Key Stage: X will be able request, by pointing, signing or verbally, more of an activity/food Y times per day/per week with/without support, within

the education institution setting, which will enable him/her to have some control over what they do or eat, which will assist him/her in developing their knowledge of their likes, dislikes and preferences, promoting their independent choice-making.

and

By the end of the term/school year/Key Stage: X will be able to point to/sign/say, on each occasion, twice a day, 3/5 times per week, with/without support, which object, activity or food she/he would like from a choice of two within the education institution setting to enable him/her in becoming more independent and being able to have some control over things that they do or eat.

Generally, the benefit to the child or young person in developing their ability to make choices concerns having more control over what happens in their life, thus becoming more independent. The above outcomes can be developed as the child or young person makes progress. For example, let us return to Jill in Chapters three and four (pp. 51 and 62) and consider the outcomes that are likely to have been formulated to support her developing the ability to make choices for snacks, drinks, and food for her school lunch. Probably the outcomes would have been similar to these, beginning with:

1st decision-making outcome: preparing for nursery
By the end of the spring term: Jill will be able to choose between a piece of banana and a quarter of an apple at morning and afternoon snack, on every occasion, without support, enabling her to have some control over what she has to eat, assisting her becoming more independent.

2nd decision-making outcome: preparing for nursery
By the end of the summer term: Jill will be able to choose between milk or water to drink at morning or afternoon snack time on every occasion without support, enabling her to have some control over what she has to drink, assisting her becoming more independent.

3rd decision-making outcome: choosing school lunch food
By the end of the autumn term: Jill will be able to choose whether to have pasta or potatoes with her school lunch, 3/5 days per week, without support, enabling her to have some control over what she has to eat, assisting her becoming more independent.

4th decision-making outcome: choosing school lunch food
By the end of the summer term: Jill will be able to choose her main course dish from the two choices on offer, on every occasion, with support, enabling her to start to have some control over what she has to eat, assisting her becoming more independent.

Outcomes for 'important' decisions

Although most decisions children and young people will learn to make can be considered everyday decisions, 'important' decisions occurring less frequently, participating in the decision-making process is a core SEND COP principle. Therefore, a young person's participation in making an 'important' decision, such as choosing a new education or training placement, needs to be encapsulated in an outcome, whether it is being able to make the choice or ensuring that the young person's views and feelings are considered. The outcome below is based on a real EHC Plan outcome, which the author was pleased to see.

> *By the end of Year 14: Jack will have been able to choose an appropriate course to attend within an appropriate post 16 provision, with support, and successfully transitioned to it.*

Given the aim of the outcome, it is challenging to make this truly follow the Time Will Often Support Benefit (TWOSB) formula SMART outcome. Nevertheless, it should contain as many of the TWOSB elements as possible and be written in as observable terms as possible. Jack's outcome could be improved by adding the benefit to Jack of attending an appropriate course in a suitable education institution. This is actually two interrelated outcomes, the first can be evaluated by his current placement, the second can only be measured as achieved after Jack has started attending college. This may be a common feature of some outcomes relating to choosing a new education or training institution. However, it would seem appropriate that the young person should be considering what successful transition to the next placement constitutes in their present placement as their current placement staff's knowledge of the young person will assist in considering what may be barriers to 'successful transition', and having the opportunity to address these as preparation for transition.

Regardless of when Jack's outcome is evaluated to ascertain the extent to which it has been achieved, it lacks specificity regarding the exact meaning of 'successfully transitioned', thereby impacting on the young person's and education and associated professionals' ability to consider if it has been achieved. Overall, the two interrelated outcomes could be made SMARTer by indicating what would constitute 'successfully transitioned', likewise adding information about the benefit of choosing an appropriate course and placement: for example,

> *By the end of Year 14 (July 2019): Jack will have been able to choose an appropriate course to attend within an appropriate post 16 provision, with support.*

> *By the end of the autumn term 2019: Jack will have made a successful transition to a course which enables him to continue to develop his independence and work-related skills*

to achieve his aspiration of living in his own supported living flat and obtaining a work placement, either paid or voluntary. This means Jack will be

- *attending every college session he should be attending*
- *arriving on time at college*
- *attending the classes he should be attending*
- *taking part in the lessons*
- *making progress*
- *building relationships with staff and students*

An outcome that is focused on participation in the decision-making process for choosing the next education or training institution or social care provision could be formulated in this way:

By the end of the autumn term of Year 14: Jill will have taken part in choosing her next placement, education or social care, with support, which means she will have

- *identified the establishments to visit*
- *chosen an object of reference/picture, symbol, sign and/or word to represent each establishment*
- *visited the establishments and taken photographs and videos of key places and people*
- *talked, using a Talking Mats style approach, with her key worker about what she liked and did not like about each establishment; the 'mat' photographed as a record of Jill's views and feelings*
- *completed the young person's decision-making framework*
- *communicated her choice to education institution staff so she can be assisted in formally communicating it to the establishments and local authority*

which will have ensured that her views, wishes and feelings have informed the decision-making process and helped her learn about making 'important' decisions which is a life skill.

Summary

In addition to the key points about outcomes highlighted in Chapter five, which related to the guidance given in the SEND Code of Practice, the current chapter has addressed the formulation and writing of SMART outcomes which follow the SEND Code of Practice guidance about the elements that should be included in an outcome, captured in the mnemonic Time Will Often Support Benefit (TWOSB). Essentially, outcomes enable a child or young person to be supported to develop their ability to do something they were unable to do, to meet the overall aim of preparing them for adulthood. The main points to remember are that outcomes have to be

- relevant, purposeful and realistic, with a direct benefit to the child or young person, and support the overall aim of preparation for adulthood
- focused on issues that can be addressed within an education or training institution
- formulated and written in terms of observable behaviours that can be measured so that it is clear when the outcome has been achieved. This can be tested by 'Hey Dad watch me while I . . .'
- SMART and structured as indicated in the SEND COP guidance (TWOSB)
- achievable, which means consideration has to be given to
    - the child or young person's acquisition of associated skills to support the achievement of the outcome, for example, communication or motor skills, or sensory tolerance
    - where the child or young person is starting from – baseline
    - the step in the skill development the outcome is focused on. This should be based on either the baseline information or the progress the child or young person has made, and must be realistic; Vygotsky's zone of proximal development can assist in working out what is achievable with or without support.

Notes

1 Available from: www.nao.org.uk/successful-commissioning/designing-services/smart-outcomes/, accessed 20 February 2019.
2 Available from: https://en.oxforddictionaries.com/definition/realistic, accessed 22 February 2019.

PART 3

THE ROLE OF EDUCATION AND ASSOCIATED PROFESSIONALS

Chapter seven

EDUCATIONAL PSYCHOLOGISTS (EPs) AND ASSOCIATED PROFESSIONALS

The starting point for reading this chapter is reflecting on your current practice as an educational psychologist (EP) or associated professional concerning supporting and enabling children's and young people's decision-making, as well as eliciting, recording and reporting the child's or young person's views, wishes and feelings about the particular issue.

Consider your practice regarding whether you

- include an age- or developmentally appropriate decision-making outcome in a report or consultation record
- promote and encourage children's and young people's participation in decision-making, such as raising this issue in meetings with parents, young person and/or education institution staff and when working directly with a child or young person
- promote the inclusion of a decision-making outcome as part of person-centred planning or the EHC Plan process
- encourage education institution staff to develop, support and enable the child or young person's decision-making
- promote and encourage use of a shared language, including widely recognised symbols such as emojis
- encourage parents to empower their son's or daughter's decision-making
- ensure that you are fully familiar with the child or young person's preferred means of communication and can understand their responses
- work collaboratively with education professionals to write effective outcomes

- harness the full potential of digital technology to support
  - children and young people
    - developing and using their decision-making ability
    - being able to communicate their choices
  - parents developing and enabling their son's or daughter's decision-making ability

Additionally, EPs should consider whether they

- promote the importance of the inclusion of decision-making outcomes with local authority SEN officers who write and manage EHC Plans
- elicit and record children's and young people's views, wishes and feelings about educational matters
- offer training to education institution staff and/or parents on developing and supporting children's and young people's decision-making

There are many commonalities between the role of an EP and associated professionals regarding supporting and enabling children's and young people's decision-making ability, and these will be discussed together. However, there are some specific considerations for EPs which will be explored separately.

Bolton (1990) cites Bruner's analogy of a bridge to describe the way in which educational psychologists practise psychology, stating:

> Bruner (1966) for instance talks of the activity of bridge building. It is not, he says, for the psychologist to suggest where the bridge is built, but to show the sort of bridge that is required, that is to suggest the most effective techniques for teaching and learning. On this account what matters is the soundness of the bridge...
>
> (p167)

The bridge metaphor can equally apply to part of the educational psychologist's role as a link between children and young people and education institution staff, parents, and local authority officers as well as health and social care professionals. Likewise, some associated professionals may consider being a bridge between children and young people and parents, education, health and social care professionals as part of their remit.

Educational psychologists and associated professionals supporting and enabling children's and young people's decision-making

This can be considered in two parts, knowledge and practice. Components of the latter overlap with some of the essential elements of the decision-making syllabus set out in Chapter five.

Knowledge

Basic knowledge includes the legislative context (Chapter three), as well as the theory and research evidence demonstrating the benefits to children and young people of being able to participate in and make decisions (Chapters one and two). All EPs and associated professionals should be fully conversant with the legal duties set out in the SEND Code of Practice and the Mental Capacity Act Codes of Practice. Germane to developing children's and young people's decision-making ability is knowing the importance of ascertaining their views, wishes and feelings and fostering their participation in decision-making. When working with young people aged 16–25 years it is imperative that EPs and associated professionals know the content of the MCA Code of Practice, Chapters 1–6, 12 and 15, the relevant sections of the MCA (Amendment) Act 2019 Code of Practice and the SEND Code of Practice, Chapter 8, which makes reference to young people making their own decisions and sets out the preparing for adulthood outcomes.

Digital technology

It is essential that EPs and associated professionals are knowledgeable about the available digital technology including specialised and readily available apps for mobile phones and tablet computers as well as emojis and other widely used symbols. Furthermore, there needs to be an awareness of how the education institution uses digital technology with its children or young people. Many children and young people with autism use Proloquo2go or similar communication apps, so becoming conversant with these would facilitate communication, likewise learning some Makaton signs. Being familiar with the education institution's decision-making curriculum, decision-making framework and process enables EPs and associated professionals to support children and young people in developing and using their decision-making ability.

Practice

Language and communication

Previous chapters have emphasised the importance of shared verbal and non-verbal language and communication. As EPs and associated professionals work with a number of education institutions it will be necessary to be acquainted with each institution's way of referring to matters, likewise each child and young person's way of expressing things, including signs and symbols. Education professionals and parents tend to be familiar with the language of the SEND COP; there is a need for everyone to become conversant with the language of decision-making, including local authority SEN officers. As argued earlier in the book, it is probably most helpful if this is the same as the language in the MCA COP, thus the same terminology is used from the earliest age. EPs are well placed to promote this in education institutions, with other education and associated professionals and local authority SEN officers; likewise associated professionals encouraging this with colleagues.

Everyday practice

The mantra 'no decision about my education without a contribution from me' is a good guide for EPs and associated professionals working with children and young people, their parents and education institution staff, as well as when liaising with health and social care professionals. Hopefully, the mantra facilitates developing and supporting children's and young people's decision-making becoming a way of thinking embedded in everyday practice, including establishing good practice for eliciting and recording their views, wishes and feelings. To realise this aspiration EPs and associated professionals working with education institutions will need to be familiar with each establishment's approach to developing and supporting children's and young people's decision-making. Furthermore, when working with the post 16 age group, the MCA COP way of thinking should also become embedded in everyday practice.

Decision-making outcomes

Previous chapters noted consideration should be given to formulating a decision-making outcome as part of person-centred planning or reviews and including this in reports, thereby indicating the need to include a decision-making outcome in the EHC Plan with the appropriate provision. From the discussions in Chapter six and earlier in the book, it is evident that writing effective outcomes may be best accomplished collaboratively to ensure the child or young person is developing all the requisite skills needed to achieve the outcome. For example, when formulating decision-making outcomes, EPs may need advice from the speech and language therapist working with the child or young person to ensure the approaches take account of the child's or young person's language and communication needs, or information may be needed from the occupational therapist for outcomes focusing on self-help or other practical skills.

It should be seen as good practice for a child or young person to have a developmentally or age-appropriate decision-making outcome, from the earliest age. These will mostly focus on everyday decisions. However, outcomes for 'important' decisions should be formulated well in advance of the time for making such a decision, for example, transition to the next phase of education, to facilitate the child or young person's participation in the decision-making process. For instance, a decision-making outcome for a young person leaving their special school at the end of Year 14 will need to be formulated no later than Year 13 May half-term to assist them in choosing their next placement, or ensuring their participation in the decision-making process if they are unlikely to be able to make the choice themselves. Similarly, a young person seeking a post 16 placement after finishing Year 11 will need a decision-making outcome formulated no later than Year 10 May half-term to encourage their participation in the process. EPs and associated professionals can promote this with education professionals by raising the issue in discussions with education institution staff, parents, children and young people during review meetings, as well as including a decision-making outcome in reports or support plans.

Observation and record keeping: views, wishes and feelings

In relation to decision-making, establishing good practice is fundamental for eliciting and keeping records of children's and young people's views, wishes and feelings, to enable these to be accurately represented to other education, health or social care professionals and/or parents (for young people aged over 18 years their consent is needed to share information). The SEND COP emphasises that children's views, wishes and feelings should be considered, but generally it is their parents that will be making the decisions. However, from the end of Year 11 young people have the legal right to make decisions about their education. Thus, meticulous recording of young people's views, wishes and feelings is essential when they are making 'important' decisions such as choosing a new education institution or training placement. This can include taking photographs of Talking Mats style approach displays showing a child's or young person's views, wishes and feelings, which can be included in reports or shown to others. Keeping a photographic record facilitates comparison over time to consider changes in preferences or check for consistency if there is uncertainty about the reliability of the child's or young person's responses. Justice Munby, cited in Chapter four, suggested that the strength and consistency of a child's or young person's expressed views, wishes and feelings was an important consideration when evaluating the weight to be given to these. This further highlights the necessity of scrupulous record keeping, ensuring children and young people are afforded their rights. However, a child's or young person's meaningful views, wishes and feelings will only be elicited if the task is undertaken with the appropriate planning and care, indicating that it takes time, and it is essential that sufficient time is set aside for it.

Atkinson et al. (2015) note that enabling and supporting young people to express their views is an integral part of the MCA ethos. The author believes this ethos should also apply to children, ensuring their right to make their views known about things that affect them. This is likely to present some challenges regarding ascertaining these for children and young people with severe and complex needs such as profound and multiple learning difficulties (PMLD). Harding (2009) highlights that eliciting the views of a child or young person with considerable support needs takes time and skill. Using the available literature, she explored how far it is possible to ascertain the views of children with PMLD. Whilst the research cited pre-dates both the implementation of the Mental Capacity Acts and the approaches that have been developed to elicit children and young people's views, including the advances in ICT, her article raises some relevant issues and considerations for EPs and associated professionals exploring the views and feelings of a child or young person with severe and complex needs. From the outset, establishing from education institution staff or parents how the child or young person expresses whether they are happy or unhappy with a person is essential, before trying to ascertain the child's or young person's views, being mindful of signs that they are not comfortable with the situation. This raises the matter of consent, particularly for the post 16 age group. It is likely that for young people with severe and complex needs their parent(s) will have given permission for the EP or associated professional to work with them as they may not have the capacity to give consent; however that does not mean that any signs of distress demonstrated by the young person can be ignored. Morris (2003, cited in Harding 2009) indicates that it is imperative that affective responses are always considered, especially if these are interpreted as negative, suggesting it is unlikely the child or young person would consent.

Harding discusses whether a view on a matter can be interpreted from an affective reaction, suggesting that a view is a reasoned position. Thus, photos of a child enjoying activities in a particular school is not the same as the child expressing their wish to attend this school. Likewise negative reactions should not automatically be considered to indicate the child or young person does not wish to take part in the activity. This is an interesting debate, however the research cited earlier in this book demonstrated that people with severe and complex learning disabilities can express a preference for food and drink when given a choice and being given choices has a beneficial effect on well-being. Also, Peter (Chapter four, p. 64), visiting a range of secondary schools, demonstrated a different response in the special school from the mainstream, suggesting affective responses can be deemed indicative of views and feelings. Justice Munby, endeavouring to determine how to give the appropriate weight to the views and feelings of individuals lacking capacity to make the particular decision, considered that the strength and consistency of response could be determinative. Furthermore, the MCA COP 'best interests' checklist highlights that a person's views, wishes and feelings may be expressed through their behaviour or habits, suggesting affective and behavioural responses should be considered by those making the decision on behalf of someone who lacks capacity to do so. Thus, there is support for EPs and associated professionals to regard affective and behavioural responses as an indicator of the child's or young person's views, wishes and feelings. Sinson (2016) provides a detailed account of how to undertake a capacity assessment; this approach could also be seen as good practice for eliciting children's and young people's views, wishes and feelings. Consideration is given to the interview environment, timing – best time of day for the child or young person – and how the interview is conducted. Emphasis is placed on the need for the EP or associated professional to be familiar with the child's or young person's communication, likewise understanding how to communicate effectively with the child or young person, including the use of technology.

Parents

Often EPs or associated professionals are the bridge between parents and education institution staff or other education or healthcare professionals. When working with children, it is routine to talk with parents; however once a young person has had their 18th birthday, they are an adult, therefore their permission is needed to speak with their parent. This raises the issue of whether the young person has the capacity to consent. The EP or associated professional will have to determine this.

There is a wealth of research spanning decades demonstrating the benefit of parental involvement in a child's education. For example, White and Rae (2016) present a review of some of the literature about parental involvement in children and young people's education; and Morris and Atkinson (2018) cite a number of research studies about parental participation with young people to facilitate effective transition planning. White and Rae explored the use of person-centred reviews involving parents and children to facilitate transition, concluding that the process could have positive outcomes for both the child and the parents. However, it was considered that parents were most likely to be involved in their child's education if they felt it was their role and felt able to do so. Parents need to be empowered to enable their son or daughter to make their own decisions or participate in the decision-making process. EPs and associated professionals could be part of this process in partnership with education professionals.

Anecdotal evidence from the author's own experience and that of other education professionals is that parent workshops are an effective way of helping parents understand the needs of their son or daughter with SEN in particular areas. A Sensory Service Manager reported excellent attendance at a Saturday parent day which helped parents understand the need to enable their son's or daughter's independence. Parent workshops have a twofold purpose: they facilitate the professional leading the workshop to impart information, but equally, or possibly more importantly, parents meet other parents with sons or daughters with similar needs and realise they are not alone, others are encountering similar challenges. The author, in her role as a home-school liaison teacher in a school catering for children and young people with severe learning difficulties, organised a monthly parents' coffee morning. To assist parents attending, the author collected some of them from their homes, and she was gladdened by the chatter in the car between the mothers as these particular parents tended to be quite isolated. These women became friends and supported each other.

For children and young people and their families receiving social care support, social workers, respite carers, personal assistants and short breaks personnel may be able to support the development of children's and young people's decision-making abilities. They will need to be made aware of the outcomes, approaches and strategies, including language and communication.

Educational psychologists

This section considers issues specific to EPs, exploring the role, individually, and at service and local authority level, with regard to developing, supporting and enabling children's and young people's with SEN decision-making ability. It will revisit some of the areas addressed above. As noted above, EPs, like other education and associated professionals, can be the bridge between education, health, social care and children and young people and their parents.

EPs are considered agents of change effecting this variously through individual conversations, supporting good practice, offering training, and influencing policy and practice locally and nationally (Roffey et al. 2018). Roffey et al. highlight EPs' involvement in the creation of SEAL (social and emotional aspects of learning) materials and writing books for educators on a wide range of topics including SEN, school leadership, mental health, behaviour and resilience. Morris and Atkinson (2018) and Roffey et al. describe EPs as advocates for children and young people, with Morris and Atkinson urging EPs to be 'relentlessly tenacious' (p6) in this role, both individually and at service level.

Individual EP's role

Knowledge

In June 2018 The British Psychological Society (Evans 2018) updated its guidance on safeguarding children and young people to encompass well-being across a range of environments and settings, including education. Chapter two noted that being able to have some control over what happens to you promotes well-being and contributes to resilience. Evans considers psychologists have much to offer in the area of safeguarding, their multi-agency working providing opportunities to influence policy at local and national levels. Evans believes that 'improved human rights for children today, will ensure that the world is fairer, safer and healthier for the future' (p06).

EPs need to be knowledgeable about the theoretical underpinnings and relevant research relating to the benefits of developing children's and young people's with SEN decision-making ability, cited in earlier chapters and below. Choosing a new educational or training placement has been highlighted as probably the one 'important' educational decision that most children and young people will make during their education. The SEND COP encourages children to participate in decision-making, however young people have the right to make their own decisions. It is essential that EPs develop their skills and strategies to promote, facilitate and support children and young people's 'meaningful participation' (Morris and Atkinson 2018, p145) in choosing their next educational or training placement.

White and Rae (2016) explored the use of person-centred reviews with Year 6 and Year 9 pupils to facilitate the child's participation in the process of considering the next stage of their education. The study focused on the participants' views of the person-centred review process, particularly whether the pupils and parents felt listened to, and considered the implications for EPs. Despite the researchers' identified limitations of the study, it provides food for thought for EPs developing their skills to promote children and young people's meaningful participation in decision-making. White and Rae noted the study supported that pupil participation in educational decisions is both possible and beneficial. The pupils were positive about being involved in the meeting and felt their views had been heard. The outcomes suggested the informal, but skilfully facilitated, nature of the meeting was helpful, as were the visual approaches utilised. The fact that all participants, including parents and children, are expected to write in front of everyone may be a barrier to participation for some families. The authors raised the issue of needing to be aware of parental level of education and literacy skills but did not suggest that the use of technology may offer a solution.

The reader may wish to consider what and how technology could have been employed to overcome any potential difficulties with the participants' literacy skills to remove this barrier to participation.

White and Rae suggest that EPs may be facilitators of person-centred review meetings as they have the necessary skills. However, given the EP shortages and time constraints, it may be that EPs train others as facilitators. They also recommended that EPs build on the visual approaches used in the meeting to ensure that the child's views are included in transition planning. Furthermore, EPs can share this approach with other education and associated professionals to promote the inclusion of children's and young people's views, wishes and feelings about educational matters. Overall, empowering others may be a more effective use of limited EP time to foster children's and young people's increased participation in decision-making.

Practice

Previous chapters have referred to the role of education professionals with regard to developing and enabling children's and young people's decision-making ability, but without specifically indicating to which educational psychologists are best suited and that their time constraints allow them to fulfil. Roffey et al. and Morris and Atkinson consider that EPs advocating for the child or young person is important, in the author's view essential, for promoting children and young people participating in and making their own decisions. What does this look like?

EP as the child's or young person's advocate

There are various ways in which EPs can fulfil the advocacy role. As noted above, EPs link with education, health and social care professionals and parents, as well as working directly with children and young people, which enables their role as an advocate. EPs have a range of tools and skills to explore children's and young people's meaningful views, wishes and feelings about educational matters, ensuring these are routinely recorded in reports and communicated to other education and associated professionals and parents. Remember, if the young person is aged over 18 years their consent is needed to share information with other people – this should become routine practice. The emphasis here is on 'meaningful'. Whilst EP reports should record directly elicited children's and young people's views, wishes and feelings, this is not always the case. Sometimes this is due to relying on third party reports such as those of education institution staff or parents, particularly if, for whatever reason, the EP has not met the child or young person. On other occasions it is because views and feelings have to be discerned through observing behaviours, which are not evident during the EP's visit to the education institution or may only become known over time. For example, ascertaining the views and feelings of a child or young person with significant developmental delay and very limited speech, language and communication skills, is more likely to be accomplished through observing their responses to different settings, experiences and activities, to build a picture of their likes and dislikes. For instance, Hugo, whose barriers to learning are autism and severe learning difficulties, prefers to be outside whatever the weather. He enjoys going for walks in the school grounds. Therefore, if a new education institution is being considered, Hugo's behaviour informs those choosing a new placement that it would have to have an outside space where he can go for walks, and they would need to ensure that his love of being outdoors could be accommodated by having a staff member available who is happy to go outside in most weathers. The EP involved in Hugo's transition review can act as his advocate ensuring that his likes and dislikes are recorded, considered and communicated to his new placement.

Advocacy is not just communicating the child's or young person's views, wishes and feelings, but also advocating for their rights regarding decision-making, including promoting and enabling their participation in decision-making about educational matters with other education, social care and health professionals as well as parents. In addition, offering advice and training to education institution staff, parents and other education and associated professionals about developing and supporting decision-making.

Decision-making outcomes

EPs have the skills to formulate and write SMART outcomes, using the Time Will Often Support Benefit (TWOSB) formula detailed in Chapter six, which they can pass on to other education or associated professionals. Ideally, this ensures there is a SMART (TWOSB) decision-making outcome, for all children and young people with SEN, from the earliest age, and this becomes the usual practice within the local authority.

Observation and record keeping: views, wishes and feelings

Ingram (2013) presents a thought-provoking discussion about how EPs interpret children's views elicited as part of an assessment of the child's presenting difficulties, suggesting they are not generally taken at face value but interpreted. She reasons this arises from EPs having various theories to explain why what appear to be insightful views may not be, or they are not helpful. Ingram acknowledges that children may find this disempowering as the child is unable to challenge the EP's analysis of their expressed views. It is concerning if EPs are routinely interpreting a child's or young person's views, wishes and feelings that are ascertained about a decision to be made, such as choosing a new educational or training placement, rather than reporting them verbatim. It is essential that the approaches used meaningfully explore the child's or young person's views, wishes and feelings. Ingram suggests cognitive behavioural approaches as they are based on a partnership with the child, enabling the child to retain more control over how their views are analysed. The provisions within the SEND COP and MCA COP imply that the views, wishes and feelings of every child or young person with SEN need to be considered.

Overall, the discussion above suggests that EPs should take time to elicit children's and young people's views and feelings using approaches that enable the EP to work together with them, refraining from routinely finding reasons to invalidate these. It would be more constructive to examine the child or young person's use of heuristics, both voiced and tacit, in their decision-making to explain their reasoning. For instance, Marvin (Chapter one, p. 16), when choosing his secondary school, articulated his overriding desire was to be with his friends. This influenced his decision-making; he was not concerned about curriculum access or taking exams. Adults could consider he did not understand that his school choice would limit his life chances and decide he should attend a school where he had full access to the curriculum. However, this would have ignored all the unspoken factors driving Marvin's thinking. Two years before he had experienced his older brother's death from the same condition aged 16, he was very aware of his own life expectancy. Thus, he could not understand the adults' obsession with curriculum access and getting qualifications. This information contextualises Marvin's responses and choice, indicating his heuristics were perhaps those any of us would apply in a similar situation, prioritising our quality of life over other factors. Marvin's views needed to be respected, given weight and not invalidated. The real Marvin did attend the same school as his friends part-time; when they left at the end of Year 11, he decided he wanted to attend the resourced school for his post 16 education.

The above discussion does not preclude consideration of consistency of response and factors that may be affecting the child or young person during the interview or generally at that time.

Everyday practice

To reiterate, an EP's approach to enabling the development of children's and young people's decision-making ability should become a way of thinking embedded in everyday practice. Routinely, EPs should be talking with parents about how they are fostering their son's or daughter's abilities to make everyday choices from the earliest age and encouraging this. This should be supported by EPs providing decision-making outcomes in their reports/ consultation records, likewise promoting the formulation of decision-making outcomes as part of person-centred planning with parents and education institutions. EPs should be aware of practical strategies, particularly regarding the child or young person being given the opportunity to have a wide range of experiences to build their knowledge of their immediate world. The decision-making syllabus set out in Chapter five provides suggestions.

To provide practical support to parents, EPs could consider

- having written or visual information (e.g. web-based podcasts)
- offering workshops for parents about developing and enabling their son's or daughter's decision-making skills
- developing materials to support children and young people with SEN learning how to make their own decisions as well as how to choose a new educational or training placement
- constructing their own checklist of experiences to build the child or young person's knowledge of the world linked to the local authority area, preferably highlighting activities and experiences that are free of charge and suitable for children and young people at different ages and developmental levels. The National Trust's '50 things to do before you are 11¾' is a good starting point for inspiration.

Partnership with others: education, health and social care professionals

As noted above, EPs liaise and work with education, health and social care professionals, and thus are well placed to explain the requirement for children and young people to make their own decisions or participate in the decision-making process. It is essential that local authority SEN officers managing EHC Plans understand the importance of including decision-making outcomes in EHC Plans, with the necessary provision from the earliest age. EPs can offer support to education institutions developing this area in various ways, such as assisting thinking by asking questions that may challenge, as well as modelling good practice in their own work with children and young people.

Educational psychology service (EPS) level

Supporting, enabling and facilitating children's and young people's decision-making ability begins at the earliest age. Education psychology services (EPS) would benefit from having expectations about the way EPs will practise with respect to this. This can be considered as an integral part of the EPS way of working with regard to the MCA requirements (Sinson 2016), including having service guidance and protocols covering

- EPs always considering formulating a decision-making outcome in reports or consultation records, raising this issue in person-centred planning or EHC Plan reviews

- the importance of eliciting a child's or young person's meaningful views in relation to 'important' decisions such as choosing a new educational or training placement, emphasising this takes time
- the need to analyse the child's or young person's use of heuristics in their decision-making to ensure important factors are not overlooked, thereby ensuring the appropriate weight is given to their views
- the need to keep meticulous records of a child's or young person's views, wishes and feelings, which may be photographs of their Talking Mats style approach display
- how to write Time Will Often Support Benefit formula SMART outcomes
- supporting parents to enable their son or daughter to
    - make everyday decisions
    - participate in 'important' decisions such as choosing a new educational or training establishment
- supporting education institutions to promote, develop and facilitate children's and young people's decision-making abilities and participation in decisions including considering decision-making outcomes

Additionally, education psychology services may wish to include fostering children's and young people's decision-making ability and eliciting meaningful views, wishes and feelings as part of supervision. Consideration should be given to the training needs of the service in this area and what should be included in the induction process for new colleagues.

Conclusion

The discussion above has explored the various roles for EPs regarding developing, supporting and enabling children's and young people's decision-making ability, from being a child's or young person's advocate to supporting and advising parents and education institutions, as well as working in partnership with other education, health and social care professionals. In addition to the key considerations for all education and associated professionals at the end of this chapter, there are some specific ones for EPs.

Key considerations for EPs

- Reflection on practice, hopefully fostered through supervision.
- Embrace the role as a child's or young person's advocate.

- Ensure sufficient time is allocated to eliciting children's and young people's meaningful views, wishes and feelings concerning 'important' decisions such as choosing a new educational or training placement.

- Always consider the heuristics the child or young person has applied to making their decision – particularly 'important' decisions – to assist in understanding their thinking and, thus, the weight that can be attributed to the choice.

- Perfect being able to write Time Will Often Support Benefit formula SMART outcomes and share this with other education professionals and parents.

- Support and, when appropriate, challenge education institution staff approaches to developing, enabling and supporting children's and young people's decision-making ability.

- Consider
    - the policies and protocols.
    - information both for EPs and for those with whom they work.
    - service level training requirements to support individual EP practice.

Summary

The chapter began by urging EPs and associated professionals to reflect on their current practice. Now, having read the chapter, consider what you will do from tomorrow to try to ensure the aspiration 'no decision about my education without a contribution from me' becomes a reality for all children and young people with SEN with whom you work.

Key considerations

- Be confident in your knowledge about the legislative and research evidence base to support developing children's and young people's decision-making abilities.

- Be a champion for including a decision-making outcome as part of person-centred planning or EHC Plan reports or in the annual review.

- Develop strategies and approaches, including resources, to support children and young people to develop their decision-making abilities.

- Ensure that thinking about developing, supporting and facilitating children's and young people's decision-making becomes embedded in everyday practice.

- Support and advise parents about empowering their son's or daughter's ability to make everyday decisions and participate in making 'important' decisions.

- Communicate with children and young people, education institution staff and parents using a shared language.
- Ensure you know how to communicate with the child or young person and understand their communication.
- Be knowledgeable about the available technology and apps for all tablet computers, mobile phones and other digital devices that enable children and young people to communicate, make choices, and support parental involvement.

Chapter eight

SUPPORTING AND INVOLVING PARENTS

This chapter draws together suggestions for ways in which education and associated professionals can promote and facilitate parental involvement to develop, support and enable their son's or daughter's decision-making ability, mooted in previous chapters, especially Chapters four, five and seven, expanding on some ideas and introducing some new considerations. References to parents in this chapter, and by implication elsewhere in the book, extend to any family member including siblings.

SEND COP 1.40 states that 'all professionals working with families should look to enable children and young people to make choices for themselves from an early age' (p28). This is an unequivocal message to education and associated professionals that there is an expectation they will support parents to develop and promote their son's or daughter's ability to make their own decisions. Despite this exhortation, education professionals must remember that the SEND COP does not permit parents or home to be written into Section F of an EHC Plan. Whilst decision-making outcomes can be written into Section E, any provision made for this in Section F must only be for the education institution element. This does not preclude education or associated professionals from discussing strategies and approaches with parents to support the development of their son's or daughter's decision-making ability at home. In fact, the author would strongly encourage this, which is the purpose of this chapter.

Before discussing the ways in which parents/families can be supported to become involved in developing and enabling their son's or daughter's with SEN decision-making ability, consideration will be given to the ways in which siblings can assist. Education and associated professionals need to be aware of the importance of siblings, likewise, understanding how a brother or sister with SEN affects their siblings; the latter issue may also need to be the focus of some of the support offered.

Siblings

Conway and Meyer (2008) capture the importance of siblings, indicating that, generally, siblings are a part of the life of their brother or sister with SEN longer than anyone else.

Siblings, if given support and information, can assist their brother or sister with SEN throughout their life. Pike et al. (2009) noted that sibling relationships are usually formed of both positive and negative interactions, providing practice for interactions in the wider world. Conway and Meyer observe there is a tendency to overlook the needs of typically developing siblings and that they have very particular issues. They highlight the lack of support for siblings, which is now, to some extent, addressed in the UK by the charity Sibs[1] representing the needs of siblings of disabled people. It has siblings' groups across the UK and an online support and information service for siblings aged 7–17 years whose brother or sister has a disability, SEN or a long-term condition.

There is now a recognition of the importance of the impact of siblings on an individual child's psychological development (Pike et al. 2009). Howe and Recchia (2014) highlight that sibling interaction can provide the background for teaching and helping as well as caregiving. The sibling relationship can promote the development of children's knowledge of their social, emotional, moral and cognitive worlds, as well as the development of understanding of others' minds (theory of mind). Chapter five in this book highlighted the importance of children and young people with SEN having a range of experiences to support building knowledge about their immediate world as part of developing their decision-making ability. Thus, it would seem, when appropriate, advantageous to involve siblings to support their brother or sister with SEN, if they wish to do this.

The efficacy of children helping other children within an educational context is evidenced in the wealth of research over more than thirty years, both with same-age and cross-age peers – the latter is likely to be of more relevance as generally there is an age difference between siblings. Some recent examples include Shenderovich et al. (2016) who undertook a meta-analysis of cross-age peer tutoring in kindergarten and elementary schools focusing on reading. The study concluded that cross-age tutoring showed small, but significant effects for tutees for some decoding and reading comprehension, but not for maths. O'Hara (2011) showed that peer mentoring can have a positive impact on the emotional literacy of a mentee with a low average level, suggesting that it could be a useful approach for pupils with SEN. Aldabas (2019) reviewed peer-mediated intervention studies where pupils with autism (ASD) had been participants, concluding that the majority reported changes in social behaviour, and a few noted improvements in communication skills. Hanze et al. (2018) demonstrated that cross-age tutoring can be enhanced by providing the tutors with training. All these studies have some implications for education and associated professionals considering involving typically developing siblings in supporting and enabling their brother's or sister's with SEN decision-making abilities, particularly the benefits of offering some appropriate training to the tutors – in this case siblings.

Supporting and involving parents

Chapters four and five made some suggestions about how to involve and support parents. The key is to understand the parent's journey, going from making all the decisions about education for their son or daughter with SEN to becoming their advocate, ensuring their son or daughter makes their own decisions or has their views, wishes and feelings taken into account if they are unable to make the decision. Sinson (2016) captures this:

> Over the years, a young person's parents will have become experts in understanding their needs to advise others about these. Parental and family life is likely to have been adapted to support the young person. Parents are likely to have concerns about the shift from them as decision makers to their young person. They may be worried that education professionals will over-estimate their young person's decision-making abilities, without understanding that their young person's level of functioning is related to the amount of support parents are giving. Parents are likely to be anxious about feeling forced to withdraw support, as this may lead to the young person no longer being able to cope. Adjusting to the new expectations is likely to present challenges, parents will need support to adapt to their changed role, and, that their young person should now be given every help and support to make their own decisions about their education and future.
>
> (p170)

Mitchell (2012) undertook a small-scale study exploring the factors parents consider when involving their young person (aged 13–21 years) with learning disabilities in making a choice in the areas of education, health and care. Although Mitchell acknowledges the limitations of her small-scale research, it provides some insight into how parents facilitate, or not, their son's or daughter's participation in decision-making. The study showed that parents' perception of their child or young person's ability to understand the relevant information influenced how far the parent enabled their offspring to make the decision or participate in the process; this was independent of their age. However, this was not always the most important factor, or even considered. Other considerations related to the parents' views about the nature of the decision, e.g. the significance or complexity, the desire to protect their son or daughter, personal beliefs and attitudes, and confidence in the practitioners. The relevant key findings from this study are that:

- Parents supported decision-making by simplifying the choices and, where possible, providing direct experience of the choice options. They presented the options based on their belief that they knew what was appropriate or best for their son or daughter.

- The ability to actually experience the choices increased their offspring's level of participation in the decision-making. It was noted specifically that, in education, where the young person was able to experience the options, e.g. choosing a college, this appeared to support the young person's involvement in decision-making.

- The lower the possible risks involved with the decision, the more likely it was that a child or young person would participate in making the choice.

- Parents play an important role as information provider to both their son or daughter and practitioners to support their offspring when making significant life choices.

- Parents were concerned about their young person's needs and wishes being understood and valued, particularly if they had impaired communication.

- Practitioners need approaches and strategies for working with parents who they believe are finding it difficult to allow their young person appropriate participation in decision-making. It is suggested that this may be a training need for practitioners.

- Parents did think they would have a reduced role in decision-making as the young person transitioned to adulthood, with a shift in the parents' role to one of advocacy for their young person.

Mitchell's study provides a starting point for considering how education and associated professionals can work positively and effectively in partnership with parents to support parental involvement in empowering their offspring's decision-making.

Working in partnership with parents

For education and associated professionals there are several fundamental components to achieving this, beginning with communication, which is the bedrock, including the education or associated professional's interpersonal skills, their ability to build trust with parents, as well as using a shared language, such as the consistent use of verbal and non-verbal representations of items and activities. Chapter five suggested that education institution staff consider adopting the now widely understood emojis and emoticons, such as smiley face ☺, sad face ☹, red heart ♥ (like), which would also need to be shared with parents. Communication is a two-way process, and it is essential that education and associated professionals are aware of the way parents and/or children and young people refer to family members, home-based items or activities, to ensure the intention of using a shared language is realised.

Next is the education and associated professionals' secure knowledge of the legislative reasons and mental health benefits, as explained in Chapters two and three, for developing children and young people's decision-making ability. The legislative context enshrined in the SEND COP will need to be understood by parents, likewise the fact that from 16 years of age the Mental Capacity Act 2005 (MCA) entitles young people to make their own decisions. Parents may be unaware that from the end of Year 11, the local authority and education professionals will communicate directly with their son or daughter with SEN rather than them, in line with the provisions of the MCA (SEND COP 1.8). Equally beneficial is parents understanding that a child or young person who has some control over what happens in their life may present with fewer behavioural issues and have better mental well-being, which in turn will have a positive impact on parents' well-being. Therefore, it is advantageous to the child or young person and their family if the child or young person has been provided with teaching and support enabling them to develop their ability to make their own decisions or show a preference.

Education professionals will need to have acquired knowledge and experience of approaches to develop and support children's and young people's decision making, likewise having an overall strategy for encouraging parental involvement in this endeavour. It is recommended that education professionals develop a repertoire of verbal and visual explanations, and similarly example scenarios, addressing issues relating to developing and enabling decision-making. There may be a need for education professionals to receive training and guidance regarding working with parents and families. Education institutions may consider developing protocols for this.

Chapter five set out a decision-making syllabus as a guide for education institution staff developing their own decision-making curriculum. To work in partnership with parents, accessible information about the education institution's approach and overall outcomes for children and young people's decision-making is essential, as well as specific strategies for them to try. This may present a challenge as parents are likely to have a wide range of literacy skills and understanding. Education professionals will need to be innovative and creative, harnessing the potential of the available ICT, including videos on the education institution website, and easy read or photographic materials to explain things.

It is important parents do not feel overwhelmed or deskilled if they find it difficult to meet, what they believe are, the education or associated professional's expectations in this area. Thus, it is fundamental that parents are provided with achievable ways of supporting the development of their son's or daughter's decision-making ability. Accordingly, there will need to be prioritisation of necessary activities education or associated professionals would like parents to undertake with their son or daughter. Chapters one and five noted the importance of experiences for developing reasoning abilities and building the child or young person's knowledge about their immediate world, essential prerequisites for decision-making.

Experiences can mean activities in the home, the local community or further afield. When considering everyday choices, children and young people can only make these if they have experienced the options. These could be the first activities that are suggested such as experiencing different foods, drinks, textures, or play activities. This could extend to immediately outside the home, so the child or young person experiences different sights, sounds, smells and weather, to further afield such as the local park, play area or shops. Chapter five indicated that the education institution may have their own enrichment checklist, like the DfE's 'My Activity Passport', which parents may find helpful. Furthermore, education and associated professionals may wish to put together their own checklist specifically for parents, highlighting activities based on free or low-cost experiences at home or in the wider local community, such as the example in Appendix 6 for children and young people with significant learning difficulties.

Everyday decisions

Earlier chapters cited research which demonstrated the benefits for individuals with significant learning disabilities of making choices about food and drink. As already noted, being able to choose food and drink and being able to make a choice about leisure activities are lifelong skills, which could be considered as essential foundation life skills. Acquiring the ability to make these choices falls within the SEND COP overall outcome of successful preparation for adulthood. Therefore, encouraging parents to let their son or daughter make these choices would be beneficial. Food is probably a good place to begin this process.

Before a child or young person is able to make choices about foods, they have to have experienced these, which is the starting point. Farrow and Haycraft (2019) looked at effective strategies to help children eat vegetables, however the approaches can be applied to all food and drink. They indicate children and young people need repeated exposures to a new food, suggesting it can take up to fifteen exposures, in some cases more, and they acknowledge that this may be both expensive and time consuming. Farrow and Haycraft discuss modelling as a strategy to encourage children to eat new foods – that is, watching other children, adults or 'characters' eat new foods – suggesting in the education setting the child or young person is seated with other children or young people who eat all their food. They note this can be just as effective in the home, implying there is a role for siblings who can be observed eating different foods as a way of encouraging their brother or sister with SEN to do the same. Farrow and Haycraft guard against eating a new food being rewarded by being given a favourite food, indicating research shows that small non-food based tangible rewards such as stickers or verbal praise are effective in motivating children or young people to try novel foods. They suggest there is evidence to support a combination of modelling, repeated exposure and small non-food based rewards as an effective approach.

Additionally, they propose setting aside time for reward based 'food adventures' (p25), that is trying new foods, away from meal times. This could be a good way of introducing new foods, providing time for the food to be explored through touch, smell and taste as part of repeated exposure, particularly as meal times can be hectic and stressful. Parents could be encouraged to find what works best for them as a family, enabling them to follow the guidelines for the effective approach, including modelling, which could involve a sibling, repeated exposure and non-food based small rewards. The author would recommend parents consider introducing 'food adventures' as a snack time, giving the activity a real context; as indicated previously, ideally, activities should be relevant, purposeful and realistic, even when creating opportunities.

Farrow and Haycraft indicate there is evidence to suggest playing messy games with food reduces fear of the food and increases willingness to try new food. The author is very aware that this is anathema in some cultures and therefore should be avoided. Although the author has advocated touching, smelling and tasting food as part of familiarisation, she views this very differently from playing games with food, and hopefully her approach could be acceptable to families from cultures where playing with food is an abhorrent idea.

Other everyday decisions include what to wear, e.g. cardigan or jumper, what to do, e.g. colouring or playing with toys, go to the park, go for a walk, or a swim. To facilitate choice-making, parents should be encouraged to consistently use the same word, sign, object of reference or photo for each activity, utilising these when asking which their son or daughter wishes to do. Again, before a child or young person can make a choice, they have to know about the options through having experienced them, which is the first stage. Just like food, the child or young person will need repeated experiences of the choices, including linking with its verbal and/or non-verbal representation. Engaging in leisure activities can be considered an essential life skill. Children and young people need to experience a wide range of these activities both at home and in the wider community. Home-based activities could include listening to music or stories to encourage the child or young person to develop preferences, playing simple card or board games, jigsaws, playing games on a tablet computer, baking or cooking, gardening or growing plants indoors, or creative activities such as painting, colouring, drawing, making models, sewing and knitting. The local authority's Local Offer website should provide information about a range of community-based leisure activities for children and young people with SEN; however understanding which section to go to can be tricky. The author's home local authority lists leisure activities under the heading 'short breaks'; other local authorities have more helpfully labelled sections such as 'stuff to do', or 'things to do'. It may be advisable for education professionals to ascertain where activities for children and young people with SEN are located on the Local Offer website, and provide parents with this information. For parents who have limited access to the internet, education institution staff could consider parents accessing the information when they visit the institution or signposting them to places such as libraries or community hubs with free internet access.

Young people aged 18–25 years

To reiterate, young people aged 18+ years are adults, and this has to be respected. Thus, at this age the young person's permission needs to be sought to involve their parents. Education professionals must have regard to the Mental Capacity Act 2005 Code of Practice; for guidance, Sinson (2016) explains the legal requirements for education professionals. It is for education professionals to determine whether the young person is able to consent to their parents' involvement for a particular issue, in this case matters relating to developing, enabling and supporting decision-making. Essentially, this means education or associated professionals cannot involve a young adult's parents without either obtaining the young person's consent or considering whether the young person can give their consent. Like all adults, young adults with SEN are entitled to have support from whomever they wish, such as other family members, relatives or friends. It may be that some young adults or their family wish to establish a Circle of Support (Foundation for People with Learning Disabilities).[2] This is a group of people who meet together to support someone to achieve their educational and life goals. Furthermore, this means the young person has other people who know their views, wishes and feelings and who can offer support for decision-making. There is a lovely fictional account of such a group in Cecelia Ahern's (2015) novel *The Year I Met You*.[3]

Many young people in this age group will reside in the parental home; support from parents or another family member would be helpful if the young adult can be encouraged to agree. For young adults living in supported living, or other residential settings, involving their key worker or supporter would be beneficial, with the young adult's agreement. As noted above, some young adults may have a Circle of Support, preferring support for decision-making from a group member.

Decision-making outcomes

Chapters five and six explored decision-making outcomes in depth including encouraging parents, children and young people routinely to consider formulating a decision-making outcome as part of person-centred planning or an EHC Plan process. Discussing a decision-making outcome with parents raises the profile of this important life skill, helping parents understand there is a need for them, together with education institution staff and education and associated professionals working with the child or young person, to focus on facilitating the development of this skill, from the earliest age, so that their son or daughter will be able to make their own decisions. Outcomes assist education and associated professionals and parents to establish what needs to happen, how and why, such as enabling a child's or young person's participation in the 'important' decision of choosing a new education institution, for example moving from primary to secondary education, or to post 16 provision. For this 'important' decision, education professionals will need to support parents to think about how their son or daughter will participate in this decision, encapsulating this in one or more outcomes. This needs time; good practice indicates this process should be started in the academic year before the transition takes place, that is in Year 5 for secondary transfer at the end of Year 6, or Year 10 for transfer to post 16 at the end of Year 11. For children and young people with EHC Plans, both these transfers have deadlines when the local authority needs to be informed of the choices, thereby providing the time-scale for the preparation needed to assist the child or young person in collecting the relevant information to make their choice. The scenario 'Jill chooses her post 18 placement' (Chapter four, p. 72) sets out a suggested timetable and process to support Jill in gathering all the relevant information to enable her to make her choice.

'Important' decisions: choosing a new education or training placement

As already noted, the majority of children and young people will have to make the 'important' decision of choosing a new education institution or training placement at least once during their education. From the end of Year 11 it is expected that young people will make their own decisions, although it is recognised that some may not be able to make 'important' decisions, such as choosing their next educational or training placement. In this instance, it is the young person's parents who will make the decision on their behalf. Even when it is likely a young person will be unable to make the decision, it is expected they will participate in the process as far as possible. Education professionals will need to explain this to parents, encouraging them to include their son or daughter in the decision-making process. As noted above, outcomes relating to choosing a new educational or training placement can facilitate this by focusing on how this can be achieved, establishing the roles parents and education and associated professionals will take on to enable this process, supported by the decision-making framework, discussed in Chapter one, providing all involved with a structured systematic approach.

Chapter four presents a series of case studies exploring the child or young person's participation in choosing a new education institution and the education professional's role in supporting and encouraging parents. These scenarios demonstrated that the education professional acted as a facilitator of and advocate for the child or young person's right to make their own decision and participate in decision-making. The education professional was presented as a source of advice and practical suggestions for parents, children and young people regarding where to locate information about education institutions and training placements, how to collect information during visits to these, as well as providing a child or young person friendly decision-making framework worksheet to guide the process.

Views 💬, wishes ★ and feelings ☺☹

From the earliest age, education and associated professionals will need to encourage parents to consider their son's or daughter's views, wishes and feelings, as well as becoming adept at observing and noting their reactions, in preparation for the eventuality of needing to make an 'important' decision on behalf of their son or daughter, if they are deemed to lack capacity to make this particular decision. It may seem premature to be talking to parents of early years or primary aged children about this, but the more parents become accustomed to thinking in this way, the easier it will be for them to follow the MCA 'best interests' checklist, if they need to do so, for 'important' decisions, once their child has reached the end of Year 11. Just as it has been suggested that education professionals think about embedding developing and enabling children and young people's decision-making into everyday practice, parents should be encouraged to do the same as far as practicable.

Information, information, information ℹ

The discussion above indicates a recurrent theme about the need for education professionals to provide parents with information, including a range of practical suggestions, relating to developing, enabling and supporting their son or daughter's decision-making ability. The case study 'Decision-making curriculum' (Chapter five, p. 92) suggested providing information, including practical advice, about developing decision-making, in a range of formats in the parent section of the school website, likewise having leaflets, USB memory sticks and DVDs. This could include step-by-step guides to developing children and young people's ability to make everyday choices, as well as how to enable their son or daughter to participate as far as possible in making decisions. Furthermore, this fictional school offered parents workshops focusing on developing decision-making and how to involve children and young people in making the 'important' decision of choosing their next placement.

Parent workshops have a twofold purpose: firstly they enable education professionals to impart information and practical advice; however, just as importantly, they are a means of parents meeting other parents whose sons or daughters share similar barriers to their learning. There are now websites offering parent support, but it remains preferable to meet other parents face to face. Parents supporting each other is very helpful. In a parent workshop the author presented in a special school, it was noticeable that one parent received advice and support from others who had experienced a similar issue with their young person. Although parents' groups are highly beneficial to the participants, holding events is a challenge as education institution staff or other education or associated professionals will wish to do this within their working hours, which is when parents are also likely to be working. The parent workshop the author presented was held on the special school premises on a Saturday, enabling working parents to attend, although it was appreciated there may have been other parents who wished to come but who worked on Saturdays or perhaps had childcare issues. A resolution to the dilemma could have been to video the workshop and upload it to the school website, thereby allowing parents to experience the content, but not the direct contact with other parents or the opportunity to have their questions answered.

Conclusion

Hopefully the discussion above has provided food for thought about how to foster and encourage parental involvement in developing, supporting and enabling their son's or daughter's decision-making ability as well as participation in making everyday and 'important' decisions from the earliest age. Unequivocally, the two most important factors for working positively and effectively with parents are the education and associated professionals' communication skills and the provision of practical and relevant information in accessible formats suitable for a range of literacy and language skills. The creative use of ICT will facilitate this, as will the focus on a shared language, including employing widely recognised signs and symbols, as the author has tried to do in this book, using Microsoft Word Segoe UI emoji font. Although the suggestions may appear onerous, it should be seen as an integral part of developing the child or young person's independence as part of the SEND COP core principle relating to preparation for adulthood.

Summary

- The education and associated professionals' communication skills and ability to build trust with parents are integral to being able to foster parental involvement in developing and supporting their son's or daughter's decision-making ability.

- Education and associated professionals should provide parents with

    - practical, relevant information about strategies and approaches, as well as associated information about the legislative context, in an accessible format.

    - information about the importance of considering children and young people's views, wishes and feelings.

- Education and associated professionals need to ensure they are using a shared language, verbal and non-verbal, including knowing how the family, child or young person refer to family members, items and activities.

- Education institution staff need to ensure they share the establishment's approach to their pupils or students making their own decisions and participating in decision-making with parents and other education and associated professionals.
- Education professionals should consider
    - uploading information to the parents' section of the education institution's website
    - utilising ICT to ensure accessibility of information and communication
    - using widely understood signs and symbols such as emojis
    - offering parent workshops which are videoed and put on the education institution's website for parents unable to attend
    - offering resources and materials to support
        - the development of decision-making
        - the child or young person's participation in making 'important' decisions.

Notes

1 Available from: www.sibs.org.uk/, accessed 22 March 2019.
2 Available from: www.mentalhealth.org.uk/learning-disabilities/a-to-z/c/circles-support-and-circles-friends, accessed 24 March 2019.
3 C. Ahern (2015) *The Year I Met You.* Glasgow: Harper Collins.

EPILOGUE: REFLECTIONS AND STEPS FORWARD

> No decision about my education without a contribution from me.

This book was born out of the author's own experience of parental assumptions about their son's or daughter's with SEN ability to make their own decisions. The proclamation above represents the author's aspiration for young people aged 16–25 years with SEN. Hopefully this book's content facilitates education professionals, in partnership with parents and associated professionals, to achieve this. The book has led education and associated professionals on an exploration of the various factors concerning developing, enabling and supporting children and young people's decision-making, from the earliest age, highlighting the legal basis for this, the Children and Families Act 2014, the accompanying SEND COP, and, when working with young people aged post 16, the Mental Capacity Acts and their Codes of Practice. Furthermore it has indicated the mental well-being benefits to the child or young person and their parents or carers when children and young people are empowered to make some of their own decisions, particularly everyday ones.

This chapter reflects on some of the fundamental issues related to developing decision-making with children and young people with SEN, proposing considerations for education and associated professionals to ponder in planning their next steps.

Decision-making

Making everyday or 'important' decisions has been clearly identified as an important life skill, but one that many children and young people with SEN will require direct teaching to acquire.

Epilogue

As a life skill it is just as essential as learning to dress, eat, drink and toilet independently. As noted above and in Chapter two, being able to exercise some control over what happens to you has a beneficial effect on well-being which, in turn, benefits parents, family members and carers as the child or young person's behaviour may become more manageable.

Every day we make myriads of everyday decisions, giving little thought to the process. 'Important' decisions, such as those resulting in long-term changes or involving significant expenditure, are probably more systematically considered with more awareness of the process. However, when developing and enabling children's and young people's with SEN decision-making ability, education and associated professionals need confidence in their knowledge of the process. Therefore Chapter one introduced the process and a decision-making framework providing a structured systematic approach to support education and associated professionals in this endeavour. Chapter five set out a decision-making syllabus from which education professionals can construct their own decision-making curriculum.

From the earliest age

The phrase 'from the earliest age' is a recurrent theme, not just because this exhortation is enshrined in the SEND COP, but because it is necessary regarding developing a child or young person's decision-making ability. At the heart of the SEND COP is the concept of preparation for adulthood; actually this is not just about children and young people, but also about parents being prepared for when their child becomes an adult. Thus, by introducing decision-making from the earliest age, not only are education and associated professionals teaching children, but educating parents as well, readying them for when their child becomes 16 years old, and then 18, lawfully an adult entitled to make their own decisions. Chapter eight noted that the parent's role changes from decision-maker to advocate as their child becomes a young person and young adult.

Overall, there are many benefits to both the child with SEN and parent by initiating parental support to develop and enable their child's decision-making ability from the earliest age. Apart from those noted above, parents become familiar with the language and concepts involved in decision-making, likewise developing their ability to observe and note their child's reactions to understand their views, wishes and feelings. Furthermore, parents can be encouraged to provide their child with a wide range of advantageous experiences and activities at home and in the local community, thereby promoting their child's knowledge of their immediate world, perhaps also similarly for their siblings. Moreover, being provided with a structured approach supporting the development of the ability to make 'important' decisions, such as the decision-making framework discussed in Chapter one, gives parents a decision-making process to facilitate their child's involvement in making their own decisions or participating in the process when they become 16 years old.

Early years education and associated professionals, such as pre-school or nursery staff and Portage Home Visitors, should routinely consider introducing a decision-making outcome for everyday decisions such as food and drink, likewise offering a range of interesting experiences and activities to build the child's knowledge of their immediate world. If children are receiving SEN support, a decision-making outcome focusing on everyday decisions should usually be considered, particularly those assisting parents at home and/or preparing the child for their transition to compulsory education – the everyday decisions they will encounter in school.

Communication, communication, communication

Throughout the book there has been great emphasis on communication between the education professionals and the child or young person and with parents and associated professionals, highlighting the need to use a shared language. 'Language' in this context denotes verbal and non-verbal representations of people, objects and activities, including objects of reference, signs, symbols, emojis and words. Communication is a two-way process; it is essential that education and associated professionals not only give information but listen to parents as well. The aspiration to use a shared language can only be realised if education and associated professionals are able to elicit from parents, children and young people how they refer to family members, objects and activities.

Communication, be it verbal, written, non-verbal or visual, is the only way education or associated professionals can impart to parents the need to support their son or daughter to develop their ability to make decisions and offer assistance with this. Thus, developing high quality communication is essential, such as well-presented, accessible written and visual information, likewise practised verbal explanations and practical demonstrations. Good communication is fundamental to building trust with parents to facilitate the education or associated professional to work positively and effectively, sharing strategies and approaches, in a way that does not overwhelm or make parents feel deskilled, as well as encouraging young people's parents to enable their son's or daughter's participation in making 'important' decisions.

Throughout the book there has been reference to using digital technology to promote children and young people's decision-making, with a proposal that education professionals and education institutions could consider adopting the now increasingly widespread emojis and emoticons. These are effectively becoming a globally understood language used worldwide enabling communication even when you are unable to actually speak the other person's language. The author is essentially illiterate in all of these – she did not understand when a friend ended a text with :)! However, the author, when researching for this book, noticed that the Microsoft Segoe UI font symbol ♿ is now frequently used in public spaces to

Epilogue

denote baby-changing facilities and the 🛈 symbol is now used at her main railway station on a sign indicating the information desk. This raises the question about whether it would be more educative and useful for children and young people if education and associated professionals used these now universally understood symbols in place of Boardmaker ones or similar?

Education and associated professional as the child's or young person's advocate

It has been mooted that education and associated professionals have a role as the child's or young person's advocate, ensuring that their right to make their own decisions is respected by others. Some education or associated professionals may find this an uncomfortable role, particularly if they are advocating on the young person's behalf for something that differs from parental wishes, for example the young person's participation in making a decision about their next educational or training placement. However, from the age of 16 years young people are lawfully entitled to make their own decisions. If they are unable to make the particular decision, young people's views, wishes, and feelings must be considered by those making the decision on their behalf. Education and associated professionals have a role to play in facilitating this by supporting parents to involve their son or daughter in making the decision, likewise helping them in ascertaining their youngster's views. When education professionals have introduced decision-making and the notion of considering the child's or young person's views, wishes and feelings from the earliest age, it is likely that parents will be more familiar with this and be open to the support and advice offered.

The education and associated professional's advocacy role probably assumes more importance when the young person has become 18 years old, to ensure that their rights are upheld, particularly regarding the issues that should be addressed at preparing for adulthood EHC Plan reviews such as education or training, independent living, healthcare and participating in society. At these reviews young people are also required to consider which decisions they wish to take for themselves and their role in decision-making (SEND COP 8.10). Independent living could be a delicate subject, but young people have the right to consider where they wish to live, and education and associated professionals should have the confidence to raise this issue with young people and, with the young person's consent, their parents. Many young people will require assistance to progress their wish for independent living such as supported living as this is accessed through social care. If the young person does not have an allocated social worker, it may be that an education or associated professional will need to support the young person in pursuing this.

Education and associated professionals need to feel comfortable and confident in their role as a child's or young person's advocate. It may be that education institutions or education support services would benefit from having a supportive policy and protocol for this role and offering appropriate supervision.

Choices

Choices are at the heart of decision-making and have been given extensive consideration throughout the book. Discussions have highlighted that the issues regarding deciding on the choices that are offered are far from straightforward. Mitchell's (2012) study reports that parents limited the choices offered to their son or daughter to avoid overwhelming them with too many options. Whilst this would seem to be a pragmatic way of enabling children and young people to have choices, any selection of options from the overall range actually available raises a number of issues. Firstly, the person, be it a parent, education or associated professional, selecting the options to be offered is effectively restricting and controlling the child's or young person's choices, prompting questions about the criteria employed to make the selection. Were the options chosen because these are the ones the selector feels are the best for this child or young person, the ones the selector themselves likes, regardless of any previous preferences shown by the child or young person, the cheapest, the easiest, or by some other criteria that do not take account of what is known about preferences? The appropriateness of limiting the options may depend on the decision being made. Chapter four discussed choosing a new educational placement and the associated issues, as, in this case, the local authority actually controls what can be considered as real options, that is, those that will be funded. Therefore, should education or associated professionals and/or parents only support young people to consider these real options, rather than all the available choices?

There are no simple answers to the dilemmas posed above, but there are perhaps some guidelines that may assist. When offering everyday choices such as food, drink, or clothing, when there are options, then those offered in school or at home must be those the child or young person is known to like so that there is a real choice. At minimum there should be a choice between two items; this would be the starting point to develop decision-making. When children or young people go to a café or restaurant there is likely to be a wide choice, some of which they may not like, but hopefully there will be things they like. In this instance, those accompanying the child or young person can direct their attention to choose between the items they do like. For leisure activity options, it is important children and young people experience a range so that they can develop their preferences. Once their preferences are established, they can be offered a choice from these. For food, drink and leisure activities, it would be good practice to continue to try to extend preferences throughout the child's or young person's attendance at the education or training institution.

Education and associated professionals, like parents, will need to reflect on their reasons for offering the particular choices. Chapter one noted the rule of thumb should be that, when

Epilogue

considering what choices to offer, the education or associated professional or parent tries to stand in the child's or young person's shoes, rather than viewing the options from their own perspective or preferences, asking themselves what choices would the child or young person wish to be given.

The notion of standing in the child's or young person's shoes can be explored by revisiting 'Rodney cooks his lunch' (Chapter three, p. 47), analysing the approaches the teaching assistants may have adopted if he had been overwhelmed by the number of options. The scenario provides some insight into their possible approaches. Ms Felix chose tuna Bolognese for Rodney based on her memory of what he had cooked last term, although there is no indication if he actually chose this himself or if it was chosen for him. However, he is known to like this, so possibly it could be considered a choice that he may have made himself. Nevertheless, her action did not afford Rodney the opportunity to actually make the choice himself, nor did she consider that he may wish to choose a different dish. Imagine you have gone out for a meal and your dining companion makes all the choices for you, how would you feel? These may be based on what your companion knows of your preferences, but this may not take account of what you actually fancy eating for that meal. You may wish to try something different or perhaps if it was cold you would like something hot, or vice versa. Perhaps this provides some insight about how children and young people with SEN may feel if they are not afforded the opportunities to make some real choices.

Consider how Ms Felix may have selected the options to offer Rodney if she had been instructed to offer him a choice of two dishes to cook. His known preferences are for white pasta dishes, either macaroni cheese or tuna Bolognese. As noted above, she did choose a dish he was known to like, but when given the opportunity to decide the options offered she may have considered this a time to provide choices that she thinks are healthier, easier to cook, or chosen by some other criteria. If the choices offered reflected her standing in Rodney's shoes, he would be shown white pasta dishes – tuna Bolognese and macaroni cheese. However, Ms Felix may have thought that brown pasta tuna Bolognese was a healthier option, offering this alongside a white pasta dish. From Rodney's viewpoint this may not have seemed like a choice – there was only one option he was known to like.

Thus, possibly the biggest dilemma is whether to limit options to enable a child or young person to make their own choice without being overwhelmed by the full range of options, which could be a hindrance. Education or associated professionals and parents considering the options from the child or young person's perspective, albeit offering limited choices, are likely to be affording that child or young person the opportunity to have some control in their life. Returning to Supreme Court judge Lady Hale's gilded cage analogy (Chapter three, p. 50), perhaps this would prompt her to consider the door of the gilded cage as open, offering an opportunity for some autonomy.

Outcomes

Whilst choices are at the heart of decision-making, outcomes are the linchpin that will focus minds on the task of empowering children and young people to be able to make their own decisions. Therefore, the ability to formulate effective SMART outcomes is essential, one education and associated professionals should endeavour to acquire. Chapter six gave extensive guidance and models; it is now a matter of practice to perfect this skill and for education and associated professionals not to be daunted by the task. Peer tutoring was referred to in Chapter eight; this approach benefits the tutor as they consolidate their understanding by having to teach the tutee. Therefore, preparing and delivering training packages is a way of assimilating the subject matter, and it is suggested those education or associated professionals who deliver training offer outcome writing training to colleagues. It is recommended that education and associated professionals ensure there is training for new colleagues. Another approach would be to work together as an education institution staff to develop outcome writing in a similar way to the collaborative problem-solving groups that run in some schools. The format of these groups is that one person brings the 'problem' to discuss, and colleagues help find solutions by pooling their collective experience. Thus, one education or associated professional could bring an outcome they are formulating for their colleagues' support to make it a SMART outcome that contains as many of the TWOSB elements as appropriate.

As noted previously, the author rarely sees decision-making outcomes in reports or EHC Plans. The structure of many EHC Plans means it is uncertain where such an outcome would fit as they are aligned to the four areas of need set out in the SEND COP. This seems to act as a tacit guide for education and associated professionals writing outcomes to address these areas directly, which a decision-making outcome may not do. Education and associated professionals should include a decision-making outcome in their reports and not be deterred by the fact that it does not readily fit one of the four areas. It should be aligned to the area of best fit, even if it seems unsuitable. The resolution is the restructuring of EHC Plans Sections B and F to accommodate decision-making, necessitating local authority SEN officers fully understanding the importance of decision-making outcomes.

Mental well-being

Research cited earlier highlighted the mental well-being benefits to individuals with significant learning disabilities if they are able to make some choices. Thus, developing and enabling children's and young people's decision-making ability is not only preparation for adulthood, but also promoting their mental well-being, which can reduce incidences of difficult behaviours. The importance of good mental health is now widely recognised with many government initiatives to improve children's and young people's well-being; however these do not include teaching children and young people to make decisions. Evidently, it has yet to be formally recognised that being able to make choices, thereby empowering children and young people to have some control in their life, also promotes their mental well-being. Perhaps the importance of this essential life skill is overlooked because typically developing children and young people seem to acquire it by osmosis. Earlier in the book the author asked if the reader could recall when and how they learned to make decisions – probably not a question that was answered, as the reader, like the author, has no recollection of learning this. Nevertheless, as practitioners experienced in working with children and young people with SEN, we know that decision-making needs to be taught, ensuring they are afforded every opportunity to have some control over what happens in their life, hopefully promoting their well-being.

Seemingly it falls to education and associated professionals working with children and young people with SEN to highlight the mental well-being benefits associated with being able to make decisions or demonstrate preferences. This is an important message to communicate to parents, and all education and associated professionals may wish to consider the most effective way of doing this, starting from the earliest age. Equally important is the local authority SEN officers' awareness of the mental well-being benefits of being able to make decisions, assisting their understanding of the need to include decision-making outcomes in every EHC Plan from the earliest age.

Next steps

The starting point for this is for the education and associated professional to reflect on their current practice with regard to developing, supporting and enabling children and young people's decision-making ability. Chapter seven posed some reflective questions, which you may wish to revisit.

Education institution staff

Additionally, it is suggested education institution staff reflect on issues such as the institution's policy and practice regarding developing, supporting and enabling children's and young people's decision-making ability, including the use of a shared language, both verbal and non-verbal representations of objects, activities and people, as well as the range of experiences and activities offered within the institution to develop their knowledge of the wider local community. Consider how this is communicated to parents and associated professionals.

Where next?

The Chinese philosopher Lao Tzu[1] wisely stated, 'a journey of a thousand miles begins with a single step', meaning taking the first step is the most important. Having reflected on current practice, do you know what you will do differently tomorrow to ensure you focus on developing, enabling and supporting children's and young people's with SEN decision-making ability?

Having read the book, education and associated professionals are aware of what the author sees as priorities in this area. To be effective, some require the whole institution or service to make changes, others can be put in place by the individual education and associated professionals. The author's suggested priorities are:

- using a shared language, verbal and non-verbal, including universally recognised non-verbal symbols such as emojis, within the education institution, with parents and other education and associated professionals
- education and associated professionals are encouraged to use universally recognised non-verbal symbols in their everyday practice, promoting the adoption of these by education institutions
- education professionals, particularly EPs, to promote the use of universally recognised non-verbal symbols by local authority SEN officers, incorporating them in EHC Plans to help make this a more accessible document for children and young people with SEN
- constructing a coherent decision-making curriculum
- using a structured decision-making framework
- formulating decision-making outcomes as part of person-centred planning or the EHC Plan process, ensuring this is included in EHC Plans
- offering a wide range of experiences and activities to build the child or young person's knowledge of their immediate world
- supporting and encouraging parents to empower their son or daughter to make their own decisions, especially everyday ones
- promoting the mental well-being benefits of children and young people being able to make their own decisions
- assisting local authority SEN officers in understanding
    - the need to include a decision-making outcome in EHC Plans from the earliest age
    - the associated mental well-being benefits for children, young people and their parents or others who educate or care for them if they are able to make some choices, enabling some control over what happens in their life

However, this does not mean any of these have to be your starting point. It is essential education and associated professionals choose their own first step that is achievable for them. Change is a process which takes time, but there has to be a starting point. Make a plan; applying a solution-focused approach may assist, this could take several forms. You could consider how you feel about your current practice, rating it on a scale of 1–10 (1 being the worst and 10 the best). Whatever you rate it at, analyse why you have not rated it one or two points higher, your reasons helping identify the first step. Alternatively, you could start the process with where you would like your journey to lead, then identify the very first step to take you there. For instance, this could be wanting every child in your group to be able to choose their own morning snack, analysing what would begin this process, using this to determine the very first step. The key to the first step is to make it a very small change, so it is both achievable and sustainable. Add the first step to your plan along with what you need to do to achieve it and a time-frame to do this in – be realistic, remember the proverb 'Rome was not built in a day'. The author finds setting herself self-imposed deadlines helps her focus on achieving her aim – she used this approach to write this book. The challenge may be persuading colleagues and parents to join you on this venture. Ideally, both are needed to achieve your goal of enabling children and young people to make their own decisions. However, if you begin to change your practice, others may follow, supporting your efforts to enable every child and young person with SEN to develop this important life skill and to be able to make decisions about their education or demonstrate preferences. Ideally, realising the aspiration 'no decision about my education without a contribution from me'.

Note

1 Available from: www.bbc.co.uk/worldservice/learningenglish/movingwords/shortlist/laotzu.shtml, accessed 28 March 2019.

Appendix 1

COMPLETED DECISION-MAKING FRAMEWORK FOR 'IMPORTANT' DECISIONS FOR EDUCATION AND ASSOCIATED PROFESSIONALS OR PARENTS: CHOOSING A NEW EDUCATION INSTITUTION

A blank version of this framework is available as an eResource.

A. Year 6 child choosing a secondary school

Teaching, supporting and enabling decision-making is an interactive process based on knowing how to communicate with the child and understanding their communication.		
Framework	**Decision-making process**	**Explanatory notes**
1 What is the actual decision that needs to be made?	Choosing a secondary school for the new academic year. Camilla and her parents are looking at the options. As Camilla is a child, her parents will make the decision and communicate this to the local authority. However, the SEND COP places emphasis on children participating in decision-making as much as possible.	This needs to be framed as straightforwardly as possible, including considering the best way to communicate the decision to be made to the child.
• Why is this decision needed?	Camilla is in the final year at her mainstream primary school, therefore, a new school needs to be chosen for the next academic year.	There is usually a reason a decision needs to be made; helping the child to understand why they are being asked to make a choice may be helpful.

(Continued)

Appendix 1

(Continued)

Framework	Decision-making process	Explanatory notes
• What happens if the child's parents do not make the decision?	As Camilla is a child, her parents will make the decision, and complete the local authority school choice form. If her parents do not make the choice, then the local authority automatically allocates a school regardless of whether she is the subject of an EHC Plan.	If there is a decision to be made, then there is usually a consequence of not making the decision such as not being considered for something or someone else choosing for you.
• Is there a timeframe in which the decision needs to be made?	For secondary school choices, local authorities usually give a deadline for receiving completed choice forms in the second half of the autumn term. Therefore, it is important to begin the process, no later than the start of the autumn term in which the decision needs to be made. It may be advisable to be considering the options in the preceding summer term.	Some decisions such as choosing a new education institution need to be made by a set date.

2. **Information about the choices**
• What are the options?
  A ◉ B ◉ C ◉
• Need to gather relevant information
  ○ How will the child be helped to do this?
  ○ Who could assist?
	Camilla and her parents are considering mainstream high schools, Castle Road High and Royal Town Academy, the enhanced resource provision at Daffodil High, as well as Bosun Lane Special School.
	
	Camilla and her parents are attending each school's open evening. Her parents have asked if
	
	• they can take photos of the front and key areas of the school to remind Camilla about each school.
	• they and Camilla could meet with the SENCo to talk about the support on offer
		To consider the choices, the child and their parents need to know what options are on offer. These need to be presented in a way the child can understand.
		
		Relevant information is information specific to the particular choice. For example, if the decision is choosing an education institution, then the relevant information will be about the establishments under consideration. Presenting the information in the most accessible format for the child is very important to support, develop and enable their decision-making ability.

Appendix 1

Teaching, supporting and enabling decision-making is an interactive process based on knowing how to communicate with the child and understanding their communication.		
Framework	**Decision-making process**	**Explanatory notes**

• What format should the information be presented in?
  ○ photos, pictures, videos
  ○ objects of reference
  ○ easy written materials
  ○ audio
  ○ via signing
  ○ by experiencing the options
	• Camilla could record this talk on her iPad to remind her.
	
	Additionally, the primary SENCo and Camilla's current TA (Mrs Evans) have helped Camilla and her parents select pictorial objects of reference for each of the choices following Camilla's visit to the schools. Camilla has chosen a picture of a sandcastle for Castle Road High, a crown for Royal High, a parrot for Bosun Lane Special School (this is the school's symbol), and a daffodil for Daffodil High. It is important everyone working with Camilla to support her participating in this decision knows how she is referring to the schools.	

⚖ 3 **Using and weighing the information** A ◉ B ◉ C ◉ ☺ ☹ 💡 • The child needs to be helped to show what they like or dislike or the advantages or disadvantages of the options.	Mrs Evans (TA) will work with Camilla to help her identify the things she likes and dislikes about each of the schools she has visited, using ☺ for like and ☹ for dislike. Camilla understands pictures, she has photos on her iPad from each school and the recording of what the SENCo told her. Also, the SENCo from each school has made a booklet for Camilla about what is on offer in the school. Using all this information, Mrs Evans will ask Camilla to indicate what she likes and dislikes, and pictures/photos representing these will be put in the appropriate column. This will be done for each school. Mrs Evans will photograph the display for each school, so Camilla's parents can see how she is thinking. Camilla seemed to like more things about Daffodil High than the other schools, she seemed to really like the resourced provision base.	This is about analysing the pros and cons of the choice, the things the child likes or dislikes about the options. For many children with SEN, this is probably best done visually such as putting pictures or symbols under a smiley or sad face emoji or variations on this, perhaps using technology. It is important to keep a record so the child can revisit their thoughts. Keeping these as a paper file or electronically may be helpful as a record of the child or young person's decision-making ability, as well as the extent to which they participated in the decision-making process.

(*Continued*)

Appendix 1

(Continued)

Framework	Decision-making process	Explanatory notes
• Having set out what the child likes and dislikes about the options, they use this information to make their choice.	Camilla will be encouraged to look at the display and count the number of things she liked for each choice and see if she can work out from this which she seems to like the most. As Camilla is a child, her choice will be given to her parents to enable them to consider her views when they are making the decision. Regardless of whether Camilla is the subject of an EHC Plan, the actual decision regarding a high school place is made by the local authority with regard to the choices on the form.	The child now looks at how they have rated each choice in terms of likes/dislikes, positives/negatives or advantages/disadvantages, and uses the information to make a choice based on this consideration. This may be challenging for some children. Generally, if there are more things under 'like' it would be expected this would be the child's choice. If the more liked option is chosen it suggests the child has probably understood the decision-making process for this particular choice. If they choose the option with the more 'dislikes', this may indicate they have not understood the process for this particular decision. However, good practice would suggest trying again on another day.
💬 4 **Communicate the decision** • The child can use any verbal or non-verbal means of communication to indicate their choice.	Mrs Evans asked Camilla to indicate which school she would like to attend. Camilla chose to use the pictorial object of reference to indicate she wishes to attend Daffodil High. Mrs Evans repeated the process a few days later to ensure this was really her choice. Again, Camilla selected the pictorial object of reference representing Daffodil High. Her parents will be informed of her choice, but as she is a child, her parents will make the actual decision.	The child can communicate their choice in any way they choose, verbally or non-verbally. It is essential the person working with the child knows the child's preferred means of communication and can understand this. Equally important is that everyone supporting children to enable their decision-making knows how to communicate with them.

Appendix 1

B. Choosing a post 16 education institution: Year 11 child aged 15–16 years at the time the decision needs to be made

	Framework	Decision-making process	Explanatory notes
	Teaching, supporting and enabling decision-making is an interactive process based on knowing how to communicate with the child or young person and understanding their communication.		
1	**What is the actual decision that needs to be made?**	Choosing a post 16 education institution for the next academic year. Camilla and her parents are looking at the options.	This needs to be framed as straightforwardly as possible, including considering the best way to communicate the decision to be made to the child.
•	Why is this decision needed?	Camilla is in Year 11, the final year at her mainstream enhanced resourced high school, therefore she needs to choose a new education institution for Year 12 and apply for a place in her chosen establishment. Young people must remain in education or training until their 18th birthday.	There is usually a reason a decision needs to be made; helping the child to understand why they are being asked to make a choice may be helpful.
		As Camilla has had her 16th birthday, she should be encouraged to participate in the process and make her own decision. In reality, Camilla is very likely to need her parents' support to help her. However, if Camilla is the subject of an EHC Plan, it will be her parents that make the choice as she has not come to the end of Year 11, and so is not permitted to make her own choice under the provisions set out in the SEND COP.	
•	What happens if the child or their parents do not make the decision?	If Camilla or her parents do not make the decision, she will be left without an educational or training placement, which for this age group would be problematic as she must remain in education or training until her 18th birthday. If Camilla is the subject of an EHC Plan, the local authority will allocate a place in a post 16 provision.	If there is a decision to be made, then there is usually a consequence of not making the decision such as not being considered for something or someone else choosing for you.

(*Continued*)

Appendix 1

(Continued)

Teaching, supporting and enabling decision-making is an interactive process based on knowing how to communicate with the child or young person and understanding their communication.		
Framework	**Decision-making process**	**Explanatory notes**
📅 • Is there a time-frame in which the decision needs to be made?	Generally, post 16 establishments have a time-frame for applications. If Camilla is the subject of an EHC Plan she must let the local authority know her choice by a set date so the new EHC Plan can be issued by 31 March, naming the education institution the local authority agrees she can attend.	Some decisions such as choosing a new educational placement need to be made by a set date.

ℹ️ 2. **Information about the choices**
• What are the options?
A ⬤ B ⬤ C ⬤
• Need to gather relevant information
   ○ How will the child be helped to do this?
   ○ Who could assist?
• What format should the information be presented in?
   ○ photos, pictures, videos
   ○ objects of reference
   ○ easy written materials
   ○ audio
   ○ via signing
   ○ by experiencing the options
	Camilla and her parents are considering City FE College and Blue Harbour Specialist College, both day placements. Camilla was not keen to consider a residential college as she wants to be at home with her family.
	
	Camilla and her parents are visiting each college. Her parents have asked if
	
	• Camilla can take photos of the front and key areas of the college to remind her about each college
	• they and Camilla could meet the course leader of the additional learning needs courses
	• Camilla could record this talk on her iPad to remind her
	
	Each college also has an electronic pictorial prospectus to show the activities on offer, which Camilla has downloaded onto her iPad. Additionally, Camilla's current teacher and TA (Ms Attar) have helped her select pictorial objects of reference for each college and how she wants to refer to them.
		To consider the choices the child needs to know what the options are on offer. These need to be presented in a way the child can understand.
		
		Relevant information is information specific to the particular choice. For example, if the decision is choosing an education institution, then the relevant information will be about the establishments under consideration. Presenting the information in the most accessible format for the child is very important to support, develop and enable their decision-making ability.

Appendix 1

Framework	Decision-making process	Explanatory notes
	Camilla has chosen the coat of arms on City College's sign and the boat from Blue Harbour College's sign; she also says 'City' for City College and 'Har' for Harbour as she is unable to say this in full. Ms Attar will let Camilla's parents, as well as other education and associated professionals who work with her, know how she refers to each college, ensuring everyone uses the same language and pictures.	
⚖ 3. **Using and weighing the information** ☺☹💡 • The child needs to be helped to show what they like or dislike or the advantages or disadvantages of the options.	Ms Attar will work with Camilla to help her identify the things she likes and does not like about each of the colleges she has visited, using ☺ for like and ☹ for dislike. Camilla understands pictures, she has photos on her iPad from each college, as well as the picture prospectus and the recording of what the course leader has told her. Using all this information, Ms Attar will ask Camilla to indicate what she likes and dislikes, and pictures/photos representing these will be put in the appropriate column. This will be done for each college. Ms Attar will photograph each display, so Camilla's parents can see how Camilla is thinking.	This is about analysing the pros and cons of the choice, the things the child likes or dislikes about the options. For many children with SEN, this is probably best done visually such as putting pictures or symbols under a smiley or sad face emoji or variations on this, perhaps using technology. It is important to keep a record so the child can revisit their thoughts. Keeping these as a paper file or electronically may be helpful as a record of the child's decision-making ability as well as the extent of their participation in the decision-making process.
• Having set out what the child likes and dislikes about the options, they use this information to make their choice.	Camilla will be encouraged to look at the display and count the number of things she likes for each choice and see if she can work out from this which she seems to like the most. She seemed to like more things at Blue Harbour College, especially being able to cook her own lunch.	The child now looks at how they have rated each choice in terms of likes/dislikes, positives/negatives or advantages/disadvantages, and uses the information to make a choice based on this consideration.

(*Continued*)

Appendix 1

(Continued)

Framework	Decision-making process	Explanatory notes
	Although Camilla is 16 years old, under the provisions in the SEND COP, it is her parents who will make the choice and communicate this to the local authority. The information from this process will enable her parents to consider her views when they are making the decision.	This may be challenging for some children. Generally, if there are more things under 'like' it would be expected this would be the child's choice. If the more liked option is chosen it suggests the child or has probably understood the decision-making process for this particular choice. If they choose the option with the more 'dislikes', this may indicate they have not understood the process for this particular decision. However, good practice would suggest trying again on another day.
4. **Communicate the decision** • The child can use any verbal or non-verbal means of communication to indicate their choice.	Camilla is asked to indicate which college it is she would like to attend; she says 'har' and gives the Blue Harbour College picture. To ensure this really was her choice, Ms Attar repeated the process a few days later. Camilla's parents will be informed of her choice. As Camilla is the subject of an EHC Plan and has not yet finished Year 11, it is her parents who will make the decision and complete the local authority's form.	The child can communicate their choice in any way they choose, verbally or non-verbally. It is essential the person working with the child knows their preferred means of communication and can understand this. Equally important is that everyone supporting children to enable their decision-making knows how to communicate with them

Appendix 1

C. Choosing a post 16 education institution: Year 12 young person aged 16 years–17 years 11 months at the time the decision needs to be made

Teaching, supporting and enabling decision-making is an interactive process based on knowing how to communicate with the young person and understanding their communication.		
Framework	**Decision-making process**	**Explanatory notes**
🚩 1. What is the actual decision that needs to be made?	Choosing a new education institution for the new academic year. Camilla and her parents are looking at the options.	This needs to be framed as straightforwardly as possible, including considering the best way to communicate the decision to be made to the young person.
• Why is this decision needed?	Camilla is in Year 12 and now wishes to have the opportunity to do catering and hospitality, which her current college does not offer. Currently she is following a life skills course with horticulture and animal care options.	There is usually a reason a decision needs to be made; helping the young person to understand why they are being asked to make a choice may be helpful.
	As Camilla has had her 16th birthday and has completed Year 11, the SEND COP now gives her the right to make her own choices. The SEND COP emphasises that young people should participate in decision-making as far as possible. Camilla should be actively encouraged to participate in the process and make her own decision. In reality, Camilla is very likely to need her parents' support to help her; she has agreed to this. As she is not yet 18 years old, her parents could still make the decision for her in certain circumstances. However, Camilla should be encouraged to participate in the decision-making, even if she is not able to make the decision. Information about her likes and dislikes should be considered by her parents if they are making the decision on her behalf.	

(Continued)

Appendix 1

(Continued)

Framework	Decision-making process	Explanatory notes
• What happens if the young person does not make the decision?	If Camilla or her parents do not make the decision she will remain in her current college until the end of the academic year she turns 18 years old.	If there is a decision to be made, then there is usually a consequence of not making the decision such as not being considered for something or someone else choosing for you.
• Is there a time-frame in which the decision needs to be made?	Generally, post 16 establishments have a time-frame for applications. If Camilla is the subject of an EHC Plan, she must let the local authority know her choice by a set date so the new EHC Plan can be issued by 31 March naming the education institution the local authority agrees she can attend.	Some decisions such as choosing a new educational placement need to be made by a set date.
2. **Information about the choices** • What are the options? A ⬤ B ⬤ C ⬤	Camilla and her parents are considering Whitebeam College and Silver Bridge Specialist College, both day placements as Camilla has stated she does not want to sleep away from home.	To consider the choices the young person needs to know what the options are on offer. These need to be presented in a way the young person can understand.

• Need to gather relevant information
   ◦ How will the young person be helped to do this?
   ◦ Who could assist?
	Camilla and her parents are going to visit each college. Camilla's parents have asked if
	
	• Camilla can take photos of the front and key areas of the college to remind her about each college.
	• they and Camilla could meet the course leader of the additional learning needs courses
	• Camilla could record this talk on her iPad to remind her.
		Relevant information is usually information specific to the particular choices. For example, if the decision is choosing an education institution, then the relevant information will be about the establishments under consideration. Presenting the information in the most accessible format for the young person is very important to support, develop and enable their decision-making ability. It may be appropriate to consider involving the young person's parents.

Appendix 1

Teaching, supporting and enabling decision-making is an interactive process based on knowing how to communicate with the young person and understanding their communication.		
Framework	**Decision-making process**	**Explanatory notes**

• What format should the information be presented in?
  ○ photos, pictures, videos
  ○ objects of reference
  ○ easy written materials
  ○ audio
  ○ via signing
  ○ by experiencing the options
	Each college also has an electronic pictorial prospectus to show the activities on offer, which Camilla has downloaded onto her iPad. Additionally, Camilla's tutor (Mr Gill) and Learner Support Assistant (Mrs Torma) have helped her select pictorial objects of reference for each college and how she wants to refer to them. Camilla has chosen the tree on Whitebeam College's sign and the bridge on Silver Bridge College's sign; she also says 'white' for Whitebeam and 'bridge' for Silver Bridge. Mrs Torma will let Camilla's parents, as well as other education and associated professionals who work with her, know how Camilla refers to each college, ensuring everyone uses the same language and pictures.	

3. **Using and weighing the information** ☺☹💡 • The young person needs to be helped to show what they like or dislike or the advantages or disadvantages of the options.	Mrs Torma, Learner Support Assistant, will work with Camilla to help her identify the things she likes and dislikes about each of the colleges she has visited, using ☺ for like and ☹ for dislike. Camilla understands pictures, she has photos on her iPad from each college, as well as the picture prospectus and the recording of what the course leader has told her. Using all this information Mrs Torma will ask Camilla to indicate to her what she likes and dislikes and pictures/photos representing these will be put in the appropriate column. This will be done for each college. Mrs Torma will photograph the display for each college, so Camilla's parents can see how Camilla is thinking.	This is about analysing the pros and cons of the choice, the things the young person likes or dislikes about the options. For many young people with SEN, this is probably best done visually such as putting pictures or symbols under a smiley or sad face emoji or variations on this, perhaps using technology. It is important to keep a record so the young person can revisit their thoughts. Keeping these as a paper file or electronically may be helpful as a record of the young person's decision-making ability, as well as showing the extent to which the young person has participated in the decision-making process.

(*Continued*)

Appendix 1

(Continued)

Framework	Decision-making process	Explanatory notes
Teaching, supporting and enabling decision-making is an interactive process based on knowing how to communicate with the young person and understanding their communication.		
• Having set out what the young person likes and dislikes about the options, they use this information to make their choice.	Camilla will be encouraged to look at the display and count the number of things she liked for each choice and see if she can work out from this which she seems to like the most and which college she wishes to attend.	The young person now looks at how they have rated each choice in terms of likes/dislikes, positives/negatives or advantages/disadvantages, and uses the information to make a choice based on this consideration. This may be challenging for some young people. Generally, if there are more things under 'like' it would be expected this would be the young person's choice. If the more liked option is chosen it suggests the young person has understood the decision-making process for this particular choice. If they choose the option with the more 'dislikes', this may indicate they have not understood the process for this particular decision. However, good practice would suggest trying again on another day.
4. **Communicate the decision** • The young person can use any verbal or non-verbal means of communication to indicate their choice.	Camilla is asked to indicate which college it is she would like to attend; she says 'white' and gives the Whitebeam College picture. To ensure this really was her choice, Mrs Torma repeated the process a few days later. Camilla's parents are supporting her and will complete the necessary paperwork on her behalf. Mrs Torma will ask Camilla if she will let her parents know her choice or would she like Mrs Torma to do this.	The young person can communicate their choice in any way they choose, verbally or non-verbally. It is essential the person working with the young person knows their preferred means of communication and can understand this. Equally important is that everyone supporting young people to enable decision-making knows how to communicate with them

Appendix 1

D. Choosing a post 18 education institution: Year 14 young person aged 18+ years at the time the decision needs to be made

Teaching, supporting and enabling decision-making is an interactive process based on knowing how to communicate with the young person and understanding their communication.		
Framework	**Decision-making process**	**Explanatory notes**
1. What is the actual decision that needs to be made?	Choosing a new placement, education or social care, for the next academic year. Jill is considering the options. As she is 18 years old, she will need to agree to her parents being involved in this process; she can have assistance from anyone she chooses, provided she has capacity to choose the person. Her tutor, Ms Roberts, has asked Jill who she would like to help her. Jill has indicated she would like her parents to assist her in making this decision.	This needs to be framed as straightforwardly as possible, including considering the best way to communicate the decision to be made to the young person.
• Why is this decision needed?	Jill is the subject of an EHC Plan so can only continue in education and training if the local authority agrees she needs more time to complete her education or training.	There is usually a reason a decision needs to be made; helping the young person to understand why they are being asked to make a choice may be helpful.
• What happens if the young person does not make the decision?	Jill is in the final year of her special school. If she does not make the decision, she will not have the opportunity to be offered a place on her chosen course. Jill is the subject of an EHC Plan; she will need the local authority to maintain this for her to continue attending a college or training placement such as a supported internship. The local authority may not agree with her choice and name its own provision or decide to cease to maintain the EHC Plan. Jill needs to be made aware that even if she makes a choice and is offered a place, the local authority may not agree to fund the placement.	If there is a decision to be made, then there is usually a consequence of not making the decision such as not being considered for something or someone else choosing for you.

(Continued)

Appendix 1

(Continued)

Framework	Decision-making process	Explanatory notes
🗓 • Is there a time-frame in which the decision needs to be made?	Generally, post 16 education institutions have a time-frame for applications. As Jill is the subject of an EHC Plan she must let the local authority know her choice by a set date so the new EHC Plan can be issued by 31 March naming the education institution the local authority agrees she can attend.	Some decisions such as choosing a new educational placement need to be made by a set date.
ⓘ 2. **Information about the choices** • What are the options? A ⬤ B ⬤ C ⬤	Jill is considering • White Sails FE College, her local FE college, offering provision for three days per week • Tansy Park FE College, in the neighbouring local authority, offering provision for three days per week • Cottage Road House, a local social services provision for people with learning disabilities, offering placements for 1–5 days. It has an associated residential respite care facility. Jill would be able to stay one night a month. • Isidore Specialist College, 50 miles from home, which could be for three or five days per week. Jill knows she would need to sleep at Isidore two or four nights per week. She understands what this means as her older sister is away at university. Jill has understood that it is the local authority who will decide if she can go there. Her parents have explained that it costs a lot more money to go to Isidore Specialist College than White Sails or Tansy Park College. Jill seems to understand this.	To consider the choices the young person needs to know what options are on offer. These need to be presented in a way the young person can understand.

Appendix 1

Teaching, supporting and enabling decision-making is an interactive process based on knowing how to communicate with the young person and understanding their communication.		
Framework	**Decision-making process**	**Explanatory notes**

• Need to gather relevant information
   ○ How will the young person be helped to do this?
   ○ Who could assist?
• What format should the information be presented in?
   ○ photos, pictures, videos
   ○ objects of reference
   ○ easy written materials
   ○ audio
   ○ via signing
   ○ by experiencing the options
	As Jill has agreed to her parents helping her, Ms Roberts suggests that Jill, her parents and Ms Roberts meet to help Jill work out what she is looking for in her next placement. The meeting identifies that Jill wants to develop her independent living skills in preparation for moving to her own flat, and that she would like options and associated work experience placements in animal care. The meeting also highlighted that Jill thinks she needs to get used to sleeping somewhere without her parents or other family members. She has been to respite carers during the daytime, but has never slept anywhere without a family member. Jill thinks she would only want to sleep away from home for two nights a week.
	
	Jill wants to visit the colleges and social care provision and has agreed her parents can accompany her. She would like her parents to help her ask questions and take photos. Jill, with Ms Roberts's support, has asked each college and Cottage Road House if she can
	
	• take photos of key areas and, for Isidore College and Cottage Road House, a bedroom, to help remind her
	• meet the course leaders and, with their agreement, record this talk on her iPad.
		Relevant information is information specific to the particular choice. For example, if the decision is choosing an education institution, then the relevant information will be about the establishments under consideration. Presenting the information in the most accessible format for the young person is very important to support, develop and enable their decision-making ability. It may be appropriate to consider involving the young person's parents. However, bear in mind, if the young person is aged over 18 years, that their consent will be needed to involve their parents. A young person aged over 18 years can choose whoever they wish to support them, if they have the capacity to make this decision. Education institution staff will need to ascertain who the young person aged over 18 years wishes to help them.

(Continued)

Appendix 1

(Continued)

Teaching, supporting and enabling decision-making is an interactive process based on knowing how to communicate with the young person and understanding their communication.		
Framework	**Decision-making process**	**Explanatory notes**
	With Ms Roberts's assistance Jill has made a pictorial checklist of the five most important things she wants to know about each establishment. This covers helping her to • learn to cook simple meals • shop for food and other household items • learn about animal care • travel independently • know where you eat lunch Each college also has an electronic pictorial prospectus to show the activities on offer, which Jill has downloaded onto her iPad. Cottage Road House website shows the activities on offer. Additionally, Ms Roberts has helped her select a way of referring to each college; she has chosen the word 'sail' and a picture of white sails for White Sails. Tansy Park is represented by the word 'park' and a picture of a flower. For Isidore Specialist College Jill says 'izzy' and has chosen a picture of a bee like the one on the college logo. Jill refers to Cottage Road House as 'house' with the photo of the house used on its website. Ms Roberts will pass this information to all the education institution staff and associated professionals who work with Jill. Ms Roberts asks Jill's permission to share this information with her parents, to which she agrees.	

Appendix 1

Framework	Decision-making process	Explanatory notes
	It is essential that everyone supporting Jill in making this decision is using the same language and pictures when talking with her to refer to the options. Ms Roberts has also suggested to Jill's parents that they note Jill's reactions during each visit.	
⚖ 3. **Using and weighing the information** ☺ ☹ 💡 • The young person needs to be helped to show what they like or dislike or the advantages or disadvantages of the options.	Following the visits Jill has talked with her parents at home and Ms Roberts in school about what she liked and disliked about each establishment. Both have used the photographs and videos that were taken during the visits to help Jill remember, as well as smiley and sad face cards. Both her parents and Ms Roberts have kept records of her likes and dislikes, and these are consistent. **Isidore Specialist College** Liked – animal care option, cooking her own lunch Disliked – the student bedroom, car journey because it took a long time. **Tansy Park FE College** Liked – everything. Teachers are nice, can do animal care and learn to cook her own lunch. Canteen was nice serving food she likes. Disliked – thought it took a long time to get there.	This is about analysing the pros and cons of the choice, the things the young person likes or dislikes about the options. For many young people with SEN, this is probably best done visually such as putting pictures or symbols under a smiley or sad face emoji or variations on this, perhaps using technology. It is important to keep a record so the young person can revisit their thoughts. Keeping these as a paper file or electronically may be helpful as a record of the young person's decision-making ability, and the extent to which they participated in the decision-making process.

(Continued)

Appendix 1

(Continued)

Framework	Decision-making process	Explanatory notes
• Having set out what the young person likes and dislikes about the options, they use this information to make their choice.	**White Sails FE College** Liked – she knows everyone and has friends there. She can learn to cook her own lunch and do animal care. She will be helped to travel independently. Disliked – Jill could not think of anything she disliked or that she would change. **Cottage Road House** Liked – Jill would be able to cook her own lunch every time she attended. The staff take you shopping for the ingredients. It is close to home and she may be able to learn to travel there by herself. Disliked – Jill was less certain about the residential accommodation. She is not very sure about sleeping away from home. Mrs Scott, course leader at Cottage Road House, explained that Jill did not have to sleep at the House if she did not want to and talked to her about perhaps just visiting the residential accommodation for tea a few times. Jill has indicated to both her parents and Ms Roberts her choice. As agreed, Ms Roberts, Jill and her parents meet together for Jill to make her choice. Jill chooses White Sails FE College and Cottage Road House, provided she did not have to sleep there. She thought going for tea would be alright.	The young person now looks at how they have rated each choice in terms of likes/dislikes, positives/negatives or advantages/disadvantages, and uses the information to make a choice based on this consideration. This may be challenging for some young people. Generally, if there are more things under 'like' it would be expected this would be the young person's choice. If the more liked option is chosen it suggests the young person has understood the decision-making process for this particular choice. If they choose the option with the more 'dislikes', this may indicate they have not understood the process for this particular decision. However, good practice would suggest trying again on another day.

Appendix 1

Teaching, supporting and enabling decision-making is an interactive process based on knowing how to communicate with the young person and understanding their communication.		
Framework	**Decision-making process**	**Explanatory notes**
4. **Communicate the decision** The young person can use any verbal or non-verbal means of communication to indicate their choice.	Jill has agreed it is best if her parents help her complete the college and Cottage Road House application form and all the paperwork for the local authority to let them know her decision.	The young person can communicate their choice in any way they choose, verbally or non-verbally. It is essential the person working with the young person knows their preferred means of communication and can understand this. Equally important is that everyone supporting young people to enable their decision-making knows how to communicate with them.

Appendix 2

CHILD OR YOUNG PERSON COMPLETED DECISION-MAKING FORM

A blank version of this form is available as an eResource.

Name: Marvin Dent Date started: 28 September 2018 Who has supported me with the decision-making process? Mrs Joseph and my parents	Decision-making process
⚑ What is the actual decision that needs to be made?	I need to choose my secondary school placement.
? Why do I have to make this decision?	I am in Year 6 – the last year of primary school.
✳ What happens if I do not make this decision?	The local authority will make me go to Trillian Academy, my parents may also decide I must go to Trillian Academy.
📅 When do I have to make this decision?	School choice form has to be sent to the local authority by 30 November 2018.
ℹ️ Information about the choices • What are the choices? A⬤ B⬤ C⬤	Clipper High, but this would be part-time. I have to have another placement, the Willow Centre or home education. Trillian Academy, this would be full-time, but it is a long way from my home.
ℹ️ What information do I need?	There are some things that are very important such as disabled toilet, a hoist, a place to do physiotherapy, a lift to get me to the upper floors. I want to know about the dining room, what food is offered, if I will have just one TA or more than one. Who will help me with going to the toilet? I am going to make a checklist of everything I want to know about.

Appendix 2

Name: Marvin Dent Date started: 28 September 2018 **Who has supported me with the decision-making process?** Mrs Joseph and my parents	Decision-making process
How will I get this information? visit places take part in activities take photos, videos talk to people record people talking to you about the choices read information use the internet to find information	Visit all three schools, Clipper High, Trillian Academy and The Willow Centre with my parents. Take photos of key areas. Talk to the SENCo. Talk to other pupils if possible. Take a video around the schools if they will allow me. Look at the school prospectus online.
Who can help me get the information? family members friends people in school/college	I want my parents to take me to visit the schools. I hope my parents will take photos and make any notes as well. I hope they will video me in the school. I hope Mrs Joseph will help me make a checklist. I hope the SENCo in each school will answer my questions.
What I like and do not like about each choice A⦿ B⦿ C⦿ ☺ ☹ 💡	This will be shown on the checklist.
💡 Which choice do I like better? A⦿✓ B⦿✗ C⦿✗ **Which choice am I going to choose?** A⦿ B⦿ C⦿ ?	13 smileys for Clipper High 13 smileys for Trillian 9 smileys for The Willow Centre
Who do I need to tell my decision? family members people in school/college local authority SEN officer social care **What is my decision?** A⦿ B⦿ C⦿ ?	I need to tell my parents what I have decided as they have to fill in the school choice form. I want to go to Clipper High and The Willow Centre. I want to be with my friends for at least part of the week. I did not like Trillian Academy.
Date completed: **15 November 2018**	

Appendix 2

Educational placement checklist

Child/young person's name: Marvin Dent

Who has supported Marvin? Mrs Joseph

	Clipper High	Trillian Academy	The Willow Centre
Disabled toilet	☺	☺	☺
Ceiling hoist	☹	☺	☺
Mobile hoist	☺ OT will lend		
Who will help me in the toilet?	☺ 1 male, 1 female TA	☹ 2 female TAs	☹ 2 female TAs
Place to do physio	☹ school will try to find a space, but it will be somewhere different each day	☺	☺
Lift	☹	☺	one-level building
Dining room	☺	☹ accessible but very busy	☹ there isn't one, pupils all bring packed lunches or have a packed lunch provided
Food on offer	☺	☹ no burgers, chips once a week ☺	
Can I sit with friends?	☺		
Same TA in lessons	☹ TAs are subject based	☹ TAs are subject based	☺ TA is also keyworker
Different TA in each lesson	☹	☹	
SEND room to go to at lunchtime	☹ it is on the first floor	☺	☺ social area for all the pupils
Can I access the science lab?	☹	☺	☹ there are no specialist rooms
ICT room?	☹	☺	
technology room?	☹	☺	
Can I use my laptop in lessons?	☺	☺	☺
How many times a week is there homework?	☺ In Year 7 twice a week	☹ In Year 7, 4 times a week	☹ 1-4 times a week
Is it a one week or two week timetable?	☺ 1 week	☹ two week	☺ individual timetable

Appendix 2

	Clipper High	**Trillian Academy**	**The Willow Centre**
Is there room for my wheelchair in the classroom?	☺ ground floor classrooms are the biggest, tend to be used for lower sets	☺	☺
How many pupils in a class?	☺ 15–18 in lower sets 20–25 other classes	☺ 12–15 lower sets, 20–30 other classes	☺ 1–5
Can I learn French?	☺	☹ German and Spanish	☹ no modern foreign languages taught
Will I be able to join school trips?	☺	☺	☹ no school trips

Appendix 3

STATUTORY 'BEST INTERESTS' CHECKLIST AND COMPLETED 'BEST INTERESTS' BALANCE SHEET

Blank versions of these sheets are available as eResources.

Zsofia's post 18 placement 'best interests' balance sheet completed by her parents

The statutory 'best interests' checklist is set out in the MCA COP, Chapter 5. A person trying to work out the best interests of a person who lacks capacity to make a particular decision ('lacks capacity') should:

MCA 'best interests' checklist	Notes
Encourage participation Do whatever is possible to permit and encourage the person to take part, or to improve their ability to take part, in making the decision.	Zsofia will be taken to visit the chosen placements, her reactions will be observed and considered by her parents to make the decision.
Identify all relevant circumstances Try to identify all the things that the person who lacks capacity would take into account if they were making the decision or acting for themselves.	Zsofia likes quiet places that are not crowded. She enjoys visiting her current college as the department is in a separate building from the main college. There are usually no more than 8 students in a group.
Find out the person's views • Try to find out the views of the person who lacks capacity, including: • the person's past and present wishes and feelings – these may have been expressed verbally, in writing or through behaviour or habits.	Zsofia likes cooking, art and craft, horse riding, going out in the community and animals. Zsofia does not like swimming, gym-type activities, sports centres and horticulture. Zsofia seems to like her weekly visit to White Crest FE College.

Appendix 3

MCA 'best interests' checklist	Notes
• any beliefs and values (e.g. religious, cultural, moral or political) that would be likely to influence the decision in question. • any other factors the person themselves would be likely to consider if they were making the decision or acting for themselves.	As parents we know Zsofia: • does not always like meeting new people, her reactions can be unpredictable • likes being among young people, preferring to go to school rather than be at home as she is during school holidays • likes quiet calm places • does not like crowded or noisy places. As her parents, we think her dislike of gym-type places and swimming pools is the noise levels. She has never enjoyed going to the pantomime at the local theatre, we have stopped taking her. She watches recorded televised pantomimes which she enjoys as she can control the sound level on the television.
Avoid discrimination Not to make assumptions about someone's best interests simply on the basis of the person's age, appearance, condition or behaviour.	
Assess whether the person might regain capacity Consider whether the person is likely to regain capacity (e.g. after receiving medical treatment). If so, can the decision wait until then?	Zsofia does not understand that she has to leave her current school and needs to choose a new placement. She will not be able to learn to do this in the time-frame.
Avoid restricting the person's rights See if there are other options that may be less restrictive of the person's rights. *This must be considered if residential placements are being proposed and from 1 October 2020 some day placements and transport arrangements in line with the provisions of the Mental Capacity (Amendment) Act 2019*	
Consult others • If it is practical and appropriate to do so, consult other people for their views about the person's best interests and to see if they have any information about the person's wishes and feelings, beliefs and values. In particular, try to consult:	Need to talk with: Mrs Roman, current teacher Mr Kovacs & Ms Charles, teaching assistants who go with her to White Crest FE College Mrs Leonard & Mr Simon, White Crest FE College staff

(*Continued*)

Appendix 3

(Continued)

MCA 'best interests' checklist	Notes
<ul><li>anyone previously named by the person as someone to be consulted on either the decision in question or on similar issues</li><li>anyone engaged in caring for the person</li></ul>*This includes education institution staff, specialist teachers, educational psychologists.*<ul><li>close relatives, friends or others who take an interest in the person's welfare</li><li>any attorney appointed under a Lasting Power of Attorney or Enduring Power of Attorney made by the person</li><li>any deputy appointed by the Court of Protection to make decisions for the person.</li></ul>When consulting, remember that the person who lacks the capacity to make the decision or act for themselves still has a right to keep their affairs private. When the Mental Capacity (Amendment) Act 2019 comes into force on 1 October 2020, it will be mandatory to consult with the young person about arrangements that may constitute a deprivation of their liberty.	
Take all of this into account Weigh up all of these factors in order to work out what is in the person's best interests.	Considering Zsofia's reactions, the curriculum offered and the environment at Portside Road FE College indicated Zsofia would probably not choose this college. She was very relaxed at Blue Wave House, she responded well to the staff there. There is a consensus from school and college staff and Zsofia's own reactions suggesting she likes White Crest FE College. Zsofia's parents know that she prefers to be at school than at home. Therefore, taking everything into account, it is probable that Zsofia would choose White Crest FE College, 3 days, and Blue Wave House, 2 days, and want to attend Blue Wave House in college holidays.

Appendix 3

MCA Code of Practice 'best interests' balance sheet

Young person's name: Zsofia Rudolf

Name of person (s) filling in the balance sheet: Mr & Mrs Rudolf (Zsofia's parents)

Option 1: White Crest FE College – 3 days per week

✓☺ What does Zsofia like about this choice?	X ☹ What does Zsofia not like about this choice?
Zsofia has already been attending one day a week, she knows the staff and students and looks forward to her weekly visit. The department is sited in a separate building from the main college, it is quiet, she does not have to walk through the main college building's crowded corridors to access her classroom.	
Zsofia likes Mrs Leonard and Mr Simon, college staff.	*Mr Simon may not be with Zsofia's group in September, Zsofia may have to get to know a new member of staff. She does not always like meeting new people, her reactions can be unpredictable. Also, she would no longer be supported by school staff who know her very well.*
Zsofia likes most of the activities she does at college. The life skills course would include many of these activities, including weekly visits to the local community.	*The college does not go horse riding, she would have to go to the sports centre or college gym once a week.*

Option 2: Portside Road FE College, Newtown – 3 days per week

✓☺ What does Zsofia like about this choice?	X ☹ What does Zsofia not like about this choice?
	The department is sited in the main college building. Zsofia showed her dislike of having to walk through the busy reception area to get to the classroom. Overall, the environment was too noisy for her.
Zsofia responded positively to the staff when they were talking with her and showing her round.	*However, despite her positive response to the staff they were unsuccessful in encouraging her to join in with any of the physical or musical*

(*Continued*)

Appendix 3

(Continued)

✓☺ What does Zsofia like about this choice?	X ☹ What does Zsofia not like about this choice?
	activities. Despite liking cooking activities, she would not join in the cookery session even though both her parents and college staff encouraged her.
The college follows a life skills style curriculum, including arts and crafts, mainly making products to sell, and cooking. There are weekly trips into the local community. Zsofia would be able to go horse riding weekly.	There is an emphasis on physical activity with sessions in the college gym or a local sports centre for all students, including a weekly swimming session for her group in the autumn term. There would be a weekly music session for all the students. Zsofia was reluctant to enter the gym area as it was too noisy for her.

Option 3: Blue Wave House, social care provision – 1–3 days per week

✓☺ What does Zsofia like about this choice?	X ☹ What does Zsofia not like about this choice?
It is housed in a purpose-built modern building with good disabled access. Spacious, calm and fairly quiet environment. In any room there are not usually more than eight young people. Zsofia can attend this provision all year, it is only closed on Bank Holidays and for just over a week at Christmas and New Year.	
Zsofia responded very positively to the staff, she willingly went with a support assistant to the kitchen to make a snack and left her parents talking with Mrs Sandy, course leader.	During the visit Zsofia only met a few staff, at this juncture it was uncertain who would be her key worker.
There is a focus on cooking, shopping for ingredients and trips into the local community, including going to cafés, as well as some arts and crafts activities. As the curriculum has some potential to be tailored, riding for the disabled and regular visits to the city farm could be included.	.

Appendix 4

SEND CODE OF PRACTICE PREPARATION FOR ADULTHOOD OUTCOMES

SEND COP paragraphs 1.39, 7.38 & 8.10

This Appendix summarises the key points about the preparation for adulthood outcomes. Education and associated professionals are reminded of the need to read the relevant sections of the SEND COP. The long-term outcomes for preparing for adulthood relate to support for:

- Preparation for higher education and/or employment, including identifying appropriate post 16 pathways. Training options should be discussed such as supported internships, apprenticeships and traineeships. This also includes addressing support to find a job, learning how to do a job such as work experience and help understanding any available in-work welfare benefits.

- Preparation for independent living, including exploring what decisions young people wish to take for themselves and planning their role in decision-making. Discussions should also include where the young person wishes to live in the future and what support they will need. Local housing options, support in finding accommodation, housing benefits and social care support should be explained.

- Support in maintaining good health in adult life, including help to understand which health professionals will work with them as adults. Planned transitions to adult services.

- Support in participating in society, including understanding mobility and transport support, and how to find out about social and community activities and opportunities for engagement in local decision-making. This also includes support for developing and maintaining friendships and relationships.

Appendix 4

Preparation for Adulthood (PfA), a DfE-funded programme delivered by the National Development Team for Inclusion (NDTi) as part of the Better Outcomes Together Consortium, refers to these outcomes as Employment, Independent Living, Friends, Relationships and Community, and Good Health. More information is available from: www.preparingforadulthood.org.uk/, accessed 28 March 2019.

Appendix 5

GUIDELINES FOR UNDERTAKING OBSERVATIONS

A brief introduction to undertaking observations is presented here, Robson and McCartan (2016) provide a more detailed discussion.

When making video recordings of children and young people, it would be helpful if education institutions have guidelines covering all aspects of this, including seeking the child's or young person's and/or parents' permission, the devices that can be used and secure storage of the recordings. Education and associated professionals will need to know the relevant aspects of data protection legislation to ensure the child's or young person's privacy is protected.

Guidelines for undertaking observations

- What is the aim of the observation? That is, what it is you wish to find out about the child's or young person's development or behaviour. In relation to decision-making, it may be their reactions to activities, experiences, the options being considered, or how they are progressing in their decision-making ability such as making a choice between two food items.

- What you are trying to find out will determine the type of observation you will need to undertake. There are several different types of observation, one or more may be more suited than others for a particular aim.

- It is important to remember that as the observer you have a limited time for which you can concentrate to continuously observe; usually 30 minutes is considered to be the longest time an adult can reliably continuously observe.

- Make sure you have sufficient paper and a pen (probably a spare one as well) with you at the time of the observation. Using an observation recording format/checklist, such as Table 5.3 (Chapter five), may assist in ensuring you record all the necessary information, thereby constructing a consistent observation process within the education institution, enabling a comparison of observations over time to assist in establishing behavioural patterns.

- Always note the date, time and location of the observation, such as the classroom, cookery room, in the park, or canteen. Likewise record where the child or young person is in relation to others and who else is present. All this information should be noted even when

Appendix 5

some of the observation is being undertaken by videoing. It may be helpful to draw a plan of the area where the child or young person is for the duration of the observation.

- If it is appropriate, and you have permission from the child or young person and/or their parent to do so, videoing may be helpful. Recordings must not be made on your own personal devices. Be very careful about recording other children or young people if you do not have permission to do so. Recordings must be securely stored, for example on the education institution intranet or cloud.

Types of observation

A. **Observation codes:** sometimes it is helpful to devise a code to help you write quickly when observing, as writing and observing can be quite difficult, and you may miss an important event because you are writing. Consider devising an agreed code, such as for behaviours, actions and locations, within your education institution, as this will make it easy for you each to understand others' observation records. The table below is presented as an example; it is strongly advised that an education institution develops its own code that makes sense to its staff.

Facial expression (e)	smile	es
	frown	ef
Language and communication (u)	laugh	ul
	cry	uc
	shout	us
	talk	ut
Big movements (gross) (m)	walk	mw
	run	mr
	climb	mcl
	crawl	mcr
Fine movements (f)	draws	fd
	writes	fw
	cuts with scissors	fsc
	cuts with knife	fkc
Actions (act)	paints	actp
	looking at books	actb
	home corner	acthc

Appendix 5

B. **Event recording**: this type of observation can be used when looking at social, emotional and behavioural reactions. It is a written narrative recorded, in chronological order, as the events happen. You write down everything the child or young person does and/or says in a given time period. If part of the observation is being videoed, it is advisable to still note what the child or young person says as this may not always be recorded clearly, particularly for children and young people with speech, language and communication difficulties.

C. **Time sampling:** this is best suited to finding out what a child or young person does at break times, or how they work in lessons. It can also look at social relationships, that is, how long the child or young person sustains interactions and with whom. You watch the child or young person at specific time intervals and note what they are doing and/or saying at that time and with whom. How often you observe depends on the aim of your observation. If you are trying to find out how the child or young person spends their time, e.g. at break times, you may choose to observe every 5 minutes for the whole of the session. In class you may observe every 5 minutes over the course of an hour to see how they are spending their time and with whom. Often this type of observation is used to compare the behaviour of the target child or young person with others in the group. It may be helpful to have an observation schedule with a code such as the example below, which will facilitate consistency within the education institution and enable comparisons over time that may establish behavioural patterns.

Time sampling observation schedule

Name   Activity   Location

Date   Time started observation   Time ended observation

Observer's name

Staff present

Time period being sampled (e.g. every 5 minutes)

Notes, e.g. noise level, light, temperature, fire alarm, weather (windy, thunder, bright sunshine)

minutes	5	10	15	20	25	30	35	40	45	50	55	1 hour
target cyp[1]												
cyp 1												
cyp 2												
cyp 3												
teacher												
other staff												

Code

cyp		
✓ on task	it interacting with teacher	pa playing alongside peer
X off task	ios interacting with other staff	comp using computer
ip interacting with peer	pp playing with peer	z observer distracted

Teacher/other staff		
ii working individually with a cyp	mm managing materials	comp using computer
ig working with a small group	or out of the room	tt talking with staff
ic working with the whole class	hsc helping with self-care	z observer distracted

1 cyp is the short way of writing 'child or young person'.

D. **Checklist:** you will need a predetermined checklist of skills to see if the child or young person has acquired the skill. To observe some skills, you may have to set up an activity to ensure you see the targeted skill; others can be observed at the natural time. For example, if you wish to see if the child or young person can choose a drink or snack at break time, this can be observed at break time. If you observe the skill, tick it on the checklist, remember to include the date and your initials so that on another occasion it can be seen what was observed when and by whom. Dating observations enables patterns of behaviour to be established over time. Good practice would be to repeat the same observation a week later to establish this is a secure skill.

Completed observation recording format/checklist

Name of pupil/student: **Victorine Moore**	Name of person making the observations: **Ms Anita Selby**
Date: **3 May 2019** Time: **1.30pm – 2pm** Location: **Year 12 classroom & ball pool**	Who else was present? Staff: **Mr Green, Mrs Gill & Ms White (classroom)** **Ms White (ball pool)** Pupils/students: **Alice, Ezra, Tom (classroom)** **Alice (ball pool)** Visitors: n/a
Activity or experience: **Choosing the Friday afternoon choice and the chosen activity**	
Communication: note how - *you communicated with the pupil/student, e.g. verbally alone, verbal supported with signing, use of objects of reference, symbols, pictures, photos* - *the pupil/student communicated with you*	
Verbal communication – words 'ball pool', 'sensory room', 'choose' + Makaton signs + ball pool, sensory room objects of reference	
Victorine communicated her choice by reaching with her left hand for the ball pool object of reference in my right hand, accompanied with a grunt. When I swapped it to my left hand, again she chose the ball pool object of reference.	

Appendix 5

Pupil/student response
Include comments related to:
verbal – record the words used by the pupil or student
non-verbal behaviour – record facial expressions, body movements, vocalisations, signing, or symbols, behaviour, length of time engaged in the activity, behaviours indicating a wish for the activity to continue or to stop
Victorine responded to being asked which activity she wanted to do by reaching for the ball pool object of reference. The question was repeated with the ball pool object of reference swapped to my left hand. Victorine again reached for the ball pool object of reference, which she was given and it was explained this was where we were now going.
When I opened the door and she saw the ball pool she gurgled – her happy sound. She became quite active, suggesting she wanted to be put in the ball pool. I had to wait for Ms White as it takes two of us to transfer Victorine from her wheelchair to the hoist. When in the ball pool she gurgled and made a 'ppp' noise – also known to indicate she is happy. After 15 minutes she began to groan – the sound she makes when she has had enough of whatever she is doing. Ms White and I took her out of the ball pool, transferring her back to her wheelchair. I took her back to the classroom where she chose a drink; she was not making any vocalisations suggesting she was unhappy about the ball pool session ending.

Appendix 6

SAMPLE 'MY ACTIVITY PASSPORT'

My Activity Passport

Name:

Date started:

	Activity: In the home	✓	Date	☺☹☹
1	Build a den			
2	Taste a new fruit			
3	Taste a new vegetable			
4	Touch something with a rough texture			
5	Dress up like a favourite character			
6	Make a sandwich			
7	Take a photograph			
8	Make a paper boat and see if it floats in the bath or sink			
9	Play a simple board or card game			
10	Listen to a different type of music from the sort you usually do			

Appendix 6

My Activity Passport

Name:

Date started:

	Activity: Outside the house (this could be in the garden or on a balcony or further afield)	✓	Date	☺☺☹
1	Watch the sun set			
2	Visit a city farm or farm			
3	Go on local public transport (bus, tram, train)			
4	Go out in the rain and feel the rain on your hand			
5	Feel the warmth of the sun on your hand			
6	Feel snow and make a snowman/snowball			
7	Roll or ride down a hill			
8	Stay away from home for a night			
9	Look at the moon and stars at night			
10	Look for butterflies/ladybirds			

Appendix 7

MECHANICS OF THE TALKING MATS STYLE APPROACH

The mat

The mat is a piece of plain material, such as felt or some other slightly textured material, probably at least the size of two A4 pieces of paper. The colour should be chosen to ensure there is a good contrast between the material and the pictures so these can be easily distinguished from the 'mat'. How big the mat needs to be will be dependent on the size the pictures need to be so that they can be easily seen by the child or young person, ensuring all can be accommodated. The minimum dimensions given enable the photographs or symbols to be a reasonable size to facilitate them being easily seen. For children or young people with visual impairments, it is advisable to seek advice from the VI specialist supporting them as to the size and/or nature of the visual image.

The pictures

As noted above, consideration needs to be given to the visual images to be used with children and young people with visual impairments. However, careful thought should be given to any visual image being used for any child or young person. Throughout the book the child's or young person's participation in the decision-making process has been emphasised, therefore education and associated professionals may need to be creative about the visual representations being employed to facilitate this. If a child or young person is unable to understand photos or other pictorial representations, then real objects should be considered such as known objects of reference. For example, if a young person has visited a post 16 establishment that provides for cooking lunch, using the known object of reference for cooking could be used to ascertain the child or young person's views about this activity in the new provision. When using real objects, perhaps the 'mat' will also need to be rethought. Maybe the mat is now a table covered with a piece of material.

Appendix 7

How many pictures?

For some children and young people, the number of items being considered will be linked to their personal checklist of things they wished to find out during their visits to each establishment. For instance, returning to the case study 'Jill chooses her post 18 placement' (Chapter four and Appendix 1D), she had items on her checklist that she wished to find out about; it is these things that she expresses her opinions about as illustrated in Figure 7.1 below.

The method

Ideally, the child or young person will place the visual symbols and/or photographs onto the mat to indicate how they feel about the particular activity. However, when working with children and young people with physical disabilities it may be necessary for whoever is undertaking this activity to place the pictures on the child or young person's behalf. It is also possible to undertake this process using digital technology. Nevertheless, the author favours this approach in the real world, if this is appropriate for the child or young person.

The process

- At the top of the mat put the photo or symbol representing the important decision, for example if this relates to choosing a new education institution then a photo or symbol representing the education institution under discussion will be placed at the top. Returning to the case study 'Jill chooses her post 18 placement' (Chapter four and Appendix 1D), Jill was considering White Sails FE College, Tansy Park FE College, Isidore Specialist College and Cottage Road House. The symbol she has chosen for each college is the symbol that will be placed at the top of the mat when discussing that college (see the example below).

- The mat is divided into two columns, the 'like' (e.g. smiley face, thumbs up) symbol at the top of one and 'dislike' (e.g. sad face, thumbs down) at the top of the other.

- The child or young person is able to put the photos or symbols under their chosen representation for like (e.g. smiley face, thumbs up) or dislike (sad face, thumbs down) to express their views and feelings.

- When the young person has finished expressing their views for this choice, it is photographed as a record and this can be presented in formal documents as such. The photographs can be appended to a child or young person's decision-making framework. When the young person is making a decision, they should be shown the photos of all of their mats to remind them of what they thought.

Appendix 7

Additionally, the mat is an indication of the child or young person's participation in the decision-making process.

Figure A7.1 Jill's 'mat' for Isidore Specialist College

GLOSSARY

ABA   Applied Behavioural Analysis, a behavioural approach used to support children and young people with autism to fulfil their potential (National Autistic Society, www.autism.org.uk/get-involved/media-centre/position-statements/interventions.aspx, accessed 28 June 2019).

'Best interests' checklist   This is the 'best interests' checklist in the Mental Capacity Act 2005 Code of Practice, Chapter 5. This checklist should be followed by parents in the event they are making an important decision about a young person's education on behalf of their son or daughter, if they have been deemed to lack the capacity to make the particular decision at the time it is needed.

CAMHS   Child and Adolescent Mental Health Service. In some health authorities it is known as Healthy Young Minds.

Child   In education, a child refers to a person aged 0–16 years who has not completed compulsory education. In general law, a child is a person aged 0–17 years 11 months.

Children and Families Act 2014   The law that covers educational provision for children and young people in England with special educational needs and disabilities.

Code of Practice (COP)   A Code of Practice is the guidance the government publishes about how a particular law should work on a day-to-day basis. A Code of Practice explains in more detail what the law means and gives practical steps. People in certain roles or jobs have to follow a particular Code of Practice. These roles or jobs are set out in the Code of Practice.

Compulsory school age   The beginning of the term following a child's 5th birthday until the last Friday in June in the school year in which the young person becomes 16 (England and Wales). In Northern Ireland, young people with 16th birthdays between 1 September and 1 July, can leave school on 30 June that year. If their 16th birthday falls between 2 July and 31 August, they cannot leave school until 30 June the following year.

Education, Health and Care Plan (EHC Plan)   An EHC Plan details the education, health and social care support that is to be provided to meet a child's or young person's SEN or a disability. It is drawn up by the local authority after an EHC needs assessment has determined that an EHC Plan is necessary. In Wales, from September 2020, this will be known as an Individual Development Plan (IDP), and in Northern Ireland, from 2020, the equivalent is a statement of special educational needs.

Emoji   A digital image in electronic communication used to express a particular idea or feeling. Emojipedia, https://emojipedia.org/, is the emoji reference website documenting the meaning and common usage of emoji characters. In Microsoft programs (e.g. Word) the Segoe UI Emoji font has representations of many common emojis.

Emoticon   An image made up of symbols such as punctuation marks, used in text messages or emails, which expresses a particular emotion, e.g. :) means happy.

EP   Educational psychologist

Glossary

FE Further Education college. A college offering continuing education to young people over the compulsory school age of 16. The FE sector in England includes general FE colleges, sixth form colleges, specialist colleges and adult education institutes.

Gillick Competency 'Whether or not a child is capable of giving the necessary consent will depend on the child's maturity and understanding and the nature of the consent required. The child must be capable of making a reasonable assessment of the advantages and disadvantages of the treatment proposed, so the consent, if given, can be properly and fairly described as true consent' (Gillick v West Norfolk, 1985).

Habilitation or Mobility Officer Trained specialists who teach children and young people with a visual impairment to move independently as well as develop other independence skills. Further information is available from rnib.org.uk/insight-online/how-habilitation-specialists-can-help, accessed 29 August 2019.

LA Local authority

Local Offer Local authorities in England are required to set out provision they expect to be available across education, health and social care for children and young people in their area who have SEN or disabilities, including those who do not have EHC Plans (see SEND COP Chapter 4). The Local Offer can be found on the local authority's website; the best way to access it is by putting the local authority name plus 'local offer' in a search engine, e.g. Camden council local offer.

Makaton Makaton is a sign language programme, based on British Sign Language (BSL) signs, designed for people with learning difficulties. Signs are accompanied with speech; the signs are presented in the order the words are spoken. www.makaton.org.

MCA (Mental Capacity Act 2005) This law is about people making decisions for themselves. The law assumes everyone can make their own decisions until it is proved they are not able to do so. It provides a statutory framework for people who lack capacity to make decisions for themselves. It sets out how decisions should be taken on behalf of someone who lacks capacity to make the decision.

MCA COP Mental Capacity Act 2005 Code of Practice, available to download free from www.gov.uk/government/publications/mental-capacity-act-code-of-practice, accessed 7 August 2019.

Object of reference Any object which is used consistently and systematically to represent an item, person, place or activity. For example, using a toilet roll to represent 'toilet' or knife and fork to mean 'lunch'. It is helpful if the object has multi-sensory properties so that it can be experienced in different ways, for example being seen, but also having a smell or particular texture, or sound.

OT Occupational therapist

Parent Any person who is the child or young person's parent or has parental responsibility or cares for the child or young person.

Portage Home Visitor Portage is a structured home teaching programme for pre-school children with SEN and their families. More information is available from www.portage.org.uk/about/what-portage, accessed 31 July 2019.

SEMH Social, emotional and mental health

SEN Special educational needs

Glossary

SENCo Special educational needs coordinator

SEND COP *Special educational needs and disability code of practice: 0–25 years.* Available to download free from www.gov.uk/government/publications/send-code-of-practice-0-to-25, accessed 7 August 2019.

SLT Speech and language therapist

Strengths and Difficulties Questionnaire (SDQ) This is a brief behavioural screening questionnaire for teachers, parents and clinicians for children and young people aged 3–16 years. There is a self-report questionnaire for children aged 11–16 years. There is further information and free to download questionnaires at www.sdqinfo.com, accessed 7 August 2019.

TA Teaching assistant

Young person Someone aged 16–25 years old. However, the definition in the SEND COP is someone who has reached the end of Year 11 and is is aged between 16 and 25 years.

REFERENCES

Aldabas, R. (2019) 'Effectiveness of peer-mediated interventions (PMI) in children with autistic spectrum disorders (ASD): a systematic review.' *Early Child Development and Care*, published online, available from: www.tandfonline.com/doi/full/10.1080/03004430.2019.1580275, accessed 22 March 2019.

Atkinson, C., Dunsmuir, S., Lang, J. and Wright, S. (2015) 'Developing a competency framework for the initial training of educational psychologists working with young people aged 16–25.' *Educational Psychology in Practice 31*, 2, 159–173.

Belsky, J. and de Haan, M. (2011) 'Annual research review: parenting and children's brain development: the end of the beginning.' *Journal of Child Psychology and Psychiatry 52*, 4, 409–428.

Beresford, B. and Sloper, P. (2008) 'Understanding the dynamics of decision-making and choice: a scoping study of key psychological theories to inform design and analysis of the Panel Study.' York: SPRU, University of York.

Bolton, N. (1990) in Jones, N. and Frederickson, N. (eds) *Refocusing Educational Psychology*. London: The Falmer Press.

British Psychological Society (2018) *Safeguarding Children and Young People: Every Psychologist's Responsibility*. Leicester: British Psychological Society.

Cannella, H.I., O'Reilly, M.F. and Lancioni, G.E. (2005) 'Choice and preference assessment research with people with severe and profound developmental disabilities: a review of the literature.' *Research in Developmental Disabilities 26*, 1–15.

CentreForum (2016) *CentreForum Commission on Children and Young People's Mental Health: State of the Nation*. Available from: https://epi.org.uk/wp-content/uploads/2018/01/State-of-the-Nation-report-web.pdf, accessed 20 April 2018.

Children's Commissioner (2017) *Briefing: Children's Mental Healthcare in England*. Available from: www.childrenscommissioner.gov.uk/wp-content/uploads/2017/10/Childrens-Commissioner-for-England-Mental-Health-Briefing-1.1.pdf, accessed 20 April 2018.

Conway, S. and Meyer, D. (2008) 'Developing support for siblings of young people with disabilities.' *Support for Learning 23*, 3, 113–117.

Department for Education (2010) *UNCRC: How Legislation Underpins Implementation in England*. Available from: www.gov.uk/government/publications/united-nations-convention-on-the-rights-of-the-child-uncrc-how-legislation-underpins-implementation-in-england, accessed 13 April 2018.

Department for Education (2014) *The Equality Act 2010 and Schools*. Available from: https://assets.publishing.service.gov.uk/government/uploads/system/uploads/attachment_data/file/315587/Equality_Act_Advice_Final.pdf, accessed 2 August 2019.

Department for Education (2015) *Counselling in Schools: Blueprint for the Future*. Available from: www.gov.uk/government/publications/counselling-in-schools, accessed 15 April 2018.

References

Department for Education (2017a) *Supporting Mental Health in Schools and Colleges: Summary Report.* Available from: www.gov.uk/government/publications/supporting-mental-health-in-schools-and-colleges, accessed 15 April 2018.

Department for Education (2017b) *Supporting Mental Health in Schools and Colleges: Case Studies.* Available from: https://assets.publishing.service.gov.uk/government/uploads/system/uploads/attachment_data/file/634728/Supporting_Mental-health_Case_study_report.pdf, accessed 15 April 2018.

Department for Education (2018) *Mental Health and Behaviour in Schools.* Available from: https://assets.publishing.service.gov.uk/government/uploads/system/uploads/attachment_data/file/755135/Mental_health_and_behaviour_in_schools__.pdf, accessed 2 August 2019.

Department for Education & Department of Health (2015) *Special educational needs and disability code of practice: 0–25 years* (January 2015). Available from: www.gov.uk/government/uploads/system/uploads/attachment_data/file/398815/SEND_Code_of_Practice_January_2015.pdf, accessed 1 April 2018.

Department of Health (2015) *Future in Mind.* Available from: https://assets.publishing.service.gov.uk/government/uploads/system/uploads/attachment_data/file/414024/Childrens_Mental_Health.pdf, accessed 15 April 2018.

Elkind, D. (1975) 'Two approaches to intelligence: Piagetian and psychometric', in Sants, J. and Butcher, H.J. (eds) *Developmental Psychology.* Middlesex: Penguin Books Ltd.

Emerson, E. and Hatton, C. (2007) 'Mental health of children and adolescents with intellectual disabilities in Britain.' *British Journal of Psychiatry 191*, 493–499.

Evans, G. (2018) 'Ensuring a safer world for children.' *The Psychologist*, June, 6.

Farrow, C. and Haycraft, E. (2019) 'Do play with your food.' *The Psychologist*, April, 22–25.

Fazel, M., Hoagwood, K., Stephan, S. and Ford, T. (2014) 'Mental health interventions in schools 1.' *Lancet Psychiatry 1*, 377–382.

Fox, M. (1993) *Psychological Perspectives in Education.* London: Cassell.

Gigerenzer, G. and Gaissmaier, W. (2011) 'Heuristic decision making.' *Annual Review of Psychology 62*, 451–482.

Gillick v West Norfolk and Wisbeach Area Health Authority [1985] 3 WLR 830, [1986] 1 AC 112 ('Gillick').

Grootens-Wiegers, P., Hein, I.M., den Broek, J.M. and de Vries, M.C. (2017) 'Medical decision-making in children and adolescents: development and neuroscientific aspects.' *BMC Paediatrics 17*, 1–10.

Hanze, M., Müller, M. and Berger, R. (2018) 'Cross-age peer tutoring: how to promote tutees' active knowledge building.' *Educational Psychology 38*, 7, 915–926.

Harding, E. (2009) 'Obtaining the views of children with profound and multiple learning difficulties.' *Education and Child Psychology 26*, 4, 117–128.

Heyman, I., Fombonne, E., Simmons, H. and Ford, T. (2001) 'Prevalence of obsessive-compulsive disorder in the British nationwide survey of child mental health.' *British Journal of Psychiatry 179*, 4, 324–329.

High Court [2017] EWHC 2729 (Fam) Re S (Child as parent: Adoption: Consent).

Howe, N. and Recchia, H. (2014) 'Sibling relations and their impact on children's development.' *Encyclopaedia on Early Childhood Development/Peer Relations* Available from: www.child-encyclopedia.com/peer-relations/according-experts/sibling-relations-and-their-impact-childrens-development, accessed 22 March 2019.

Ingram, R. (2013) 'Interpretation of children's views by educational psychologists: dilemmas and solutions.' *Educational Psychology in Practice 29*, 4, 335–346.

Jacobs, J.E. and Klaczynski, P.A. (2002) 'The development of judgement and decision making during childhood and adolescence.' *Current Directions in Psychological Science 11*, 4, 145–149.

Johnston, H. (2012) 'The spiral curriculum: research into practice', non-journal article available from ERIC, ERIC Number ED538282, retrieved from: https://files.eric.ed.gov/fulltext/ED538282.pdf, accessed 4 January 2019.

Knightsmith, P. (2019) 'Breaking down barriers.' *The Psychologist*, September, 34–37.

Kostikj-Ivanovikj, V. and Chichevska-Jovanova, N. (2016) 'Relation between quality of life, choice-making and future expectations in adults with intellectual disability.' *Journal of Special Education and Rehabilitation 17(3–4)*, 29–45.

Kurtycz, L.M. (2015) 'Choice and control for animals in captivity.' *The Psychologist 28*, 11, 892–894.

Law Society (2015) *Identifying a Deprivation of Liberty: A Practical Guide.* Available from: www.lawsociety.org.uk/support-services/advice/articles/deprivation-of-liberty/, accessed 8 June 2018.

Levin, I.P., Bossard, E.A., Gareth, G.J. and Yan, H. (2014) 'The combined role of task, child's age and individual differences in understanding decision-making processes.' *Judgement and Decision Making 9*, 3, 274–286.

Mager, R.F. (1972) *Goal Analysis.* Belmont, California: Fearon Publishers Inc.

Marks, S.B. (1998) 'Understanding and preventing learned helplessness in children who are congenitally deaf-blind.' *Journal of Visual Impairment and Blindness 92*, 3.

Mental Capacity Act 2005 Code of Practice. Available from: www.gov.uk/government/uploads/system/uploads/attachment_data/file/224660/Mental_Capacity_Act_code_of_practice.pdf.

Mitchell, W. (2012) 'Parents' accounts: factors considered when deciding how far to involve their son/daughter with learning disabilities in choice-making.' *Children and Youth Services Review 34*, 8, 1560–1569.

Mitchell, W. and Sloper, P. (2011) 'Making choices in my life: listening to the ideas and experiences of young people in the UK who communicate non-verbally.' *Children and Youth Services Review 33*, 4, 521–527. https://doi.org/10.1016/j.childyouth.2010.05.016, accessed 30 November 2017.

Morris, R. and Atkinson, C. (2018) 'The role of educational psychologists in supporting post-16 transition: findings from the literature.' *Educational Psychology in Practice 34*, 2, 131–149.

O'Hara, D. (2011) 'The impact of peer mentoring in pupils' emotional literacy.' *Educational Psychology in Practice 27*, 3, 271–279.

Patalay, P. and Gage, S.H. (2018) 'Trends in millennial adolescent mental health and health related behaviours over ten years: a population cohort comparison study.' Available from: www.researchgate.net/publication/327458032_Trends_in_millennial_adolescent_mental_health_and_health_related_behaviours_over_ten_years_a_population_cohort_comparison_study, accessed 1 March 2019.

References

Pike, A., Kretschmer, T. and Dunn, J.F. (2009) 'Siblings – friends or foes.' *The Psychologist 22*, 6, 494–496.

Public Health England (2016) *The Mental Health of Children and Young People in England.* Available from: https://assets.publishing.service.gov.uk/government/uploads/system/uploads/attachment_data/file/575632/Mental_health_of_children_in_England.pdf, accessed 22 April 2018.

Robson, C. and McCartan, K. (2016) *Real World Research*, 4th edn. Chichester: John Wiley and Sons.

Roffey, S., Hobbs, C. and Kitching, A. (2018) 'Educational psychologists influencing policy and practice: becoming more visible.' *Educational and Child Psychology 35*, 3, 5–7.

Royal College of Psychiatrists (2019) *Briefing: Children and Young People with Mental Health Problems and Access to NHS Treatments.* Available from: www.rcpsych.ac.uk/docs/default-source/improving-care/better-mh-policy/parliamentary/rcpsych-briefing---children-and-young-people-with-mental-health-problems-and-access-to-nhs-treatments---copy.pdf?sfvrsn=2e924943_2, accessed 1 July 2019.

Shenderovich, Y., Thurston, A. and Miller, S. (2016) 'Cross-age tutoring in kindergarten and elementary school settings: a systematic review and meta-analysis.' *International Journal of Educational Research 76*, 190–210.

Sheridan, M.D. (1975) *The Developmental Progress of Infants and Young Children.* London: Her Majesty's Stationery Office.

Sinson, J.L. (2015) *No Decision about My Education without me. A Guide for Parents and Carers Helping Young People (16–25 Years) Make Their Own Decisions about Their Education. Understanding the Mental Capacity Act 2005 and the Mental Capacity Act Code of Practice.* Available from: www.natsip.org.uk/doc-library-login/mental-capcity-act-2005-1/861-01-no-decision-about-my-education-without-me, accessed 26 January 2019.

Sinson, J.L (2016) *Applying the Mental Capacity Act 2005 in Education. A Practical Guide for Education Professionals.* London: Jessica Kingsley Publishers.

Supreme Court (2014) P v Cheshire West & Chester Council; P & Q v Surrey County Council [2014] UKSC 19 (Cheshire West).

UNICEF (undated) *United Nations Convention on the Rights of the Child.* Available from: https://downloads.unicef.org.uk/wpcontent/uploads/2010/05/UNCRC_united_nations_convention_on_the_rights_of_the_child.pdf, accessed 13 April 2018.

White, J. and Rae, T. (2016) 'Person-centred reviews and transition: an exploration of the views of students and their parents/carers.' *Educational Psychology in Practice 32*, 1, 38–53.

Whittaker, J.V. (2014) 'Good thinking! Fostering children's reasoning and problem solving.' *Young Children 69*, 3, 80–89.

Wilson, K. and Devereux, L. (2014) 'Scaffolding theory: high challenge, high support in academic language and learning.' *Journal of Academic Language and Learning 8*, 2, A-91–A-100.

Wood, D., Bruner, J.S. and Ross, G. (1976) 'The role of tutoring in problem solving.' *Journal of Child Psychology and Psychiatry 17*, 2, 89–100. https://onlinelibrary.wiley.com/doi/epdf/10.1111/j.1469-7610.1976.tb00381.x, accessed 28 December 2018.

RESOURCES

Action on Hearing Loss: charity that provides free confidential impartial advice to people who are deaf, their families, friends and professionals. www.actiononhearingloss.org.uk

Barnardo's: the oldest children's charity in the UK. Among its services is a specialist advocacy service to give children and young people a voice. Advocates are independent and their role is just to explain the child or young person's wishes. They can accompany children and young people to meetings where decisions are being made, ensuring they are involved in decisions that affect their lives. www.barnardos.org.uk/what-we-do/protecting-children/childrens-rights-advocacy

Beat: charity providing support to individuals experiencing an eating disorder, and their loved ones. It also offers advice to education and associated professionals through its 'worried about a pupil' website section, including the signs to be aware of suggesting an eating disorder. There are free helplines for adults, young people and students, as well as information about eating disorders. www.beateatingdisorders.org.uk/

BILD: British Institute of Learning Disabilities: a charity that promotes the rights of people with learning disabilities to be valued equally, to participate fully in their local communities and to be treated with dignity and respect. It offers training and other services to the organisations who provide services and the people who give support. www.bild.org.uk

CHANGE: a human rights organisation led by disabled people working to build a society that treats people with learning disabilities equally and is inclusive. www.changepeople.org

Child Bereavement UK: a charity supporting families and professionals when a child is facing bereavement, or a child passes away. Services include a helpline providing support and information for families and professionals as well as training for schools and professionals. In some areas face-to-face support is offered such as for individual or groups of families. www.childbereavementuk.org

Circle of Support: a group of people who help someone with a learning disability. A circle of support is about bringing together lots of people to support someone who has a learning disability. Circles can help to plan things such as helping someone to find a job, finding new friends, moving out of home. www.mentalhealth.org.uk/cy/node/2232

Contact a Family: a UK-wide charity offering advice, information and support to families with disabled children including a free telephone helpline and local parent groups as well as an online community. https://contact.org.uk

Council for Disabled Children: an umbrella body for the disabled children's sector which brings together professionals, practitioners and policy-makers from education, health and social care, as well as voluntary and community organisations, to provide a voice to champion the rights of children, young people and their families and challenge barriers to inclusion. The organisation envisages a society in which disabled children's and young people's rights are respected. It provides a range of services including training, support and resources.

Resources

Down's Syndrome Association: a charity that offers advice and information to people with Down's syndrome and their families. www.downs-syndrome.org.uk

Family Fund: UK-wide charity providing grants to low-income families bringing up disabled or seriously ill children and young people. It aims to provide items and services that could not otherwise be afforded by the families to help improve quality of life, realise their rights and remove some of the barriers they face. The charity is funded by the four UK governments as well as private donations. www.familyfund.org.uk

HeadMeds: a Young Minds website providing information for young people about both the twenty-one most common mental health medications and mental health conditions.

KidsMatter: an Australian mental health and well-being initiative set up in primary schools and early education and care centres. It was developed by mental health and education and care services staff and is a partnership between education and health sectors funded by the Australian government and beyondblue. There is a section devoted to helping children develop decision-making skills. Although the advice is mainly suited to mainstream pupils, some ideas, advice and guidance are appropriate to children and young people with SEN. www.kidsmatter.edu.au/mental-health-matters/social-and-emotional-learning/making-decisions

Mencap: a charity working in partnership with people with a learning disability which provides services to support people to live how they choose. It provides information and advice for people with learning disabilities, families and carers. The website has an easy version for people with learning disabilities accessed from the main website via a blue button in the top right. www.mencap.org.uk.

Mind: a mental health charity. www.mind.org.uk

MindEd: provides free mental health e-learning and advice for all adults with a duty of care for children and young people. www.minded.org.uk

My Activity Passport: an editable checklist of activities children and young people can enjoy and learn from, produced by the Department for Education. www.gov.uk/government/publications/my-activity-passport

nasen (National Association of Special Educational Needs): a membership organisation, with charitable status, to provide training information and resources for education professionals with the aim of promoting the development of children and young people with SEN. www.nasen.org.uk

nasen SEND Gateway: an online portal for education professionals, hosted by nasen, providing access to information, training and resources to help meet the needs of children and young people with SEN. www.sendgateway.org.uk

National Autistic Society: a charity for people with autism. It provides information support, pioneering services and campaigns for a better world for people with autism. www.autism.org.uk

National Deaf Children's Society (NDCS): UK-wide charity for deaf children (offers support to age 25 years). The charity aims to work to overcome the social and educational barriers that hold back deaf children and young people. It offers a range of services to families, children, young people and professionals including a free telephone helpline for parents, children and young people and a dedicated website for deaf children and young people. www.ndcs.org.uk

National Development Team for Inclusion (NDTi): a not for profit organisation concerned with promoting inclusion and equality for people who risk exclusion and who need support to lead a full life. Particular interests are in issues around age, disability, mental health, children and young people. www.ndti.org.uk

National Elf Service: aims to bring the latest evidence-based research each week in the areas of mental health, learning disabilities and education. www.nationalelfervice.net (mental health and learning disabilities) or www.educationelf.net

National Youth Advocacy Service (NYAS): a rights-based charity operating in England and Wales for young people and adults, providing support for children and young people in care or with disabilities. It offers a variety of services including individual advocacy, a range of information, advice and support to enable a child or young person's views to be made known when decisions are being made about them, as well as an advocacy helpline. www.nyas.net

NatSIP (National Sensory Impairment Partnership): a partnership of organisations working together to improve outcomes for children and young people with sensory impairments. The website offers a wide range of resources related to sensory impairment. www.natsip.org.uk

Preparing for Adulthood: Preparing for Adulthood is an NDTi programme, working with the DfE and partners to ensure young people with SEND achieve paid employment, independent living, housing options, good health, friendships, relationships and community inclusion. Preparing for Adulthood programme provides expertise and support to local authorities and their partners to embed preparing for adulthood from the earliest age. It has three strands of work covering the development and implementation of good practice, best practice and information sharing and regional support in relation to all preparing for adulthood outcomes. www.preparingforadulthood.org.uk

Rethink Mental Illness: mental health charity which helps by challenging attitudes and changing lives and policy. It directly supports people through crises and to live independently. It offers advice and information. www.rethink.org.uk

RNIB: a charity supporting people with sight loss, providing advice and products to enable independence. www.rnib.org.uk

SANE: a mental health charity working to improve the lives of anyone affected by mental illness. It aims to raise public awareness and combat stigma. It provides care and support for people with mental health problems, their families and carers. www.sane.org.uk

SCOPE: a charity providing support, information and advice to disabled people and their families. www.scope.org.uk

SENDIASS (SEND information, advice and support service): a statutory service provided by English local authorities to provide free information, advice and support to parents of children with special needs or disabilities and young people themselves (SEND COP Chapter 2). Information about the service can be found on each local authority's website; the best way to access this is probably by putting the term sendiass plus local authority name into a search engine, for example sendiass camden council.

SENSE: a charity supporting and campaigning for children and adults who are deafblind or have sensory impairments. www.sense.org.uk

Resources

Sibs: charity to support children, young people and adults who are growing up with or have grown up with a sibling with disabilities or SEN or a serious long-term condition. Services include information, support and training on sibling issues for adult and young siblings (7–17 years), parents and professionals. For siblings aged 7–17 years there is a dedicated website offering online support and information. www.sibs.org.uk

Winston's Wish: a charity supporting children and young people following the death of a parent or sibling. Services include face-to-face support for children individually or in groups, a helpline offering support to parents, family members and professionals supporting a grieving child, and resources and information including specifically for school staff. www.winstonswish.org

Young Minds: a child and adolescent mental health charity committed to improving the emotional well-being and mental health of children and young people. www.youngminds.org.uk

INDEX

Page entries in *italics* denote figures

activities 31, 58, *81, 84,* 115, 120; 'My Activity Passport' 87, 94, 105, 117, 118, 164; *see also* experiences
Additional Learning Needs and Education Tribunal (Wales) Act 2018 5, *54, 55*
Avon Longitudinal Study of Parents and Children (ALSPAC) 37
aspirations 47, 85
associated professionals 9, *84*; and communication 145; as young person's advocate 66-7, 68, 174; understanding legal duties 3-8, 145; working in partnership parents 91, 162, 169; working with education professionals 57, 143, 150; *see also* language and communication
Atkinson, C. 148, 149, 150, 151

Beresford, B. 16, 19
'best interests' checklist 69, 96, 149, 168, 204; 'best interests' balance sheet 69, 207-8; views, wishes and feelings 59, 149; *see also* views, wishes and feelings
brain development *see* child development
British Psychological Society *see* The British Psychological Society
Bruner, J.S. 17, 144; *see also* scaffolding
Bruner's hypothesis 17, 30, 82

capacity: definition of 6, 21
case studies 9; Alberto greets adults 128-9; Arthur's choice-making 41-2; Decision-making curriculum 92-7; Developing Jill's decision-making ability 62-3; Friday afternoon choice (part 1) 60-1; Friday afternoon choice (part 2) 111-4; Jill chooses her post 18 placement 71-3; Jill makes a sandwich 51-2; Marvin's high school choice (part 1) 16-7; Marvin's high school choice (part 2) 29; Peter and Zsofia choose their secondary schools 64-5; Rodney cooks his lunch 47-9; Zsofia's post 18 placement 68-70
CentreForum 36, 39
Cheshire West 7, 49
child: definition of 8, 222
Children and Families Act (2014) 3, *54-5*; *see also* Mental Capacity Act 2005; SEND Code of Practice

children and young people 8 *see also* child and young person
Children's Commissioner 37
child development 18-9; brain development 18, 30, 86; heuristics 19-20, 154, 156, 157, reasoning abilities 18-9, 30, 31, 86, 163
choices 16-17, 26-7, *81, 84,* 97-8, 175-6; criteria for limiting 17, 22; criteria for selecting 16-7, 97; definition of 16; guidelines for offering 97-8, 175-6; limiting 17, 31, 175; reasonable choices 50-1; unwise choices 22
Circle of Support 166, 229
cognitive ability *see* child development reasoning abilities
communication 116, 162, 169, 173-4; communicate the decision 23, 24, 25, 29-30, 181, 184, 185, 188, 189, 192, 193; *see also* language and communication
compulsory school age: definition of England and Wales 8, 222; definition of Northern Ireland 8, 222
Convention on the Rights of Persons with Disabilities *54-5*
consistency 24, 59, 60, 88; between education institution staff and others 114, 117, 119; in use of language 20; of responses 102, 105, 115, 147, 149; within the education institution 117, 118, 213
curriculum 98-9, 119; decision-making 92-105, 118, 119; definition of 98; EYFS curriculum 107; life skills curriculum 88; spiral curriculum 31, 82, 88; Victorine's decision-making curriculum 102-5; *see also* decision-making syllabus

decision-making 44, 46-7 50, 171-2; as a cognitive process 15, 18; as a life skill 2-3, 16, 26, 27, 31, 42, 87, 98, 166, 171-2, 178, 180; four components of 21, 23; participation in 6, 27, 44, 58-9, 63, 96, 114, 143, 151, 161; *see also* decision-making outcomes; language; outcomes
decision-making framework 22-30, 31, *84*; education and associated professionals or parents completed for important decisions 181-99 child or young person form 'important' decisions 73-7, 200-3

Index

decision-making outcomes 5, *81*, 91–2, 98, 99, 135–9, 143, 146–7, 153, 177; and EHC Plans 28, 42, 46–7, 58, 63, 91, 108–9, 120, 143, 146–7, 159, 166–7 177; and person-centred planning 42, 58, 120, 143, 144–7, 166–7, 179

decision-making syllabus 81–120; essential components *84*, 97–119; overarching components *84*, 85–92; scaffolding 81, 85; *see also* teaching

decisions: educational decisions 57–8, 151; everyday decisions 22, 57, 61–2, 77, 78, 118, 164–6; everyday decisions definition of 21; 'important' decisions 16, 22, 23 31, 63–4, 167–8; 'important' ('more serious or significant') decisions definition of 21; unwise 22

deprivation of liberty *see* Mental Capacity Act 2005

digital technology 10, 118, 144, 145, 179; assistive 30, 47, 89; *see also* emojis

education institution 9; choosing an education institution 64–78 167; secondary transfer 64–6, 181–4; post 16 transfer 66–78, 185–99

education professional(s) 8–9; and communication 145; role as young person's advocate 66–7, 68, 77, 78, 114, 167, 174; role as facilitator 67, 77, 167; role of 11, 70, 77–8; working with associated professionals 57, 77, 143, 150; understanding legal duties 3–8, 145; working in partnership with parents 71–3, 91, 162, 169; working in partnership with the young person 71–3; *see also* language and communication

educational psychologists (EPs) 8–9 150–7; and communication 145, 146–7, 149 and Gillick competency 53; and digital technology 10, 144, 145, 178, 179; as young person's advocate 151, 152–3, 156; eliciting children's or young people's views 147–9, 153–4; everyday practice 154–5; formulating decision-making outcomes 144, 146–7, 153; partnership with others 91, 155; role of 144, 150–7; working with parents 149–50, 155; *see also* decision-making outcome

educational psychology service 155–6
emojis 10, 24, 89, 143, 145, 162, 173, 179, 222
emotional well-being *see* mental health
Equality Act 2010 46, 47, *54–5*
ethos 50, *81*, *84*, 85–6, 92, 119; and mental health 40; definition of 85; MCA ethos 148;
environment 62, *81*, *84*, 90–1, 100, 120; ambience 90; importance of 42; non-classroom spaces 90, 94, 120; use of scents 26, 63, 90, 95

everyday practice 3, *81*, *84*, 33, 61, 78, 115, 117–8, 119, 146, 168, 179
every day practice 117–8
experiences 62–3, *81*, 82, *84*, 86–8, 94, 98, 113; role of 18, 30–1; *see also* activities

Farrow, C. 164–5
Fazel, M. 36, 39
from the earliest age 1, 3, 20, 42, 47, 54, 62, 82, 88, 168, 172–3
fuzzies and performance 121, 130, 132, 134

Gillick Competency 20–1, 53, 54, 223
Grootens-Wiegers, P. 23

heuristics *see* child development
Hey Dad test 130–1, 132, 134, 139
Human Rights Act 1998 *54*, *55*

'important' decisions *see* decisions
information 4, 19, 21–3 24, 27–8, 73, 74–7, 168–9; accessible 24, 46, 73, 163, 169, 173, 179, 182, 186, 190, 195; children's right to 45–6; using and weighing 22, 25, 28–9, 183, 187, 191, 197
Ingram, R. 153–4

Johnston, H. 82
Justice Cobb 20–1
Justice Munby 59, 147, 149

KidsMatter 61, 230

Lady Hale: gilded cage quote 50, 176
language *81*; of decision-making 11, 20, 22, 31, 146
language and communication *84*, 89–90, 92, 100, 103, 111, 113, 119, 156, 158; consistency 92, 95, 109; emojis *see* emojis; Makaton 84, 100, 103, 111, 113, 145, 223; non-verbal 89, 162, 165, 173; shared language 20, 67, 77, 89, 96, 119, 143, 146, 158, 162, 169, 13, 178, 179; *see also* language
Law Society guidance 2015 49–51
learned helplessness 3
Liberty Protection Safeguards *see* Mental Capacity (Amendment) Act 2019
local authority (LA): allocation of education institution places by 26–7, 66, 175; communicate directly with young people 70, 163; local authority officers 9, 146; local authority SEN officers and EHC Plans 91, 144, 155, 177; Local Offer 45, 66, 67, 69, 70, 72, 165, 223
Local Offer *see* local authority

Mager, R.F. 121, 130
Makaton 52, 84, 93, 100, 103, 111, 113, 145, 223; see also language and communication
Mencap 2, 230
mental capacity see capacity
Mental Capacity Act 2005 2, 4, 6, 20, 23, 166, *55*; and Children and Families Act (2014) 4, 58; deprivation of liberty 49; deprivation of liberty definition 7; Deprivation of Liberty Safeguards 7, 49; five principles 6; see also 'best interests'
Mental Capacity (Amendment) Act 2019 7; 2, 4, 7, 205, 206, *55*; and Children and Families Act (2014) 4, Liberty Protection Safeguards 7
Mental Capacity Act 2005 Code of Practice (MCA COP) 6-7, 11, 146; decision-making process 17, 20-2; see also 'best interests'
Mental Capacity Act (Northern Ireland) 2016 8, *55*
mental health 33-42 177-8, 179; and children and young people with SEN 38; and education 2, 39-42; decision-making and positive impact on 2, 33, 40, 41, 163; definition of 34; functional guideline 34; mental well-being 177-8, 179; impact of poor 37, 39 prevalence of mental health issues 35-8; prevalence of mental health issues for children and young people with SEN 2, 38
mental well-being see mental health
Millennium Cohort study 37
Mitchell, W. 17, 161
'My Activity Passport' see activities

NatSIP (National Sensory Impairment Partnership) 96, 231
No decision slogan/mantra 11, 17, 54, 58, 146, 157, 171

object of reference 223
observations: guidelines for undertaking 211-6; time sampling observation schedule 214
observations and recording *84* 114-5; observation and recording format/checklist 116, 215
opportunities *81*, *84* 101, 117; creating 115, 128
options see choices
outcomes 106-114; key points about 109, 139; language of 130-2; formulating; five step process for writing 132-5; SEND COP; SMART (see also SMART) *84* 121-39; TWOSB formula 132; see also decision-making outcomes

parents 9, *81*, *84*, 118-9, 149-50; definition of 9; parent workshops 92, 96, 150, 168-9, 170; supporting and involving 159-70

partnership with others *84*, 91-2; see also associated professionals; education professionals
preferences see choices
photographs: taking 10, 117, 118, 197; see also digital technology; information
preparation for adulthood 3, 40, 45, 46, 87, 106, 119, 172; outcomes 87, 106, 209-10; see also outcomes

reasoning abilities see child development
Royal College of Psychiatrists 34, 38

scaffolding see teaching
Special Educational Needs and Disability Act (Northern Ireland) 2016 5, *54*, *55*
SEND Code of Practice (SEND COP) 3, 4; children and young people making their own decisions 46-7, 54; education and associated professionals' duties; outcomes 106-9; views, wishes and feelings 59, 154
SEN officers see local authority
siblings 91, 159-60, 164; Sibs charity 160, 232
Sinson, J.L. 7, 69, 149
SMART: achievable; measurable; realistic, specific; time-bound 122-9; see also outcomes
spiral curriculum see curriculum
Strengths and Difficulties Questionnaire 37, 224
Supreme Court see Cheshire West

Talking Mats: Jill's 'mat' for Isidore Specialist College 221; mechanics of 219-21; taking photographs of 147, 156 Talking Mats style approach 10
Teaching 109-10, 111, 113; scaffolding 82-4, 110
The British Psychological Society 151
TWOSB formula see outcomes

UN Convention on the Rights of the Child (UNCRC) 21, 44, *54*, *55*

views, wishes and feelings 44, 147-9, 152-4, 156, 168; giving weight to 5, 44, 59; see also SEND Code of Practice; Mental Capacity Act 2005 Code of Practice
Vygostsky: zone of proximal development 82, 126-7, 128, 139

young person 166; definition of 8, 224
zone of proximal development see Vygotsky

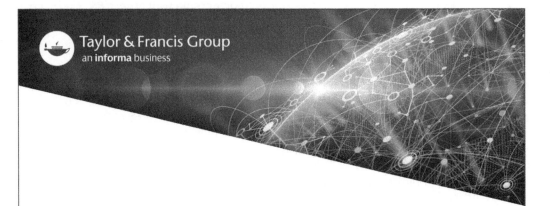